D1272873

Argumentation Theory and the Rhetoric of Assent

Edited by David Cratis Williams
and Michael David Hazen

Argumentation Theory and
the Rhetoric of Assent

The University of Alabama Press   Tuscaloosa and London

PN
4181
.A68
1990

Copyright © 1990 by
The University of Alabama Press
Tuscaloosa, Alabama 35487–0380
All rights reserved
Manufactured in the United States of America

The paper on which this book is printed meets the minimum requirements of Ameri-can National Standard for Information Science-Permanence of Paper for Printed Li-brary Materials, ANSI A39.48–1984.

Library of Congress Cataloging-in-Publication Data

Argumentation theory and the rhetoric of assent / edited by David Cratis Williams
    and Michael David Hazen.
        p.   cm. — (Studies in rhetoric and communication)
    Consists of papers thoroughly revised and heavily edited by original authors as
well as editors after having been presented at two Wake Forest University argumen-tation conferences, held at Wake Forest in Nov. 1982 and Nov. 1984.
    Includes bibliographical references.
    ISBN 0-8173-0509-2 (alk. paper)
    1. Forensics (Public speaking)—Congresses.   I. Williams, David Cratis,
1955– .   II. Hazen, Michael David, 1947– .   III. Series.
PN4181.A68   1990
808.5′1—dc20
                                                                                    90-34221
                                                                                    CIP

British Library Cataloguing-in-Publication Data available

Contents

Preface

The essays included in this volume grew out of the Biennial Wake Forest University Argumentation Conference. Since the fall of 1982, the Department of Speech Communication and Theatre Arts at Wake Forest University and the University Debate Team have co-sponsored the Argumentation Conference with the hope of establishing a recurring informal, small colloquium on argumentation theory at which both established and aspiring scholars in the area can present ideas to their colleagues with the prospect of the sort of intensive give-and-take critiques rare in larger conferences. This volume contains select essays that grew out of that interchange. Thus, while it is not a "proceedings" of the Wake Forest conferences, it is an outgrowth of those conferences.

The essays in this volume coalesce around the general question of "When, if ever, is assent justified?" And, as Professor Cox astutely notes in his introduction, such a question immediately leads into considerations of argument and power. In these considerations, many differing perspectives are represented in this volume: aesthetic and symbolist approaches, rationalistic and formalistic approaches, field theory perspectives, orientations toward various conceptualizations of a public sphere, etc. The final assemblage, while perhaps not providing any definitive answers, presents the reader with articulations of many of the fundamental quandaries implicated in criticism, quandaries regarding not only of justifications assent but also of critical methods and their implication in issues of power, of consensual, subjective, and formalistic approaches to argument evaluation and their implication in issues of power, and ultimately of the political role of argument criticism itself as it becomes embroiled in the issues of assent and dissent, in the constitution and reconstitution of various publics.

Argumentation Theory and the Rhetoric of Assent is intended not as a primer on argument theory but rather as a look at contemporary American approaches to a philosophy of argumentation and argument criticism. As such, the essays contained in this volume probe the implications of both current practices and theoretical approaches: the objective is not to map the terrain argumentation theory has traversed in recent years but rather to plot a route for the direction in which argumentation studies should move. The concluding essays by James Arnt Aune and G. Thomas Goodnight confront these concerns explicitly.

In a volume of this nature, which has been several years in the making, valuable contributions have been made by far too many people to acknowledge them all. Certainly the other participants and critics at the Wake Forest conferences—Tim Hynes, Robert Mielke, Walter Ulrich, Helen Warren, Kathy Harbart, Alan Gross, Joe Wenzel, and Michael Lewis—contributed significantly to the intellectual exchange that fomented these essays. To them, we owe our deepest gratitude and appreciation. Many graduate students, and former graduate students, at Wake Forest have also been instrumental in the successes of the conferences and in the production of this volume; we especially want to thank Bob Chandler, Lisa Honeycutt, Craig Rickett, Judy McClendon, and Carol Bibby for their assistance. Additional support, both financial and moral, was provided by Wake Forest Provost Edwin Wilson, the Research and Publication Fund, the Department of Speech Communication and Theatre Arts, chaired by Don Wolfe, and the Debate Program, under the leadership of Alan Louden and Ross Smith; in fact, it was through the auspices of the Debate Program that the Wake Forest Argumentation Conferences began. Finally, we want to thank Robbie Cox, Tom Goodnight, and Charlie Willard for their unswerving support from the outset. They not only presented papers and served as critics and respondents but also encouraged others to participate in the conferences. It is they who have set the tone of open intellectual exchange that has become the hallmark of the Wake Forest conferences, and it is to them that we tip our hats and say on behalf of all participants in the conferences, thank you.

DAVID CRATIS WILLIAMS   MICHAEL DAVID HAZEN
Kirksville, Mo.   Winston-Salem, N.C.

1

Introduction
Argumentation Theory
as Critical Practice

J. Robert Cox

The essays in this volume explore a new and exciting terrain in argumentation studies: the relation between "assent" and social practices. The authors, participants in the Wake Forest University
conferences on argumentation, have tried to be sensitive to the implications of asking, "When, if ever, is assent justified?" In doing so,
they urge us to understand assent as a function of argument's sociality or participation in the world of *praxis*. The Wake Forest essays thus serve—in their more provocative moments—as commentaries on Roland Barthes's observation, "Once uttered, speech enters
the service of power" (1982, 461).

But is anything new in this? Traditionally, the study of argument
has focused upon the formation of judgment toward the end of action. On this assumption, assent to a statement is acceptable if "it is
cast in terms of a possible unanimity between rational minds: this is
the Enlightenment narrative, in which the hero of knowledge works
toward a good ethico-political end—universal peace . . . [or] justice"
(Lyotard 1984, xxiii–xxiv). The capacity to achieve such a consensus
has been held by both traditional theorists and modernists as a humane mode for mediating power.

Yet, it is this very possibility that commentators have increasingly brought into question. We find an "eclipse" of the public by
technical reason (Dewey 1927) as well as systematic distortions in
the free converse of persons (Habermas 1970). We suspect media society or a "society of spectacle" (Guy Debord) may no longer be able

to sustain the traditional project of rational consensus. For these reasons, Lyotard believes a postmodern culture is distinguished by its incredulity toward the meta-narratives of the culture, such as the possibility of an assent of rational minds (xxiv).

But incredulity cannot sustain *res publica* and it is "the public's thing" that a theory of argumentation seems to require. In abandoning the project of modernism—the attempt to integrate Reason and *praxis*—theory thereby breaks faith with the normative rationale for argument. It is appropriate, therefore, that the first Wake Forest University Conference on Argumentation returned to this question: "When, if ever, is assent justified?" And this, Professor Goodnight suggests, is to ask no less whether knowledge and action can be productively conjoined; whether people still have the words to say what they believe and act upon what they say.

In addressing such questions, the participants in the Wake Forest University conferences faced two problems that appear throughout contemporary argumentation studies: (1) the problem of developing a justification for the normative dimension of argumentation theory—that is, the set of criteria that allows us to answer the question, "When is assent justified?"; and (2) the necessity of providing an account of the relationship between normative theory and argument practices. The participants would immediately point out, of course, that these two problems may not be separable. Efforts to articulate a justification for normative theory are themselves implicated in the problem they seek to solve; and, to the extent such efforts are based in a description of argument practices, they raise questions about material conditions and consequences of discourse—about power. Thus we return to Barthes's observation.

Most of the Wake Forest essays address this central problematic—the relationship of rational assent to power—in some fashion. A few make clear that argumentation theory inevitably becomes a "critical" practice in which criticism is taken both as a mode of theory-construction and as the telos of theory itself. A theory of argumentation would be a normative rationale for a critical praxis, an effort to resist or to recover those conditions that either retard or sustain the production and authentication of truthful, just, and effective discourse.

Interest in the justification of the normative dimension of argumentation theory has, in a sense, become a "problem" as a consequence of the field's rejection of formalism. Taken as a focus of traditional theory, Barthes's caution would be unnecessary. Neo-Aristotelianism understood "argument" as speech that was guided by *phronesis* or practical wisdom; it sought agreement from members of a community and thus served as a humane agency for mediating power. In this view, rational assent, as a Will to Truth, implied a commitment to human betterment (the latter on the assumption and as the product of such "rational" assent). Thus (to misread Nietzsche), the Will to Truth and the Will to Power were unitary.

As a theoretical and practical domain, the traditional study of argumentation focused on appeals to "conviction," that discrete faculty of mind distinguished in some unaccounted-for way by its rational quality. Argument became an applied logic, differentiated from formal logic mostly by virtue of its applied status. In its objectives and methods, the field of argumentation studies, by mid-twentieth century, had become the "study of the logical forms underlying ordinary language claims, disputes, and debates" (Cox and Willard 1982, xxi).

The normative dimension of argumentation theory under the assumptions of such "applied formalism" was clear. Laws of logical form were supposed to guide the analysis of the manifest (rhetorical) content of thought. The task of the critic was plainly given—to uncover the underlying, "real" structure of an argument and to evaluate its form accordingly.

Admittedly, some scholars held that such a normative structure revealed a tragic element of human argumentation. Arguers inevitably fail to fulfill the demands of rational decision-making. The material world intrudes too much: issues are ambiguous and value-laden; furthermore, arguers often must arrive at judgments under severe constraints of time and the availability of data. "Rational" assent is, therefore, an ideal and seldom a material trait of human argument. In our best moments, we seek but can never fulfill the criteria for justified assent.

For the most part, however, those working in the tradition of applied formalism showed little interest either in personal or social conditions that sustain reasoned discourse or in the material consequences of discourse. On an assumption of isomorphism of rational form and the psychology of judgment, critics devoted themselves to an explication of this "applied" form in discourse.

In the last two decades, however, argument has become less of an *a priori* subject. Critics have seemed increasingly to follow Toulmin's (1958) call for study of *argument-in-use*.[1] Initially, scholars found much to value in their own rhetorical heritage. Karl R. Wallace (1963), Donald C. Bryant (1973), and Carroll Arnold (1970), for example, proposed that *rhetorical* practices constituted (or could constitute) "good reasons" for rational assent. And, in the newly translated *The New Rhetoric: A Treatise on Argumentation* by Belgian philosophers Perelman and Olbrechts-Tyteca (1969), argumentation theorists appeared to discover a basis for such interests: the variable agreement or "adherence" of audiences offered a rationale for the normative dimension of argumentation theory.

An audience-centered view of argument, along with the allied "rhetoric-as-epistemic" movement (Scott 1967, 1976; Brummet 1976, 1981, 1982), seemed to offer a liberating basis for argumentation theory. Such perspectives fit nicely the ideological temper of American scholarship: Arguers compete for assent in the social marketplace, and audiences—as social referees—provide a way to discriminate among claims.

But it may not be immediately clear that the problem of providing a justification for the normative dimension of theory has been solved. Such a solution would have to assume that consensus, on the whole, provides a sufficient ground for assent. Does it? Wayne C. Booth, for one, would ask, "Am I not now forced to accept any piece of silliness that any fanatic wants to advance provided only that he can get somebody to assent to it?" (1974, 106).

In turning from applied formalism, then, have theorists settled for an uneasy truce between subjectivism and a consensus theory of truth? In comparison we might consider a related controversy in the realm of literary theory. Critics such as Graff and Lasch have charged that, in abandoning "form," certain avant-garde art has no firm *locus* for its claims. Their complaint illustrates a familiar contradiction in the subjectivist position: In exposing dominant reason as illusory, a work leaves "no means of legitimizing [its] own critique of injustice and exploitation" (Graff 1978, 21). Such abandonment of form is peculiarly susceptible to charges of resignation. Signs (stripped of their significations) become the basis of a social integration in which "even guardians of 'reality' admit that existence is an illusion, that distinctions between truth and falsehood have lost their meaning, and that it is futile to try to change the world or even to try to understand it" (Lasch 1978, 46–47).

Does a theory of argumentation, modeled on the same epistemological assumptions, run a similar risk of perpetuating a "society of spectacle?" A good number of the Wake Forest participants apparently think so. Yet most of these essays also acknowledge Rorty's cautions regarding an illusory quest for "foundations" of theory: The attempt of metaphysicians from the Greeks to Descartes, Russell, and Husserl to "break out into an *apxn* beyond discourse is rooted in the urge to see social practices of justification as more than just such practices" (1979, 390). In their essays for this volume, McKerrow, Croasmun, and Willard, for example, raise disturbing questions about both consensus theory and idealist criteria for justified assent.

It is within this context that McKerrow approaches the problem of justification in the first essay for this volume. Following Booth's (1974) discussion of "systematic assent," McKerrow examines the theoretical grounds for the concept of what he terms "pragmatic justification," a condition in which a listener has been given reasons sufficient to grant his or her adherence to the claim. His reliance upon the concept of adherence departs, however, from Perelman's use; McKerrow seeks to ground the "warranted assertability" of claims in the principle of coherence and in broader concerns of cultural norms and assumptions. This approach anticipates a fuller discussion of social formation which Aune and Goodnight address at the end of this volume.

Croasmun also addresses the "consensus" justification of argumentation theory in his incisive essay in this volume. Particularly troubling is his suggestion that the norm of consensus erodes the efficacy of dissent and perhaps the very possibility of persuasion. To avoid this possibility, he believes, the normative dimension of theory must be grounded in some criterion beyond the beliefs of "society," "community," or "others." Croasmun wants to argue for a "realist view of rhetorical epistemology," one that values inquiry into "the one world that is shared in some way by all living beings."

Yet, it is unclear how Croasmun would accomplish such a "realist" justification of normative theory. Much of his argument consists of familiar disclosures of the inconsistencies in the subjectivist or consensus position. His dispute with Brummett (1976, 1981, 1982) and Scott (1967, 1976), however, may be interesting for another reason. In shunning both relativism and foundationalism, Croasmun illustrates a type of *argument practice* that moves toward "criticism and inquiry."

Is our question, then, properly put by framing the problem of justification in epistemological terms, for example, "Should we ground assent upon the agreement of an audience or on a realist view of the world?" Here, Croasmun merely points in the general direction he would go: "To strive for *standards* of persuasion, to believe knowledge claims can be compared and evaluated, to have a rhetoric that is more than merely self-referential." Yet, this clearly differs from McKerrow who urges us to proceed from some sense of a pragmatic justification (as opposed to "epistemic justification"). The difference, McKerrow proposes, is that the former makes no assertion guaranteeing the truth of the claim. Pragmatic justification merely asserts that "within the particular context in which the claim is appraised, the belief in the claim, or the adoption of the action, is *warranted*" (1986b).

Would the problem of developing a justification of the normative dimension of theory be better defined by distinguishing rhetorical practices from epistemology? If so, we would ask, "What do arguers evoke as commonplaces of reasoning in particular settings, and how are these perceived to be guarantors of judgment?" The objective of such an orientation would be (after Toulmin) to investigate how socially situated persons argue, change, or arrive at judgments, and what these persons articulate as rationalizations for their assent.

Such concern for "pragmatic justification" fundamentally alters the project of argumentation theory. Among other things, it brackets the question of formal epistemology. And it provides, in principle, an account of not only arguers' grounds but also the nature of argumentation *theory* as also a kind of practice (a "critical" practice, as I shall argue).

Two related research programs arise out of this turn: (1) A description of the social bases of validity claims. For the most part, this has been conducted out of what Swanson (1977) terms the "critical stance" in the "mundane" world, that is, argument practices of the parties in dispute are taken as an explanandum of justification for assent. And (2) an extension of this interest to a reflection upon the social assumptions and conditions for the occurrence of argument practices *as such*. It is this "reflective stance" (Swanson 1977) that is the focus of many of the essays from the Wake Forest University conferences.

Argument scholars generally have viewed the normative dimension of assent from the first perspective: Argumentation is a study of "justified" assent, but the normative basis of this assumption is located in argument practices. Justified assent is located in *praxis* in the larger sense of what Von Wright calls "form of life." "The [set of presuppositions of argument] is not propositional knowledge . . . ," he suggests. "Giving grounds, . . . justifying evidence, comes to an end;—but the end is not certain propositions striking us immediately as true, i.e., it is not a kind of seeing on our part; it is our acting . . ." (1972, 57). On the further assumption that these *social* bases for arguers' judgments can be identified, the theoretical task is given: It is, as Toulmin (1958) originally proposed, the study of "the ways of arguing which have established themselves in any sphere, accepting them as historical facts . . ." (257).

Two organizing perspectives have guided this effort: (1) the study of *arguing* as a communicative practice; and (2) the acceptance of argument practices as the *epistemic procedures* of rational enterprises or "fields." Studies derived from both perspectives are now quite commonplace. Our understanding of the symbolic form and function of arguing in conversation and in fields such as law has grown as a consequence. The focus on practices, nevertheless, raises other questions—questions about the social assumptions and conditions for the occurrence of argument—that cannot be answered from within the first research program. The remaining essays in this volume have, therefore, tried to approach the problem of normative theory from a more reflective stance, by asking about the possibility of "justified" assent as such.

Among other things, the focus from this "reflective" perspective reveals that arguers engage in *an effort toward change,* not merely an effort to align themselves with a prior consensus. An implication of many of the Wake Forest essays is that argument is an agency of transformation as much as a mode for certifying truth. This is certainly the perspective that Jasinski believes argument scholars should bring to their study of assent: We must attend to "the ways symbolic action produces transformations (change, assent . . .) in assumptions, beliefs, practices, and affiliations." Jasinski tries to account for this by describing *form* as a process of "inferencing." Here, he draws on Burke's view of form as the structuring of audience consciousness, as a process of anticipation. The force of an argument is realized "when the inferential form articulated in the symbolic practices of a social actor enters the concrete historical world populated by rhetorical audiences, marked by problems and exigencies (themselves constituted, to some degree, by discourse) and structured by institutions, traditional practices and other constraints." Argument becomes an agency for change precisely as audiences participate in symbolic form—when they "anticipate" or are "moved along" through the potential of form and are thereby transformed.

Jasinski explicitly relates this account to material assumptions of the occurrence of argument: "form" allows insights into the way actors "assess the claims being made in light of pressing circumstances, historical traditions, new possibilities, social interests, and personal motives." Thus, the crucial task for argumentation scholars is an understanding of how the major categories of form contribute to social power. This, in turn, is the particular focus of essays by Lake and by Kauffman and Parson.

The basis for assent, Lake believes, lies in material and performative dimensions of "ritual." Actually, he is less interested in what constitutes a "sound" argument or what is the normative basis for claims per se. This is because Lake distinguishes an arguer's discursive claim and the *persona* of the implied arguer who seeks assent to the "claim enacted." In the idea of *personae*—Lake takes the case of the warrior—ritual enacts as well as urges the adoption of certain traits. The warrior *personae* is both "an argument for and the embodiment of a set of ideal Native American attributes." Human agents (in the *personae* of arguers) seek both assent and participation *in* a transforming vision: "Be as I am." Here, the criterion is not truth-seeking but performativity, "becoming." The relevant assumptions on which assent to a *persona* depends are social conditions: Is the cultural world view consonant with the *persona*? What is the value this world view has for ritual action?

Kauffman and Parson also attempt to reveal the relation between social conditions of argument and the normative dimension of argumentation theory. They focus on the role of metaphor and the social assumptions underlying its authority in public argument. Metaphor is important because it is a vehicle for the evocation and suppression of "presence" in discourse. That is to say, it may either heighten awareness of an issue or repress actual differences between arguers. Arguments with greater presence "invite participation in a controversy and encourage the intellectual risk taking necessary to overcome dogma and produce assent."

By following this line of thought, Kauffman and Parson reveal the social constraints and consequences of "arguing" as a communicative practice. This is particularly evident in their discussion of the role of faded or "dead" metaphors in shaping thought. Such metaphors—since they habituate our minds to particular points of view—suppress presence; they hide their interestedness in "the routine and the mundane."

Such "distancing" devices are forms of discursive *praxis* and the study and critique of them become—in an important sense—the study and critique of power. Kauffman and Parson point out, for example, that discussions about nuclear war technology take place in terms that often remove the public from the discussion. Former Secretary of Defense Robert S. McNamara has noted: "the potential victims have not been brought into the debate yet. . . . The average intelligent person knows practically nothing about nuclear war— the danger of it, the risk of it, the potential effect of it." The dead metaphors in which such discussion occurs suppress our awareness of choice in such vital matters. And, in the absence of the voices of critics such as Kauffman and Parson, such metaphors function as "powerful conservators of dogma, giving substantial presumption to the way things are and placing the burden of proof on those who would depart from the existing order."

Weiler turns to a similar question in his own study of argument forms in literature. In an insightful reading of Mann's *The Magic Mountain*, Weiler focuses on the critical questions we must ask if we take Booth seriously regarding the ability of fiction to produce the kind of knowledge that helps us judge when we should change our minds (1974, 12). (Weiler's analysis of the dialogic form of Mann's novel is a particularly insightful demonstration of Weiler's own thesis regarding "form" as a mode of arguing.)

Jasinski, Lake, Kauffman and Parson, and Weiler thus illustrate an important organizing perspective that has guided recent efforts to identify the social bases of "justified" assent. The argument critic includes such topics as inferencing, ritual, metaphor, and literature as appropriate subjects for inquiry because such practices constitute "arguing." And it is arguing—whether as implied *persona* or as dead metaphors—which contributes significantly to the rhetorical power of human discourse.

The same question ultimately arises in studies that employ the second perspective: "field theory." Though the theoretical parameters for this construct have not been agreed upon ("Special Issue" 1982), the work of describing the epistemic procedures and standards employed in fields has proceeded. The *Journal of the American Forensic Association* (1986), for example, reports studies of the ways of arguing in small claims courts, the different fields involved in the debate over Laetrile, appellate reasoning in First Amendment cases, and argument in the legislative process.

These studies also illustrate Willard's distinction (in the present volume) between epistemology and *epistemic* practices. The social ground of reason, for Willard, is an "epistemic" problem. This is an inquiry into local practices or the internal constitution of social domains. This allows us to leave aside epistemological diagnoses—the problem of "a privileged overarching discourse commensurable with, and capable of arbitrating among all particular discourses."

Field theory appears to offer an attractive program for argumentation studies. By restricting its focus to a description of argument-in-practice, it promises an account not only of recurring forms but also of a field's standards for valid or "strong" argument. Yet, such studies have not offered (and, in principle, may not be able to offer) what McKerrow has called "social critique—an examination of the merit of argument as it fosters or hinders social practices" (1986a, 185). McKerrow cites a 1986 study of the problems that occur when ordinary arguers appear in a rule-governed setting (small claims court) for which they lack formal training. Though the authors provide an account of the ways of arguing in this forum, they do not comment on broader questions of social good or equity. McKerrow notes only that the social consequences of this power relationship is a subject presumably left for future study (1986a, 185).

Yet, this may mask a more important question. Can the usual methods of field studies account for the social consequences of unequal power relations? Can such a perspective provide a means for commenting on inequity? Such questions concern the normative basis of criticism itself, a concern that field theory may not be able to address.

This is especially troublesome for an emerging interest in the "public sphere" and in public moral argument. Here, the absence of a norm-criterion opens criticism to a paradox: On the one hand, the focus upon practices is a liberating move against *a priorism;* it contains an openness to varied and innovative resources for human reasoning. Yet, beyond *intra*-field standards, such an account does not appear to be able to say what argument practice should be "aimed at." Within this perspective, criticism has no normative dimension. It is, in the words of the leading proponent of field theory, merely "a mode of epistemology that aims at illuminating the effects of assumptions" (Willard 1982b, 47).

The remaining essays from the Wake Forest conference try to address this concern in a more explicit manner. Some attempt to extend the field's interest in arguing to a reflection upon the social assumptions and conditions for the occurrence of argument as such. And this, I think, begins to offer an account of argumentation theory itself as a kind of practice, a "critical" practice competent to address the sociality of argument.

Rowland, for one, locates the critical basis of theory in the "shared purpose" of argument. Echoing Rescher, he understands such a purpose in terms of pragmatic utility: "The critic does not attempt to justify the evaluative standards as a form of knowledge, but uses them because they serve his or her needs." The general purpose of argument, Rowland then suggests, is to solve problems. Hence, the criteria for criticism should reflect those characteristics that make it more likely that an argument will "solve a problem."

This move is, potentially, a useful one against the infinite regress of what Weimer (1979) calls "justificationism." It is the futile attempt to find some sure ground of knowledge or a final premise for reasoning. Rowland (like Willard) rejects such epistemological assumptions for the assessment of assent. He urges, instead, that this assessment be viewed as an interpretation of purposive action.

But what is the nature of such action? Does Rowland's formulation of "action" contain some social or communally shared purpose in arguing? Such an assumption would permit us to address the conundrum of field theory: the absence of norms for settling *inter*-field disputes. Yet, Rowland seems to draw back at this point. Interestingly, it is Rowland who gives us a paradigm of such disagreement: a dispute between environmentalists and corporations over plans to drill for oil in the Arctic National Wildlife Refuge. What, then, would be the "shared purpose" of decision-making in this case? What commonplaces of judgment inform the purposive action of groups in a dispute of this paradigmatic sort? Rowland *is* clear in stating that the bases for assessment of assent would not be derived from "what is accepted as a social truth." Instead, they would be drawn from what he believes are field invariant norms of informal logic—the presence of evidence, coherence, and the use of expert knowledge. Yet, as Willard makes clear in his essay in this volume, public actors are also divided by substantive differences that do not depend on errors of reasoning.

A theory of argument, therefore, that is derived solely from the micro-units of argument forms and fallacies may very well fail. It cannot solve the problem of the "undecidability" of pragmatism's social position (Lentricchia 1983, 3). What is in dispute is precisely the question of social utility: *What ought we value as the general welfare or public good?*[2] And this, it turns out, can be decided only in the course of communal discussion and judgment, i.e., in arguing.

This returns us to the heart of our inquiry: the relation between reason and social practices. And, on an idealist level, at least, we may be able to sketch a justification for normative theory in this social or communal supposition of argument. "Rationality," McKerrow proposes in his opening essay, "is grounded in cultural perceptions of what constitutes appropriate standards of individual and community conduct." Most of the Wake Forest essays, in fact, suppose just this sort of normative reference to a "public sphere."[3]

But, this also returns us to the material problems we had noted in the beginning. Dewey (1927) and, more recently, Habermas (1971), have warned of a segmentation of interests and an "eclipse" of the public. The ascendancy of technical reason,[4] in particular, has tended to erode the competence of moral/practical reason in the public realm. Often, Willard observes, "the guarantors of ordinary knowledge claims are explicit and implicit tapestries of power, politics, authority, prestige, and rationales." And argument, although it participates in this tapestry, is shaped by its own sociality in turn. If argument is infested with the guilt of its own collusion in power (Barthes 1982), then some account must be offered of the relation between a normative theory of the *public* and argument practices as such.

Does this mean the study of argument collapses simply into a study of power? No. The Wake Forest participants clearly prefer to chart another course in linking normative theory to the study of practices. For Willard, this means *defining the public sphere itself as an argument field.* Among other things, this invites us to reconsider public "knowledge" as an epistemic concern—"a package of discourse competencies which aim at the appraisal of expert discourse." This move recalls Toulmin's observation that what we take to be rationality is an attribute of the "procedures by which the concepts, judgments, and formal systems currently accepted in [human activities] are criticized and changed" (1972, 135). Rationality is not just a social product but is contingent upon a certain kind of discourse, specifically, criticism. McKerrow's pragmatic justification (and Weimer's nonjustificationist position) similarly locates rationality in criticism. Thus, as many of the essays in this volume suggest, argumentation theory itself becomes critical *praxis* as it identifies the social assumptions and conditions that are necessary for "justified" assent.

The two concluding essays in this volume address this conjunction of theory and critical practice: Aune's reading of conventions for the production of discourse and Goodnight's proposal for criticism of dominant forms of "public" communication. Aune takes as a starting point the communicative dilemma in Marxism. This dilemma inheres in an analysis of class struggle in the absence of a political or rhetorical theory that would explain *agency*, or, "how the working class struggles and gains power." Aune proposes, in turn, that the study of argument should identify the ways in which dominant forms of argument relate to modes of production and the social formation "in the most general way." Here, Aune introduces a note of caution. Ideological criticism may well make us aware of the relationship between discourse and power; capitalism, however, is "ultimately determining only in the sense of establishing general patterns and rules for argument." An exclusive focus on ideology and ideological critique falls prey both to Booth's (1974) claim of "motivism" and to post-modernism's thesis that we are "imprisoned in a one-dimensional society of spectacle." This leads the critic to ignore the reality of actual struggles and the argument practices of historically real persons and groups.

The various perspectives within Marxism, however, fail to make the rhetorical turn that would link *theoria* with practical discourse. (This is especially true of the Frankfurt School.) And, though a Gramscian "counter-hegemony" privileges the role of rhetorical communication, Aune notes it too lacks a theory of the production of discourse and of audience effects. Only in Eagleton's program (1981, 1983) do we find a way from the Marxist tradition back to argumentation studies. Eagleton takes rhetoric to be the mode devoted to "analyzing the material effects of particular uses of language in particular social conjunctures" (Eagleton 1981, 101). The perspective of a Marxist reading of assent, then, would foreground class struggle—rather than consensus—and would accompany it with a theory of discourse production and effects.

Aune's contribution to an account of the relation between normative theory and argument practices is his effort to understand the latter in terms of the rhetorical dimensions of hegemony; it is a reading of "dominant theories of rhetoric as attempts to describe, explain, and occasionally criticize hegemonic techniques." Our initial question, "When, if ever, is assent justified?" is thus recast as a question regarding the conjuncture of discursive practices and the nature of the social formation in which such practices arise and which help to determine their impact.

In a similar fashion, Goodnight takes the task of theory to be "critique." In the last essay of this volume, Goodnight attempts to describe such contemporary practices as mass media programming and public opinion polls in light of their rhetorical presuppositions and values. Such criticism would interpret discourse in frameworks pertaining to "forms of life obfuscated by its selective representation" and "expose the 'surrogate' qualities of such depictions thereby providing difference and room for alternative discourse." Goodnight's task is to recover those practices that can resist the erosion of a genuinely *public* space in which citizens can both "formulate and authenticate their own discourses."

As it develops along such lines, argumentation theory may therefore enable us to articulate the social assumptions that are necessary for recovery of moral-practical reason. Such theory would appear to include an affirmative moment and also a critical or deconstructive phase. Affirmatively, theory is an effort to say what justified assent must assume. And this much, at least, is clear from the Wake Forest essays: An account of the normative dimension of argumentation theory can no longer envision argument practices in terms of technical form—as a "correct" set of sentences—or as an epistemological problem, for example, as a dispute between consensus and verificationist criteria. In most of these essays, the problem of justified assent is subsumed by some larger psycho-social or historical structure—ritual, fields, the social formation, or public sphere. In each case, the critic struggles to define a space in which argument is again competent to address social ends or moral purpose.

By foregrounding the concerns of *praxis*, argumentation theory may also be able to avoid a temptation in the affirmative phase of theory—what Rowland termed the "dream of a perfectly rational, re-energized public sphere." By this, I take it he means some totalizing vision of the public, a form of consensus regarding "first premises" that overdetermine arguers' assent. Argumentation theory as a critical practice thus cautions us against the tendency of any mode of discourse to rule out alternative discourses. It is the unique position of a theory of argumentation that criteria for its normative dimension cannot be lodged outside of its own *praxis*.

For this to be possible, theory seems to require that a critical moment be incorporated in its practice. Since assent assumes its own sociality, the critic must be able not only to identify the set of conditions that are historically and socially necessary for the occurrence of "discursively competent publics" (Goodnight), but also to identify what systematically distorts the possibility of such publics. As Goodnight, in an earlier essay urged, "If the public sphere is to be revitalized, then those practices which replace deliberative rhetoric by substituting alternative modes of invention and restricting subject matter need to be uncovered and critiqued" (1982, 227). The theory of argumentation as a critical practice is such an effort. Theory articulates for historical agents those ways that they (we) may aid in recovering the conditions that sustain the production and authentication of humane, just, and effective discourse.

Notes

1. The turn from "applied formalism" has been chronicled in Cox and Willard 1982, xxii–xxv.

2. Cf. Max Horkheimer's discussion of the capacity of classical theories of reason to address "ends" in *Eclipse of Reason* (New York: Contiuum, 1947), pp. 3ff.

3. Rowland, of course, addresses "three approaches to the problems of the public sphere—dialectic, audience centered and field theory." He claims these are inadequate; what is needed, Rowland argues, is evaluation based on traditional tests of informal logic. It is these "tests," nevertheless, that rely upon a sense of "purpose" that returns us to an interest in social or cultural bases for critical interpretation.

4. As McCarthy puts it, in his insightful study of Habermas, "The real problem . . . is not technical reason as such but its universalization, the forfeiture of a more comprehensive concept of reason in favor of the exclusive validity of scientific and technological thought, the reduction of *praxis* to *techne*" (1978, 22).

Part I

Rationality and Assent

2

The Centrality of Justification
Principles of Warranted Assertability

Raymie E. McKerrow

The principal thrust of Wayne Booth's *Modern Dogma and the Rhetoric of Assent* (1974) is exemplified in his observation that *"being reasonable in practical affairs is more like a process of systematic assent than systematic doubt"* (104, italics mine). The "social test of truth" that enables systematic assent to replace the traditional systematic doubt of Cartesian rationality is expressed in equally simple terms: "It is reasonable to grant (one *ought* to grant) some degree of credence to whatever qualified men and women agree on, *unless* one has specific and stronger reasons to disbelieve" (101). Given this degree of reasonableness, the search for standards of "systematic assent" has a specific context in which to operate—only when the grounds for such assent are questioned is it essential to determine whether belief or action would be justified. The assumptive ground for such "systematic assent" is also expressed in Gilbert Harman's (1980) "Principle of Conservatism": "One is justified in continuing fully to accept something in the absence of a special reason not to" (46). The converse of this position is to recognize the futility of holding a belief when the reasons one has adopted prove to be groundless. In Harman's terms, this is expressed as a Principle of Positive Undermining: "One should stop believing P whenever one positively believes one's reasons for believing P are no good" (39).

The concept of *pragmatic justification* assumes the same premise as that which grounds both Booth's discussion of systematic assent and Harman's discussion of the principles involved in "changing one's view." In a series of essays (McKerrow 1976, 1982, 1986b, 1987a, 1987b) the concept has been articulated as one that provides a *rhetorically grounded* theory for the warranted assertability of arguable claims. Used in this context, warranted assertability does not mean that "truth" has been found. Neither is the process of seeking warranted assent one of certifying the truth of a claim. Rather, it means that a listener has been given reasons sufficient to grant adherence; systematic assent is warranted by the information at hand. A warranted assertion is time-bound and context-bound: later events may indicate that an idea once considered to be "good" or well founded no longer has that status.

Whatever else may be said about the nature of arguing as a human activity, the role of justifying one's claims assumes a central place in the analysis of argument. This essay examines the theoretical grounds on which justification rests. Six principles of pragmatic justification will be discussed, beginning with an analysis of the types of claims to be justified in warranting assent. Principles Two and Three ground justification in the realm of the contingent (truth seeking but not truth certifying) and the criticizable (the act of criticism produces stronger claims on one's potential adherence). Principle Four places the process of justification within a contextual frame of reference—criticism occurs in terms of the "field" or "community" standards that are operative and relevant to the claim in question. Principles Five and Six complete the theoretical review and focus attention on the requirements of coherency and rationality in producing justified claims.

PRINCIPLE ONE: Pragmatic justification encompasses both beliefs and values.

There is a very real difference in being justified in believing that something is the case, and in being justified in taking a certain action based on that belief (McKerrow 1986b). Most of our attention in argument studies has been focused on values leading to appropriate actions, rather than on beliefs leading to appropriate judgments, as these concepts are understood and used in everyday language. Fisher, for example, argues for a "logic of good reasons" based on warrants that justify "belief, attitude, or action—these being the usual forms of rhetorical advice" (1978, 378). The five criteria proposed, however, focus almost exclusively on value judgments, as does the "end" sought: "to insure that people are conscious of the values they adhere to and would promote in rhetorical transactions, and to inform their consciousness *without dictating what they should believe*" (383). Thus, from a general sense of "good reasons" functioning to promote both belief and action, the analysis narrows to the promotion of values—the realm of practical rather than theoretical reasoning. Chaim Perelman's and L. Olbrechts-Tyteca's "new rhetoric" (1969) also supports the value emphasis by focusing attention on ending value disputes in the realm of philosophy: "its emphasis is on argumentative techniques that will support a practical judgment" (McKerrow 1986b, 214). As Ray Dearin (1986) notes, "justification, for Perelman, concerns choices, actions, intentions, and decisions" (177). Practical reasoning, in Perelman's view, deals with actions or behaviors, not propositions (Dearin 1986, 177).

Rescher's promotion of a "plausibility index" (1976, 1979; McKerrow 1987a, 1987b), on the other hand, is oriented toward theoretical reasoning or the support of propositional statements. Lehrer's (1978) doxastic system and Chisholm's (1978) and Lucey's (1976) scales of epistemic appraisal also are attempts to guide the evaluation of beliefs about what we can be said to know (McKerrow 1982). Each of these "systems" was advanced to ascertain the "truth status" of claims. Hence, to utilize them in the analysis of a claim's justifiability alters their original intent.

The distinctions drawn above between practical and theoretical reasoning can be highlighted as follows:

PRAGMATIC JUSTIFICATION

Practical Reasoning	Theoretical Reasoning
—Values	—Beliefs
—Behaviors	—Propositions
—Action	—Adherence

Where practical reasoning is oriented toward the conclusion that a particular behavior is justified, theoretical reasoning provides the basis for adherence to the proposition. Judgments concerning practical and theoretical issues may converge—one may both adhere to the proposition "We should close Maine Yankee" and act on that belief by voting for its closure. On the other hand, judgments may diverge, as intimated in the beginning discussion of this principle. An action may be right according to the standards of theoretical reasoning, without being justified in a practical sense. From a purely theoretical perspective, one might build a reasonable case for the claim "We should impeach the President of the United States." Given a belief in the correctness of the proposition, one might also be dissuaded from taking action by the costs involved—the political support base may not be present to support a case on the grounds provided (for example, in Reagan's case, the Contra affair may have produced the alleged "smoking gun," but there is no certainty that its presence would have prompted impeachment proceedings). The discrepancy between belief and action may be more striking: a person can accept the claim that cocaine is an addictive drug yet continue to use the substance. The belief is an insufficient motive for a change in behavior.

By encompassing both practical and theoretical issues, pragmatic justification operates as a generic concept identifying the processes that occur in accepting a belief or a value. As such, it provides a broader conceptual framework than either Perelman's sense of justification (limited to values) or Rescher's "plausibility indexing" (limited to propositional support). Pragmatic justification functions as a "contentless" concept; as a descriptive term, it names a process rather than a universal standard for what may pass as "justified."

PRINCIPLE TWO: Pragmatic justification is distinct from epistemic justification.

Epistemic justification aims at guaranteeing that a particular claim is true. Pragmatic justification, on the other hand, "makes no assertion *guaranteeing* the truth of the claim. What it does assert is that, within the particular context in which the claim is appraised, the belief in the claim, or the adoption of the action, is *warranted*" (McKerrow 1986b, 210). While it borrows some of the ideas found within the "justified true belief" debate, the concept does not share the same aim. The assessment that a claim is "warranted" also separates justification from "mere belief" (Moser 1985). If a hierarchy were established, mere belief (untested and untried) would be the most "primitive" state, with pragmatic justification a further step, and epistemic justification the final step in the process of truth-certification. Pragmatic justification need not, however, meet the rigorous standards required of "knowledge" considered in epistemic terms to be a rational process that produces an adequate ground for belief or action.

Corrigible Nature: A corollary of this principle is that warranted assertions are *corrigible* or *defeasible.* Claims to knowledge based on such assertions can be wrong either because later information reveals earlier judgment was based on insufficient data or because the claim to knowledge rests on a careless and incomplete review of the available information. Rescher (1982) distinguishes between the *correctness* of our assertion, and the adequacy of our *conception* related to the assertion: "There is a significant and substantial difference between a true or correct *statement* or *contention* on the one hand, and a true or correct *conception* on the other. To make a true contention about a thing we need merely get *some one particular fact* about it straight. To have a true conception of the thing, on the other hand, we must get *all of the important facts* about it straight" (113).

Given this difference, it means that to have correct *conceptions*, one must have more data than may be available at any one time. Hence, one holds conceptions "tentatively, subject to a mental reservation of sorts—a full recognition that it may ultimately prove to be mistaken" (113). Toulmin (1958) discusses the standards for knowing when one has correct conceptions (the fullest picture possible) in terms of a difference between *improper* and *mistaken* claims. Annis (1978) terms the distinction one of *excusable* versus *nonexcusable* claims. In both cases, the key is whether the appropriate *performance conditions* have been spelled out and executed prior to making the claim. Thus, one may be excused or mistaken only if the claim's truth-status has been checked thoroughly. "Negligence in the performance of one's duty is not an excusable reason for holding false beliefs as justified. A reporter who does not confirm information with other sources may be in the uncomfortable position of presenting" *nonexcusable* or *improper* claims (McKerrow 1987b, 219).

PRINCIPLE THREE: Pragmatic justification is nonfoundationalist.

If one were debating the issue of epistemic justification, the claim would be offered that most theories require some sort of "given" or "taken for granted" premise on which all others rest. To fail in this regard would entail an infinite regress, with no argumentative claim ever being able to assert that it is grounded in some firm, inviolable premise. The problem, of course, is that the assertion of a premise as "taken for granted" is simply to sidestep the entire issue of the need for a firm foundation that is known with certainty. The analysis of everyday arguments does not require the rigor of epistemic justification, as noted in Principle Two. Hence, whether it is "foundationalist" in the terms argued by epistemic justificationists is irrelevant. Nevertheless, one can argue that pragmatic justification is not premised on a "foundationalist" argument that entails an infinite regress: "Pragmatic justification is a *functional* concept which aims toward epistemic justification. It provides a conceptual basis for the assertion that a person's adoption of a belief has been assessed by criteria appropriate to the context. The claim may be true, but its truth status is not the result of a person's decision to adopt the claim as a single true belief (foundationalism), or as part of a true belief set (coherentism). In this sense, it embraces Weimer's [1979] nonjustificationist position, in that it 'locates rationality in criticism'" (McKerrow 1986b, 210).

More specifically, if there is a sense of "foundation" (that does not imply epistemic justification as a goal) applicable to argument analysis, it is *criticism*. Nor is the criticism tied to a narrow "instrumental rationality." If we are to embrace a belief or commit to an act, it must be because *all* factors affecting judgment are taken into account. As Willard (1985) points out, "critics must surrender . . . the pose of objectivity, of disinterested impersonal, uninvolved judgment" (33). Wander (1985) is even more pointed in asserting the social role of the act of criticism: "The task of criticism in our time is to raise real issues and to assist in the creation of publics able to and, in the interests of human survival, willing to rise above parochial concerns" (357). Justifying adherence to claims involving "real issues" is the beginning point of a critical act. Individual beliefs and actions, no less than community ones, participate in the creation of larger "publics."

Evolutionary Nature: Given the corrigible nature of our knowledge, the role of criticism is perceived in *circular* rather than *linear* terms. A spiral may be an appropriate metaphor, as the role of criticism is to seek improvement in the overall quality of judgments made. As a corollary to Principle Three, the circularity permits error and acknowledges the tentative nature of the beliefs we come to hold as justified. The reasoning process turns back on itself as we evaluate the success of our processes of decision-making. Rather than perceiving our reasoning in a forward-looking linear fashion, the act of criticism involves checking the efficacy of our practices. If they turn out to be sufficient, little change in the *methods* of reaching conclusions will be necessary. If, on the other hand, our track record is abysmal, and our beliefs and actions turn out to be consistently groundless after the fact, then major changes in our procedures for accepting them in the first place will be required. Truth-certification, to the extent that it serves as the ultimate goal of epistemic justification, proceeds in an evolutionary manner. Pragmatic justification, as a practical way station in the continuum between mere belief and apodictic certainty, is where the most work will be done in improving methods of analysis and decision-making. In a more technical discussion of the same issues, Rescher (1979) lays out the fundamental pattern in a question-answer format:

Q. What legitimates systematization? **A.** Its relative success *vis-à-vis* the alternatives. **Q.** How is this success established? **A.** By the record—i.e. inductively. **Q.** But how is induction itself to be legitimated? **A.** With reference to systematicity—i.e. as constituting an efficient route to the systematization of our information. The circle is clear here: systematization validates induction, induction substantiates systematization; inductive methods validate the systematizing rationale of inductive reasonings while inductive reasonings support the recourse to inductive methods. (114)

As Rescher goes on to point out, the circularity of the legitimation process and the changes in methods that may result do not weaken the reasoning process: "The circularity at issue is not vicious or vitiating—it is simply a part of that self-supportingness that is a requisite of any adequate cognitive instrumentality" (114). The evolutionary nature of the process also takes the "sting" out of circularity: If the "record" is not positive, then changes are forced in the manner in which ideas are arrived at, or the theories that are used to validate ideas are altered. If our prediction that others will respond favorably to us or our ideas is wrong, an appraisal of how we arrived at the decision is in order. We seek consistency in making accurate predictions, building on past procedures to improve our record. In the past, we have discarded those procedures that prove to be worthless in arriving at accurate judgments. The intellectual landscape is littered with theoretical procedures and concepts purporting to explain natural events. The "sciences" of phrenology, homeopathy, numerology, and other methods have long since been discredited as workable means of improving the historical record. As Rescher (1979) notes, "science has won the evolutionary struggle among various modes of methods of cognitive procedure" (110). The same process of evolutionary development applies to methods of decision-making used in more pragmatic, everyday life situations.

A caveat is in order regarding the "end-result" of an evolutionary process. There is a sense of "ultimate perfection" that permeates the task of improving our decision-making procedures. As in the case of "ultimate truth" in a truth-certification process, there is little likelihood that one will actually achieve perfection. Nevertheless, the opposite is equally untenable—being satisfied with inappropriate or ineffective procedures for making judgments. No one seriously wishes to glorify a consistency that produces falsehood. As procedures are improved, the results are not necessarily any "truer" than before, but the rationale for accepting them should be better grounded. Sloppy procedures do sometimes result in proper claims; sophisticated procedures likewise may produce mistaken or excusable claims. The probability of lessening improper claims is higher with more sophisticated and systematic methods of appraisal and judgment. In addition, the evolutionary nature does not necessarily mean that procedures will synthesize into one "grand design" for justifying arguments. While synthesis may occur in one or more disciplines (Toulmin [1972] argues that this is already the case with atomic physics), it is not an essential aim of such evolutionary development. A "legalistic model" for justifying arguments may work well within the judicial community but may be inappropriate if applied within an academic community.

PRINCIPLE FOUR: The assessment of justification is contextually based.

Contextually grounded beliefs are those which have the approval of a specific audience or community. If held as "contextually basic" (Annis 1978), the beliefs are not questioned by the members; hence to articulate them does not require additional justification. Such beliefs are not "foundations" for granting epistemic status to claims but have sufficient credence to warrant their use in support of community beliefs or actions. When beliefs are not so grounded, they must meet the approval of the community. The standards of approval are those which have met with pragmatic success in the community or field of inquiry. If a person is successful in meeting objections to a claim, it does not mean that the claim is therefore "true" in some final sense. What it does imply is that the requisite performance conditions for making the statement have been met. "Seen in this manner, contextualism is architectonic—it serves as the organizing vehicle within which the operation of pragmatic justification moves forward" (McKerrow 1987b, 219). As one changes contexts, the criteria for justification shift also to whatever is required in the new circumstances. Thus, arguing in a bar over the guilt of an alleged person and arguing in court over the same issue will require meeting different standards of acceptable argument. As one enters "interfield" arenas, one accepts the standards of the new, more "global" community. The same corrigible, evolutionary standards apply to the methods utilized in the global arena.

Methodologically grounded: The corollary this suggests, as should be evident from the preceding discussion, is that the process of justification is based on an analysis of *methods* used to justify beliefs and values. Rather than focusing on the *content* of propositions, the process of justification attends to the manner in which decisions are reached. The advantage this change in focus offers lies in the generic applicability of methods to a wide variety of propositional statements. Rather than ascertaining the viability of single propositions and attempting to improve on their truth-status a methodological focus turns our attention to the criteria and procedures for accepting broad classes of propositions. In Toulmin's (1958) language, methods may be "field-invariant" or "field-dependent." The primary difference would be in their applicability within or across different communities or fields.

PRINCIPLE FIVE: Coherency of beliefs is a major test of their justifiability.

If contextualism serves as the organizing vehicle for assessing the applicability of certain criteria, coherency provides the necessary standard for such assessment. The *systematization* of our beliefs in terms of attributes such as *wholeness, cohesiveness, functional regularity,* and *functional efficacy* provides the basis for determining whether the methods of reasoning are adequate. As noted elsewhere (McKerrow 1987a, 1987b), these attributes function as topoi for determining the coherency of our ideas. The more inferential links that can be said to "fit together" the stronger the rationale for accepting the belief in question. Conversely, the more anomalies there are in the belief set, the weaker the judgment will be (Bonjour 1985; McKerrow 1987b).

There are three corollaries that relate to the judgment of coherency. The initial one relates to the role of *plausibility* in the assessment of beliefs and values. The second concerns the role of *induction,* and the final one assesses *evidence* as it applies in the process of justification.

Plausibility analysis: The determination of a coherent set of beliefs begins with their status as plausible truth-candidates: "A proposition's membership in a p-set [set of plausible propositions] means that this thesis has a supportive foothold in our deliberations— someone or something (some appropriate source) vouches for it. . . . These data are 'givens'—yet they are not given as *truths* but merely as adequately qualified *truth-candidates;* they are simply *purported* or *alleged* truths which—considering the source of the allegation— are in a fair way of being able to make good the claims to truth made on their behalf" (Rescher 1976, 8). This summary contains two concepts worthy of further comment. First, plausibility relates to the *source* of the claim, not to the claim itself. In this fashion, it is differentiated from probability analysis. Where probability assesses the chances of an event occurring from the available alternatives, plausibility assesses the quality of the source that vouches for the claim (Rescher 1976, 28; see McKerrow 1987a, 1987b). While they have different aims, both may be considered in the overall assessment of an argument. Thus, a highly reputable source may assert a claim that is plausible, but not probable; conversely, a disreputable source may assert a highly probable claim.

Rescher interprets "source" in fairly broad terms. A source may be a person (expert or not), oral tradition, common knowledge, memory, sense-perception, conjecture, inferential reasoning, axioms, or any other authorizing principle that provides probative support for a thesis. As an example, we can cite Rescher's (1976) discussion of axiomatic sources:

Suppose a certain group of axiomatically stipulated theses to be such as to stand upon different footings of epistemic firmness or solidity. For example, some are virtually of the status of definitions, others are solidly established principles, and still others are of the status of hypotheses or conjectures. A grading scheme such as the following may now be supposed:

4/4 = 1.00: definitions, quasi-analytic theses
3/4 = .75: fundamental principles, near-uncontestable theses
2/4 = .50: well-supported theses
1/4 = .25: hypotheses, conjectures, "theories" (23)

While in actual practice one need not establish formal gradients for the probative value of various sources, the principle is clear: some sources are better than others in terms of supporting the plausibility of a claim. We implicitly accept the principle in honoring claims published in the *New York Times* and *Washington Post* over those in the *National Enquirer.*

There are several guidelines for the assessment of a set of plausible truth-candidates. First, the lowest rank that can be arrived at is "never to be less than that of the least plausible thesis operative in the derivation" (italicized in original). Second, when conflict occurs between two plausible candidates, the more plausible will be accepted. Third, the overall assessment cannot be less than the least plausible of those in the set. Fourth, logic's negation rule (which prohibits P and not-P from coexisting) does not apply in this context. Fifth, where probability analysis may yield a lower probability in a distribution table of alternatives, plausibility analysis may be additive (Rescher 1976, 12–55). Finally, the analysis fits within the framework established by Booth and Harman: "A positive presumption always favors the most plausible contentions among the available alternatives. It must stand until set aside by something yet more plausible or by direct-counter-evidence" (Rescher 1976, 55; McKerrow 1987a). Systematic assent is the rule rather than the exception.

The goal of plausibility assessment is to determine the most consistent possible set of beliefs among a group of potentially inconsistent contenders. When faced with alternatives that cannot *all* be equally correct, the task is to find those alternatives that, when combined, produce the most consistent subset from among the possibilities. Rescher offers a complex and rigorously analytical process for the determination of these "maximally consistent subsets" [m.c.s.] of a set of propositions. An example, adapted from Rescher's account of plausibility indexing (the assigning of values to plausibility accounts) may clarify the process, as well as indicate the analytic rigor involved. Assume the following set of propositions and assigned values:

	Proposition			Plausibility Index Value
1.	p	v	q	.5
2.	p	⊃	r	.8
3.	q	⊃	r	.2
4.		~r		.8

From the perspective of formal logic, this "p-set" yields the following subsets of maximally consistent propositions:

Retain	Reject	Retain	Reject
S_1 = 1, 2, 3	4	.5, .8, .2	.8
S_2 = 1, 2, 4	3	.5, .8, .8	.2
S_3 = 1, 3, 4	2	.5, .2, .8	.8
S_4 = 2, 3, 4	1	.8, .2, .8	.5

In analyzing these subsets, two general principles apply: (1) high plausibility alternatives should not be rejected in seeking consistency within a subset; and (2) low plausible alternatives should not be retained in seeking consistency within a subset. Given these, S_1 and S_3 force the rejection of highly plausible alternatives (as indicated by the "value" attached), hence are not acceptable subsets to work with. S_2 and S_4 both contain the highest plausible alternatives, hence emerge as *inevitable consequences*—either subset can be used as the basis for further exploration of the issue. As promised above, the account also demonstrates the logical rigor required if one follows Rescher's guidelines exactly. While the formal application of m.c.s. is not essential in ordinary argument analysis, the basic principle, that logical options do exist that are more plausible than other accounts, is nonetheless an appropriate one to retain.

Plausibility, as these comments suggest, is an essential component in the process of systematizing knowledge. Given the existence of inconsistent sets of propositions, the reductive process of plausibility assessment seeks to eliminate excess baggage, as it were, as either false or as insufficiently supported by sources. As Hilpinen (1982) notes, in Rescher's approach, "our knowledge is not 'justified' by the data (in the traditional sense of justification), but *extracted* from the data by a process of systematization and error elimination" (38).

The role of induction: In the context employed here, induction takes on added significance. Rather than seen as formal logic's "weaker" procedure because of its inherent inability to provide certain conclusions, induction is accepted for what it does offer—"the best *available* answer" from among possible alternatives (Rescher 1980, 7). Instead of being viewed in traditional argument terms as a form of reasoning that goes from specific to general (an incorrect view anyway), induction is used to assess the "fit" between what is already known and what may be the case. Thus, it serves a central role in systematizing knowledge. Seen as a "question-answering" technique rather than as an *"inferential* (conclusion deriving) procedure,"* induction becomes a tool for estimating the best fit or systematization of information at hand: "Induction is a matter of obtaining the optimum truth-estimate in terms of the systematic best fit secured through plausibilistic cogency" (Rescher 1980, 19–20, 27). The criteria for systematicity, referred to earlier, serve as the basis for assessing inductively arrived at conclusions. As an example: "In the absence of explicit counter-indications, a thesis about unscrutinized cases that *conforms to a uniformity present throughout the data at our disposal* is more plausible than any of its regularity-discordant contraries—and the more extensive this pattern-conformity, the more highly plausible the thesis" (Rescher 1980, 41). The forms may be simple generalization, statistical reasoning, sign reasoning, curve-fitting processes, or even philological analysis. In each case, criteria such as uniformity, simplicity, regularity can be applied to assess the probative value or plausibility of the induction. Seen in this perspective, induction serves a *regulative* function rather than a *constitutive* one (Rescher 1980). The distinction is a critical one, as it moves induction from its traditional argumentative role of creating new knowledge to one of managing knowledge, including observations that take us beyond the present information, so as to provide an adequate explanation.

Evidence: In all cases of reasoning to justified beliefs, there will never be a case in which all of the necessary data are available. Thus, following the basic rationale for inductive leaps, there will always be an "evidential gap" between "the *assertoric content* of an objective claim—the range of what we become committed to in making it— from the *supportive data* we ever actually obtain for it" (Rescher 1982, 10). This claim does more than simply recognize that rhetorical claims are contingent. The contingency of such claims is "a fact of epistemic life" (Rescher 1982, 14). If we were forced to make decisions on the basis of the assertoric content of claims, we would never be able to come to a conclusion. For this reason, Rescher distinguishes between "use-conditions" and "truth-conditions": the former are "indications of the circumstances in which a sentence is warrantably assertable"; the latter "detail the ontological (world oriented) circumstances that must obtain for a sentence to be true" (Rescher 1982, 3). From a pragmatic perspective, the "use-conditions" are satisfied in the employment of the information in ordinary living, while the "truth-conditions" may or may not be sufficient. Rescher's "use-conditions" are no more than the performance conditions necessary to avoid improper or nonexcusable claims. The gap between use and truth conditions is further support for leaving argument analysis at the level of pragmatic justification, rather than insisting on the truth conditions of epistemic justification. Argument analysis can incorporate truth conditions as part of the analysis—"What does it take for the statement to be true?" is a legitimate question. Nevertheless, determining whether the use conditions have been satisfied is the central task of such analysis.

PRINCIPLE SIX: Pragmatic justification is a rational concept.

The consideration of rationality is an appropriate final principle, as it makes little sense to examine pragmatic justification if the processes involved lead inexorably into irrationality. However, what is *not* meant by "rationality" is easier to demarcate than what *is*. In the first place, rationality is not restricted to mechanistic tools for the analysis of logical validity claims, nor is it the sole province of scientific method. Nor is rationality dominated exclusively by the tenets of theoretical reason, while "practical reasoning" operates in a different sphere. Rather, *rationality is grounded in cultural perceptions of what constitutes appropriate standards of individual and community conduct.* Witchcraft rituals are as rational as episcopal rituals—both are grounded in the cultural mores of the society that sanctions their existence. Within this context, pragmatic justification operates as a decision-making process that embraces three senses of rationality with regard to belief and action: *methodological, moral,* and *prudential*. Each of these can be seen as a discrete type of rationality. Considered as a whole, they function as interdependent forms of rational acceptance.

Methodological rationality: The *procedures* we employ to determine justifiability constitute a rational process. Rationality is inherent in following through on the dictates of such parameters as uniformity and cohesiveness in the assessment of plausible beliefs. Rationality also is inherent in adhering to the dictates of a community-based set of performance conditions for asserting that something is the case. To act in total disregard of either is to act irrationally, or to assert claims without rational warrant. Furthermore, correcting improper procedures and testing different methods to improve the quality of judgments made are rational actions.

Moral rationality: Moral rationality refers to the "goodness" implicit in the claim. As Ehninger (1968) observed, the final judgment of the "validity" of an argument lies in the person's own sense of moral obligation to acquiesce when the opposing argument is seen as stronger than one's own position. Moser (1985) argues in similar terms: one has an obligation to accept those claims that, on the basis of the evidence available, are more valued as moral claims, or are conducive to the individual or common good, assuming that one "has a preference for morally advantageous belief" (219).

Prudential rationality: This form of rationality is a response to a "what's in it for me?" or "what's in it for us?" kind of question. Acceptance has to be seen as advantageous in some manner, over and above simply enhancing one's moral goodness. Prudence would appear to dictate that acceptance, at minimum, is going to leave unaltered one's own social status in the community. By accepting, one would not be prudent if one's psychological or even financial well-being were put in jeopardy (Moser 1985, 216).

Organic unity: In the best of all possible worlds, methodological, moral, and prudential rationality converge in support of a single claim. The question "should I believe or act?" is not decided in terms of truth-certifying judgments alone. One's moral sense, as well as prudential sense of well-being, also may be invoked in making determinations about what to believe or how to act. The same distinctions may be applied at the community or societal level as well. For belief or action to be considered "rationally permissible" only one of these forms of rationality need be justified.

Even when all three forms are justified, belief or action is not necessarily easy to determine. As parts of an organic whole, the three senses of rationality may not be equally "advantageous." A conflict between one or more of the types of rationality is always a possibility. A claim may be morally defensible but not methodologically supported. It may be supported by methodological assessment but not be in one's best prudential interest. Moser (1985) offers a solution to the potential conflict between/among these possibilities. Beginning with the assumption that an individual's own preferences should govern the decision, Moser sets forth an analytically rigorous decision principle based on an "all things considered" view of rationality:

AR. If a rational obligation of one sort—call it O_e—prescribes that S should believe that p, and a rational obligation of a different sort—call it O_m—prescribes that S should deny (withhold) that p (and S has no other particular rational obligations bearing on his [her] believing, denying, or withholding that p), then S is **ATC** [all things considered] rationally obligated to fulfill O_e rather than O_m if and only if (i) the fulfillment of O_e is more likely than the fulfillment of O_m, on S's total evidence, to satisfy S's superior preference, (ii) the fulfillment of O_e is more likely than the fulfillment of neither O_e nor O_m on S's total evidence, to satisfy S's superior preference, and (iii) S is capable of coming to recognize the truth of (i) and (ii) from reflection on his evidence. (225–26)

Put more simply, if one has a conflict between two rationally defensible positions, one chooses that which is more likely to satisfy one's own preferences. The same logical principle, devoid perhaps of the rigor of biconditionality, would apply at the community level. Given a conflict between prudential and moral rationality, the community should choose that which, all things considered, is most likely to promote its "superior" preference in the given instance. A decision in such conflict cases does not mean that a person is any less rational; it only means that the person has been forced to choose between competing preferences and has made that choice known to others. The decision by Fawn Hall to assist Oliver North in the shredding of critical documents as the carefully concealed Contra-related actions became public could be assessed in terms of such a conflict—to choose personal loyalty does not imply irrationality; it only suggests what preferences one has chosen.

Rationality is a multifaceted concept. While it includes a methodological dimension, it possesses value-laden implications as well. To employ an "all things considered" principle in choosing between competing rational preferences implies an understanding of both one's own value hierarchy and that of the community (what is the "superior" preference?). While it might be rational to argue for a standard that is in some way independent of community or personal values, even the establishment of such a criterion implies a value judgment about how decisions will be reached. Whether a standard of rationality is considered independent, or as an integral part of the context, it cannot be separated from the value structure of the person or the community. What is articulated in the foregoing principle acknowledges the contextual nature in which rational processes are employed, as well as the multifaceted nature of rationality itself.

Conclusion

Whatever else is said about rhetoric or argument, the concept of justification holds a central place. Set forth as a series of principles of warranted assertability, pragmatic justification does not limit analysis to the dictates of technical reason. Nor does the concept commit us to an analytic epistemology aimed at producing apodictic claims. Pragmatic justification encompasses both beliefs and values, is truth-seeking rather than truth-certifying, is nonfoundationalist with respect to its truth-seeking status, is contextually based, is assessed by recourse to the coherency of belief sets, and is a rational process. While its centrality does not impute a privileged status over other approaches to the analysis of arguments, the process of justification is an integral part of the act of criticism.

Given the above set of principles, justification is the heart and soul of systematic assent. The principles advanced in this essay comprise a theoretical grounding in which one presumes that there is a reason for questioning the adequacy of a claim. Justification comes into play only when the "principle of conservatism" appears inapplicable, and one has a reason to doubt. One's orientation, and this is the thrust of Booth's perspective, moves from doubting everything to a positive appraisal of the grounds for assent. Where assent is possible, one can presume that the requisite performance conditions for advancing a claim have been met. Where assent appears to be questionable, one can evaluate the adequacy of the information and the methods by which it is presumed to be justified, within the context of the principles of pragmatic justification. The evaluation should yield a claim that one has sufficient warrant or grounds to assert or reasons why assent is problematic. Where prior assent proves to be wrongfully given, one can evaluate the conditions under which the claim was advanced to determine whether assent was granted to an "excusable" or "nonexcusable" claim. Seen in the context of these possibilities, the "principles of warranted assertability" function as the grounding for a reasonable approach to everyday decision-making. Freed from the strictures of a formal mechanism for deciding what to believe and how to act, the principles provide a suitable, and better suited, alternative perspective on the justification of claims.

3

Realism and the Rhetoric of Assent

Earl Croasmun

> If what is good, what is right, what is true, is only what the
> individual "chooses" to "invent," then we are outside the traditions
> of civility. We are back in the war of all men against all men.
> —Walter Lippmann (1955, 134–55)

In his survey of rhetorical scholarship more than a decade ago, Michael Leff noted a desire of theorists to seek "Ariadne's thread," a unifying theme running through the literature, a hope that some rhetorical macro-theory will lead "into a position of theoretical clarity" (Leff 1978, 91). The clash of competing macro-theories since Leff's article makes it clear that, for many, just any thread will not do. Specifically, the metaphor of Ariadne's thread suggests two requirements for a macro-theory of rhetoric. First, when Theseus entered the labyrinth he had a sword to slay the minotaur as well as a thread to provide direction. Second, Ariadne's thread led him out of the labyrinth as well as in. Presently the most prevalent and accepted (often implicitly) macro-theory is rhetorical relativism or rhetorical consensus theory. This essay argues that consensus theory should be rejected, as it does not deal adequately with minotaurs and other problems one can encounter in life. The most sharply drawn alternative, rhetorical objectivism, will then be shown to fail the second requirement: while an objectivist theory may help deal with the minotaur, it does so in a way that can leave one forever inside the labyrinth. One alternative, used as a point of contrast throughout this essay, is rhetorical realism.

The current battleground in the ongoing clash of relativists and objectivists, and the backdrop of some discussion here, is the rhetoric of inquiry. Scholars from many disciplines are now aware of argument study. "[T]he rhetoric of inquiry turns toward details of argumentation in substantive fields of research" (Nelson and Megill 1986, 31).[1] My goal is not to favor or oppose this rhetorical turn but to examine what Lyne and Howe (1986, 145) call its unfortunate and unnecessary "focus on relativism in its various guises (including loose interpretations of paradigms, perspectivism, Weltanschauungen, etc.)."[2] Simons's fear after the Iowa Conference on Rhetoric of the Human Sciences was that "what Rorty and others defend in the name of pragmatism and community will become an unfettered relativism, incapable of error-correction" (Simons 1985, 58). This result has already become popular with rhetoricians, but relativism lies not in the basic project of the rhetoric of inquiry—only in one possible approach. A stronger realism is needed, a realism that makes inquiry central to epistemology. Realism sees inquiry as most valuable when viewed as inquiry into the one world that is shared in some way by all living beings.

A useful contrast for rhetorical realism is the rhetorical consensus theory of truth, or "consensus theory." Beginning with Robert Scott (1964), it has mainly been developed by him and Barry Brummett, although Richard Vatz and others can be included. Vatz (1973) agrees with Brummett and Scott on most points discussed here, and if he is slighted in mention it is only due to the greater amount of writings from Brummett and Scott. The frequency with which these names are mentioned should also not mislead the reader that only three people hold these views.[3] Brummett, Scott, and Vatz are chosen because they give the clearest, most consistent, and best-argued defense of relativism based in rhetoric. They explicitly argue for views that others often take for granted. Even those who neither agree nor disagree with them (for example, Warnick 1983, Blair 1987, Foss and Gill 1987) tend to cite them as the main authors of consensus theory.

Just as realist epistemology had to go beyond naive realism, rhetorical relativists such as Brummett, Scott, and Vatz have gone beyond naive relativism. Differing from Rorty's contrast of study of social practices to a concentration on epistemological issues, rhetorical relativists tie the two together and place social practices at the heart of epistemology. By keeping a sense of external reality rather than focusing only on language they differ from some postmodernists.[4] The sophistication of their view, which helps avoid self-referential paradoxes and other pitfalls of naive relativism, comes from seeing language-symbol systems as an unavoidable barrier between people and objective reality, and from "arguing for the ontological primacy of the symbolic, from which reality and experience are derived." At a very basic level they see all truth and knowledge as rooted in social practice: "For the consensus theorist, then, consensus within a community shapes reality into what it is, and it is purely an act of faith or imagination to posit that there is an objective reality somewhere." When asked for a definition of truth, Brummett answers "for me, it's consensus" (Brummett 1986, 95, 94, 96). Rhetorical relativists answer the question of when, if ever, assent can be justified by finding justification in existing beliefs and social practices or nowhere at all.

A serious and consistent relativism has several problems: it denigrates dissent, it only entails intersubjectivity to the extent that it entails nihilistic subjectivity, it accounts for persuasion only in behavioristic or sophistic terms, and it reads history incorrectly. Consensus theory fails the first test of rhetorical epistemology: it does not deal with the minotaur.

The Problem of Dissent

A consensus epistemology says that people *ought* not hold minority, unpopular, or dissenting views, as was argued by Orr (1978, 270). Rhetorical relativists define and test for truth by consensus. Truth is agreement. "If nobody else shares the meaning that I give to sensory data, then I will usually conclude that those meanings are not *true*, and I will try to grasp the meanings others give to that experience" (Brummett 1976, 34). To be in a minority or view things differently is to be wrong.

Importantly, Brummett *acknowledges* the problem of dissent and responds that univocal consensus of an entire society or culture is not needed for intersubjective validation. "[O]ne has a wide variety of groups with which one *could* identify. . . . Although one often *does* agree with the majority of those in one's consensual groups, nobody argues that one *should*. One could also only accept the consensus of a minority" (1982, 428). "The majority's view of reality is true *for them*," he says, "but the minority's view is true *for the minority*" (1980, 12). Thus one can confirm *anything* by careful choice of a referent group. Intersubjectivity collapses to pure subjectivity and becomes pragmatically empty. Assent is warranted whenever one wishes to assent. For a minority, even *a minority of one*, believing makes it true "for them." The circular precept is that one should believe that which one does believe.

According to consensus theory one should confirm values and beliefs by testing them intersubjectively, but one also has the privilege of selecting the "others" for an acceptable consensus; anyone else can be ignored. The result is like trying someone for a crime but allowing them to select their own jury. It is easy to see the consensus-conferring referent groups chosen by true believers of any ideology: beliefs are confirmed by those who already agree with the beliefs being "tested." If consensus theory is believed, "Am I not now forced to accept any piece of silliness that any fanatic wants to advance," Booth (1974, 106) asks, "provided only that he can get somebody to assent to it?" Zarefsky (1976, 4) notes the obvious: "If whatever an audience may be induced to believe is granted the status of knowledge, the meaning of 'to know' would seem debased, to say the least."

Let me be clear: I am not saying that consensus theorists would agree with the above. Brummett in particular steadfastly distinguishes *inter*subjectivity from subjectivity. However my point is a clear *result* of Brummett's only *defense* against the problem of dissent. It is the only interpretation of his phrase "the consensus of a minority" that is not oxymoronic. It is a result of any view that says "Perhaps intersubjective theorists have been content too often to argue that views of reality are true if created intersubjectively in social groups. It is more consistent, however, to say that a view of reality is true *for that group*" (1980, 6). This view of intersubjectivity cheapens the currency of consensus by allowing any group or person to manufacture their own version. This manufactured consensus would not have to bear any value outside the confirming "group" since only the group members would need accept it as legal tender. A person could limit his referent group for validating and testing ideas to include only Democrats, only teenagers, or *potentially only himself*. Any standards of other groups, people, or communities would be irrelevant.

Fragmentation of validating consensus leads to another problem: it cuts against the very idea of intergroup or intercultural discourse. At best, discourse with other groups would be polite conversation with no real discussion of differences in values or beliefs. Why seek assent from those not in one's own referent group? They live in a "separate reality." Consensus theory makes existing views given and static.

At other times consensus theorists try to avoid an extreme subjectivism where one could accept only oneself as a valid consensus test. Scott and Brummett in particular deflect common criticisms of relativism (such as "you cannot condemn Nazis") by *broadening* the idea of consensus or validating group. "It would be a mistake to narrow the concept of community, to picture a person's relevant ethical community as the two or three hundred most significant people of his or her childhood. Communities that generate ethical standards must be seen as interlocking and continuous rather than as discrete" (Brummett 1981, 297). Different cultures exist, but Scott suggests they have "permeable membranes" (1976, 265). We should judge across social boundaries, for we are "in community" with the world.

Brummett argues that community membership is not voluntary.

"Because the self is a field of selves, *having been made* by other people places a person firmly, it might be said irreversibly, within a community and thus within its ethical jurisdiction" (1981, 297). There is no choice. One need not agree with the community and one has no option to choose another to "identify" with. Brummett says communities are not formed by individuals who *choose* to join them. The community is prior and controlling, and the "individual is thus derived from the social" (1986, 92). This principle is true even for dissenters and critics: "But even the defiant criminal is still *subject* to moral judgment by his or her community because membership in the community is durable; it cannot be willed away" (1981, 297). Gone is any responsibility for moral beliefs; one must discern and adhere to existing community standards.

Positing a universal community or interlocking permeable communities makes a distinction between subjectivism and intersubjectivism *only* by returning to majoritarian rule. The implication is that one *should* agree with the consensus. The fact that "the community" disagrees with some person or group brands that person or group as wrong. Dissenters are irreversibly "in" this community and should "get in step" with the community drummer rather than listening to their own. The contradiction with Brummett's refutation of the problem of dissent is clear: one is necessarily within a community and should adhere to the community standards. Dissenters cannot leave the community and are subject to its judgments. This view of dissent is also inconsistent with other aspects of consensus theory: they are still relative values that come from what people happen to believe regardless of what those beliefs are, but the task of individuals is to discover this consensus and live by it rather than "create" their own reality. Commitment and responsibility for choices are lessened and the problem of dissent reemerges. This line of argument is the *only* response by Scott, Brummett, Vatz, or others to equating consensus theory with subjectivism.

The net of consensus can be cast in a broad or narrow sweep. The first alternative leads to majoritarianism, a charge which consensus theorists take seriously and try to avoid. The second leads to fragmentation and solipsism, a charge which the same people try to avoid. They admit the gravity of *each* charge in turn, but refute it only by jumping to the other alternative.

The Problem of Persuasion

Consensus theory has a serious gap for any view stressing the importance of rhetoric: there is no clear stance on the nature or *possibility* of persuasion. How does one support or attack a claim, or persuade an audience of an ethical belief? Consensus theory gives a simple answer: truth is agreement. One looks for a factual presence or absence of consensus. Symbols are ontologically primary. "For rhetorical relativists, the creation of standards or criteria thus becomes part of the consensus process" (Jerry 1987, 122).

The ideas of intersubjectivity and being *persuaded* to accept one consensus over another pose a requirement for consensus theory: there should be some idea of *what counts as a good reason*. Without some standard one is left with what Scott terms "mere" or "vicious" relativism, and what both Scott and Brummett try to avoid. Scott defends relativism based in "the fabric of social commitments" and attacks what he calls a "vicious" relativism that disregards communal standards (1976, 263–66). Brummett sanctions moral judgment of others and *opposes* those who would be "a sort of moral chameleon" and who argue that "communicators should *understand* each other's position *in lieu of* judging others" (1981, 292, 291).

The standard of rhetorical relativists is to base judgment on the judgment of others, without identifying how one chooses the "others" with whom to concur, so assent is always-and-only justified if we observe others assenting. This perspective on persuasion omits the very elements Booth makes central to his definition of the rhetoric of assent: "the art of discovering *good* reasons, finding what *really warrants* assent because any *reasonable* person *ought* to be persuaded by what has been said" (Booth 1974, xiv, emphasis added). Consensus may be true or false: the fact of a consensus can create a presumption of truth but it is a rebuttable presumption that for Booth does not have the "ontological primacy" of a literal consensus theory of truth. "It is reasonable to grant (one *ought* to grant) some degree of credence to whatever qualified men and women agree on, *unless* one has specific and stronger reasons to disbelieve" (Booth 1974, 101, emphasis in original). Consensus theory excludes the word "qualified" and then teaches that there *are* no stronger reasons.

Picking up on a now-popular example, Brummett suggests that "If consensus did not make a belief in the flat earth true for Croasmun and Cherwitz (and for me!), it is only because we have been *persuaded* by the round earth consensus" (1982, 427). He accepts one consensus and rejects another. But *why*? Brummett is confronted with a "flat earth consensus" and a "round earth consensus," and he chooses to believe the latter. Does he seek out and align himself with the round earth consensus because it fits his preexisting beliefs? Does he join for sociological reasons and then simply adhere to whatever its earth-shape world view happens to be? Does he count up the numbers of people on each side? Or does he agree with "round earthers" because he thinks that there are some good (extra-consensual) reasons to believe that the earth is indeed round even if others disagree?

Railsback (1983, 353) tries to avoid this example by trivializing the relationship between language and the world, noting that the statement "the earth is round" is not true in a language where "round" means "#." This is irrelevant, since Railsback, Brummett, and I seem to agree on the meaning of "round." Were I confronting someone who spoke this strange new language I would try to ascertain if there was an equivalent to my English word "round." If "*" means "round," I would change my claim to "the earth is *." Railsback's emphasis on the language of claims is also inconsistent, since she (1983, 358) discusses the implications of the ancient Greeks' actually saying "the earth is round" although they surely did not speak English.

People cannot be persuaded to accept a consensus *because* it is a consensus. There must be a criterion beyond examining the beliefs of "society" or "the community" or "others," for one is left (like flat earth and round earth consensuses) with choices of multiple, *competing* consensuses. "[C]onsensus theorists argue that ultimately it is a *consensus* that determines 'justification' or 'sufficiency'" (Brummett 1982, 427), but if justification itself is *determined* by consensus how can one ever judge that any specific consensus is more justified than another? If all beliefs are true for those who believe them, beliefs become *self*-justifying; changing one's mind is necessarily unjustifiable. Flat earth groups have their own little "consensus," which makes their view seem to them "justified" and "sufficient." Consensus theory raises this sociological oddity to ontological primacy.

Obviously "people are *persuaded* to rally with one consensus or another," but Brummett's only basis for persuasion (except for consensus appeals, just discussed, and objective bases, which he rejects) is a reference to "vacuous appeals to airy principles or to neurotic fears and ambitions" (1982, 428–29). He does *not* point to these as exemplars of ethical persuasion, but they are the only ones given. To choose such a basis for the rhetoric of inquiry either demeans the former term or makes the latter hollow. Taken seriously, the position of rhetorical relativists on persuasion collapses to discussing "things that aren't there," for they despair ever knowing things that *are* there. "Brummett's theory purports to tell us something exciting: it purports to tell us how we know things about the world. But all it really does is to define the problem out of existence" (Harpine 1985, 103). Neither a sophistic rhetoric nor a purely behaviorist account of persuasion is adequate for a theory of inquiry.

The Results of Relativism

A major argument used to support consensus theory is the oft-repeated claim that rejection of relativism leads to evil, to tyranny, "to the Inquisition" (Brummett 1982, 430). Consensus theorists claim that belief in an objective reality leads to a feeling of certainty in one's own *present grasp* of that reality. Thus armed with Truth, they contend, objectivists may commit atrocities or other actions they consider (objectively?) undesirable. Before addressing this claim, one should note that the Inquisition is a damaging choice of examples. Rorty uses the basic tenets of consensus theory, not realism, to argue that Galileo was no more true or rational in his views on astronomy than was his Inquisitor, Cardinal Bellarmine (Sayers 1985, 92). If one believes that those who disagree (including Galileo) are "irreversibly" members of "the community" and within its "ethical jurisdiction," that this situation "cannot be willed away," that the individual is "derived from the social," and that the consensus of the community is immune to contradictory standards, "justified," "sufficient," and in fact "ontologically primary," the implication is clear. "The neo-marxists of the Frankfurt school have been prominent in attacking 'realism,' 'truth,' and 'objectivity' as propagandistic concepts which justify the 'scientific' exploitation of the powerless by the powerful. Yet historical examples from the time of Bellarmine to the time of Stalin show that powerful states have been allergic to realism. They have preferred that science not only serve the interests of the community, but preserve its cherished beliefs rather than challenging them" (Davenport 1987, 378). Relativists offer no reason a believer in Absolute Truth would be more tyrannical or evil than a defender of Absolute Community Consensus.

The first response to the social dangers of nonrelativism is that, before assessing the merits of this argument, a reader of the literature will quickly notice a deficiency. The indictment, an assertion of historical and sociological fact, is unsupported! In Brummett's 1982 article he outlines the position in one paragraph but gives no support or examples. He only says that the dangers of nonrelativism "have been argued elsewhere," with a footnote to his 1981 article on ethics, but the subject is not raised in that article. He defends his version of relativism against standard attacks ("relativism is self-refuting," "it requires acceptance of all standards," etc.), but the specter of rampant nonrelativism is never discussed. Scott too takes for granted that nonrelativism is untenable. Although he outlines the assertion in greater detail he again leaves the factual claim unsupported. Even his phrasing begs the question: he argues that "contingency" is preferable to "the spirit of axiomatic detachment"

(1976, 264). It is an open question, of course, whether the beliefs that we "construct" our own world, that any view we hold is correct "for us," and that there are multiple and contradictory "truths" and "realities" do indeed lead to contingency and toleration of dissent. It is also doubtful that "axiomatic detachment" is the only alternative to relativism.

McCloskey (1985, 39–40) defends relativism without such assertions, and in fact he acknowledges the opposite view that realism can be an antidote to irrationalism. His defense of relativism, however, amounts to suggesting that ideas do not have consequences. He ends up in the position that Fuller (1989, 133–51) calls "antitheory," a view that theory does not matter.

A second problem with the relativists' fear of realism is that they misconstrue realism. Their frightful scenarios begin with some person being dogmatically certain, beyond any doubt, of knowing Absolute Truth. As Orr (1978, 266) and others note, this is a false depiction. To feel that some aspects of reality have independent status and claims about reality can be true or false or partially true says nothing about *which* claims are true. The relativist confuses belief in *an* objective reality with belief in the absolute truth of claims on the *nature* of that reality. The only reason for this leap to absolutism is a passing suggestion that some might be "tempted," and even this temptation is not handled consistently. Scott (1967, 10) claims, "Accepting the notion that truth exists, may be known, and communicated leads logically to the position that there should be only two modes of discourse: a neutral presenting of data among equals and a persuasive leading of inferiors by the capable." Brummett (1984, 119) sometimes denies this "logical" temptation: "to be convinced of something need not entail dogmatic conviction."

It is more likely that acceptance of a chance of error, belief that one can move closer to or farther from the truth, would reduce the dogmatic, unreflective reification of beliefs. For example, I am convinced that either Jimmy Hoffa is still alive or he is not. I do not know *which* is true, but I am sure that one is and the other is not. I can understand how one person might believe that Hoffa is dead and another that he is alive, but I do not see how both can be correct in the same way at the same time without an incredible obfuscation of the claim.

Accepting some aspects of reality as being independent of our grasp of them, combined with the observation that there *is* in fact universal agreement on virtually no truth-claims, makes one thoroughly aware of human fallibility and the impossible-dream status of absolute certainty. At the same time, seeing one's beliefs concerning reality as having a referent, beyond a social reality constructed within one's own mind, leaves the possibility of improving, of acquiring greater insight and accuracy. To claim on the other hand that we can have no knowledge without absolute certainty, to say that our beliefs are not much but "they are mine, and they are *the only beliefs I have,*" invites dogmatism and a closed mind. In Brummett's own words, they are "like Lyndon Johnson's presidency, the only values the relativist has. Furthermore, those values are true for him or her and his or her group, just as values of cannibalism or of absolutism are true for cannibals and absolutists. Because values are true for the relativist, and because those are the only sort of values people have, the relativist has the same moral responsibility or motivation that anybody else has" (1981, 294–95). Combining this with impossibility of certainty leads to a deep epistemic pessimism. Not only would we have no basis for our beliefs but we would have no hope of ever having one. There would be no chance, not only for human perfectibility but also for improvement. Consensus theory means "this is as good as it gets."

Rhetorical relativism praises intersubjectivity yet robs it of any function or value; why seek intersubjective validation if we feel that in principle and *of necessity* everyone else is equally in the dark? It would stifle intersubjective testing and comparison. Obviously there are different ways of seeing the world; the question is whether any of them (and which ones) can be defended as better. To move from competing *views* of reality to "multiple, contradictory realities," to condone the argument-evasion of "that may be true for you but not necessarily true for me," implies that discussion and intersubjectivity lack value.

Praising intersubjectivity and depriving it of any use leads to a third shortcoming: the case for relativism is advanced by starting on nonrelativistic premises. Consensus theory places value on tolerance and open-mindedness. When Brummett contends that we can justifiably evaluate and oppose the ethical beliefs of others, he stresses that one would not be condemning a past act but suggesting future improvement, always "with an openness to counter-persuasion" (1981, 295). A reviewer suggests Scott and Brummett argue for tolerance from pragmatic self-interest ("I'll be polite if you will"), not as a moral value, but while it is an interesting and frighteningly amoral view it is not the one found in Scott (1967, 16) or Brummett (1976, 39–40).

My point is not that consensus theory appeals to tolerance without strictly "justifying" it within the theory; if relativism is taken seriously there is no persuasive force to values like "contingency" and "tolerance." Vatz says, "No situation can have a nature independent of the perceptions of its interpreter" and feels that this "clearly increases the rhetor's moral responsibility. . . . [T]he rhetor is responsible for what he chooses to make salient" (1973, 154, 158). But if no situation has *moral* implications beyond the rhetor's own perception then a rhetor has no moral responsibility but a *self-willed* one.

Using the value of tolerance as an argument *for* rhetorical relativism requires value judgments on how people *ought* to behave toward others. A person can say "I like intolerance; it is true *for me*," and it is hard to find an answer in consensus theory. A relativist can say "I do not like intolerance" or "many in our community do not like it, and we therefore have the right to judge you," but not much more. Seaton (1980, 284) notes the result: "If all opinions are valid, then a resolution of disputes through a search for the truth is impossible, and resolution through either fraud (the option of at least some of the Sophists) or force appears as the alternative. In any case, debate and free discussion are useless, and, if they are retained by a society, can be defended only as non-rational preferences."

If I disagree with someone on an important matter I could try to persuade him to change his mind, ignore him, trick him, bribe him, or try to kill him. Consensus theory would eliminate the first option since "community standards" are the only bases for persuasion. The fact that we disagree in the first place means one of us rejects the community consensus or we differ in our grasp of it. Ignoring people only works for matters that are unimportant or do not involve conflicting interests. If this is true, one is left only with undesirable choices, and "if there is no common ground between two individuals or groups for discussion of some strategic moral issue, a struggle to the death is at least as plausible and as likely a result as is tolerance" (Devine 1987, 138). It may be, as Rorty suggests, that force sometimes *is* the only solution (Davenport 1987, 393). A realist rhetoric of inquiry, however, would suggest that there is indeed some common ground for debate and commensurability of arguments. Perspectives can be compared and theories "can be critically discussed, and shown to be erroneous, without killing any authors or burning any books," leading Popper (1976, 292) to conclude that *"critical reason is the only alternative to violence so far discovered."* In contrast to some who tie argument and power together, this view would see argument as an alternative to power. Even in matters where power issues are highly relevant, symbolic use of power can to some degree be substituted for actual use of power (see, for example, Tucker and Wilson 1980, 42–51). A serious relativism undercuts this very idea of critical reason. A consensus theorist must always depend on the kindness of strangers, while having no reason to hope that their world has kindness as a socially constructed value.

Finally there is a fourth problem with the claim that non-relativism is socially harmful: it is factually wrong. The claim is one of historical and sociological fact and rather than detail their case Scott and Brummett leave proof to the reader's sense of history. They fail this test. It is popular in rhetorical circles to call someone "positivist." Relativists sometimes use the term in the manner of "Communist" thirty years ago. This usage creates an interesting problem for defenders of relativism: they never show that adherence to positivism produces the feared horrors and atrocities. Discussions of ethics inevitably get around to "Nazi examples," and I will not make an exception, although racism and Marxism-Leninism examples would do as well. Interestingly, positivism was a grave threat to the rise of fascism. Far from being complementary, the two ideologies were incompatible. "For them [logical positivists], the rigors of empirical verification were the antidote against the wild and far from merely academic metaphysics that was popular in Europe at the time. This is the reason for their great success, and the reason for Hitler's condemnation of them" (Solomon 1977, 200). On the other extreme, Lenin too feared and fought against positivism (Putnam 1981, 124). This is not a defense of positivism but it suggests that rejection of relativism does not necessarily lead to the feared consequences.

I do not know of many atrocities where the perpetrator felt philosophically or ethically *compelled* to commit such acts. Many atrocities are committed for expediency however; they are done to eliminate a barrier or get a political, economic, or personal gain and there are no strongly held moral beliefs *preventing* the expedient act. Thus Hartung (1954, 123) calls Nazis relativists: "[T]he German program of genocide [was] directed against certain peoples whose way of life differed somewhat from theirs. They, too, argued for cultural relativity, but can hardly be accused of practicing the tolerance which cultural relativists insist ought to be practiced." Patterson (1973–74, 126) uses South African apartheid and treatment of American Indians to prove that relativism "can easily be used to rationalize inaction, complacency and even the vilest forms of oppression."

The preceding analysis assumes a consistent relativism. The problem is worse with a partial or limited relativism. When pushed, one may avoid "Nazi examples" by saying "you have to draw a line *somewhere*." Arguing that tolerance of difference and openness to persuasion are *a priori* values, not themselves needing consensual validation, would be an example of an inconsistent relativism. This drawing of a line opens the door to using relativism as a rationalization or persuasive cloak for one's biases. Relativism becomes a jack-et to be worn when useful and discarded when uncomfortable. Drawing a line means selecting a point where it is to be drawn, and Bryan (1983, 643–95) argues that in practice relativism is often used for political ends. A facade of tolerance and openness is used, and a line is drawn according to the user's own interests and ideology. To say I can sometimes adhere to consensus theory to justify my actions but can at other times "draw a line" with no basis in consensus theory for when or where the line *should* be drawn means I can selectively use consensus theory to justify any action I desire.

An *absence* of firmly held epistemological or ethical belief, both in theory and in historical perspective, can be as bad as or worse than even extreme cases of absolutism. As argued earlier, serious relativism leads to epistemic and ethical pessimism. People change their minds but have no good reasons for doing so; they cannot possibly move "closer" to truth or a better grasp of reality. Such a philosophy leaves a vacuum, a void, but nature abhors a vacuum and people need *some* basis to judge truth and justice. The void can be filled by "dogmatic authority, mystical revelation, and blind faith" (Gupta 1974, 76). Pessimism inspires practices like drug cults, religious extremism, astrology, and other "regressions to the Dark Ages" (Kekes 1976, 3). "Disbelief in the power of human reason, in man's power to discern truth, is almost invariably linked with distrust of man. Epistemological pessimism," says Popper (1963, 6), "is linked, historically, with a doctrine of human depravity, and it tends to lead to the demand for the establishment of powerful traditions and the entrenchment of a powerful authority which would save man from his folly and his wickedness."

This controversy is on factual claims of history and human behavior and it requires the analysis of experts in these fields who, for example, have studied in depth the theoretical basis of fascism. Clearly relativists have little claim to humanitarian value for their theory. It is easy to defend relativism in the abstract but quite different to defend it in practice. The defender can preach tolerance and exhort others to practice it but has no reason to expect these hopes to be fulfilled, and far more importantly, undercuts any *ability* to appeal to such values while being consistent with the theory.

Relativistic views are popular in rhetoric today. Consensus theory directly advocates and defends rhetorically based relativism but it has a dilemma: if "consensus" is loosely interpreted then intersubjectivity becomes solipsism. If there are high standards for conferring consensus status and consensus is a general societal acceptance, then those who dissent are judged to be wrong. Not only is this an interesting and damaging dilemma but *both* horns of the dilemma have been propounded by writers discussed here. In either case consensus theory would stifle inquiry and make it empty. Also, rhetorical relativists talk much of persuasion but are in no position to explain how persuadees decide what consensus to accept. More importantly, they leave no basis for how people *should* decide between competing views. The appeals certainly could not refer to an "objective reality." Finally the claim that relativists are more socially responsible is unsupported and may be thoroughly wrong. In short, it appears that rhetorical relativism is not justified. It fails the first requirement of a rhetorical epistemology: it does not help people cope with problems; it does not slay the minotaur. Inquiry needs a firmer, more functional basis.

The Problem of Overreaction

Too strong a commitment to searching for some objective foundation of truth can, on the other hand, cause one to reject the legitimate insights that a realist rhetoric of inquiry provides for disciplines that have tended to be "antirhetorical," and to opt for what some call the "logic of inquiry." In rejecting relativism one can go to the opposite extreme of seeking objective foundations for all knowledge. Cherwitz and Hikins, in their recent book, have hinted at such leanings. Miller, for one, detects that "Cherwitz and Hikins have been moving toward an increasingly rigid objectivist stance in their discussions of rhetoric as epistemic" (Miller 1987, 433). They have gradually moved toward openly embracing objectivism and foundationalism. In the past, Cherwitz and Hikins sought to avoid objectivism (see, e.g., Cherwitz and Hikins 1983, 253). Cherwitz in particular states that "the existence of an independent and 'objective' reality, as an *ontological* claim, does not imply a physicalist or objectivist *epistemology*" (Cherwitz 1984, 220). Keith and Cherwitz however are concerned with having a more "coherent view of objectivity" (1989, 207) while avoiding the need to take a position on questions of foundationalism, absolutism, and incorrigibility (1989, 204). But Hikins and Zagacki explicitly "support both a version of foundationalist epistemology and an objectivist ontology" (1988, 201). Hikins's search for foundational truths is understandable given his flirtation with the concept of *a priori* truths as a basis for a theory of rhetoric: "The theory of synthetic *a priori* judgments (or one like it) could provide the foundation for a full-blown rhetorical epistemology" (Hikins 1981, 14; for an opposing view of the synthetic *a priori* concept see Hirsh 1982).

Hikins and Zagacki propose a view of knowledge that "is not akin to the old notion of direct realism" (1988, 219), although in their book "Cherwitz and Hikins articulate a variation of direct realism" (Arnold 1986, ix) and the authors themselves interject at one point that "[t]he philosophical notion of 'direct realism' which anchors this claim will be discussed fully in Chapter 6" (Cherwitz and Hikins 1986, 95). But Hikins and Zagacki hold views very *close* to "old" direct realism when they maintain (1988, 203, 215–18) that reality *presents* itself directly to humans. In arguing for a *presentationalist* view and against representationalism they *expressly reject* the view that "human knowledge is symbolically or otherwise mediated" (1988, 203). Some of the problems with Cherwitz and Hikins's direct realism have been argued by Miller (1987) and Croasmun (1987). Aside from these specific arguments against direct realism, it should be noted that this presentationalist view of Hikins and Zagacki on its face directly contradicts any claim that language is the "vehicle of all intellection" and that "all knowledge is inherently linguistic" (Cherwitz and Hikins 1982, 149, 148), and the claim of Keith and Cherwitz that "there must be something objective about language" itself (1989, 202). A more general defense of representationalism as an essential part of a realist epistemology is provided by Bartley (1987).

The least desirable of all possibilities, however, is that some people may choose to opt out of the debate, seeing the controversy over consensus, objectivism, and realism as distant, unimportant, overburdened with philosophical concepts. Mackin, for example, wants to avoid "unnecessary philosophical argument about the nature of reality and the ways of knowing reality"; he "is not concerned with whether or not the intentional experience is true to an objective reality beyond language" (1987, 1). "Truth is correspondence to the foundational terms of the local dictionary, not to an unmediated reality" (Mackin 1987, 5). Unlike objectivists who wish to get "beyond language" for their knowledge foundations, this view follows deconstructionists in denying or ignoring that which lies beyond language. Foundations are found in language. The pains taken by consensus theory to blend symbolic and nonsymbolic reality together are brushed over or ignored. An explicit desire to shun anything beyond a study of language as foundational comes from Miller (1987, 444): "what is perhaps most significant about *Communication and Knowledge* is how amply it demonstrates the impossibility of abstract theorizing beyond the ambiguities of language and the lack of common sense it takes to even try." To opt out of the debate, to ignore all but language, is to bask in the very relativism that consensus theory tries to overcome. It means avoiding the labyrinth completely, preferring to look at the word "labyrinth." It has been suggested that deconstructionists are disappointed political activists who have "retreated from the political realm into the arena of literature, content to undermine truth and language instead of political structures" (McKinney 1987, 329). No less a figure than Scott warns against transcendental extremes of those who prefer "to be inside the funhouse instead of the prisonhouse" of language (Scott 1988, 235). If Theseus were a deconstructionist he would have no reason to enter the labyrinth to combat the minotaur but once in he would not have sought Ariadne's thread. He may have even seen all life as an endless labyrinth with no escape. An objectivist Theseus would not feel the need of a thread or other mediation; the way out of the maze would directly present itself in *a priori* and unmediated fashion.

Conclusion

Some rhetorical objectivists seek the security of a solid foundation for knowledge, by arguing either that language itself is objective or that people have direct contact with objective reality unmediated by symbols. Rhetorical relativists seek foundational security as well, by basing judgments on social consensus. Full elaboration of a rhetorical realism, a view that would shun foundationalism in favor of criticism and inquiry, is far beyond the scope of this work and must come another day. The general nature of such an alternative, however, should be clear. One can reject foundational epistemology without following Rorty in rejecting all epistemology. The case for an anti-foundationalist view of inquiry does not require starting from scratch, as Bernstein (1971, 175–76) has found elements of such thought in the works of Peirce, Quine, Popper, Sellars, and Feyerabend. Some of the works and authors cited in this essay, and in particular Popper, Orr, Booth, and Zarefsky, provide a basic outline for a realist, nonrelativist, nonfoundational, non-objectivist, non-positivist rhetorical epistemology that should be further elaborated and clarified in the future.

At the Iowa Conference, McGee and Lyne (1987, 388–89) outlined four directions one can be led by the rhetoric of inquiry idea and expressed preference for one that seeks "to test knowledge claims" in order "to determine what should be treated as fact. It is a very standard, traditional rhetoric." Nelson (1987, 206) states the obvious when he affirms that "the first philosophical task for rhetoricians of inquiry is to explain how rhetoric is reasonable and how reason is rhetorical. In general terms, this involves arguments that rhetoric legitimates good standards of persuasion." To strive for good *standards* of persuasion, to believe knowledge claims can be compared and evaluated, to have a rhetoric that is more than merely self-referential are precisely the goals that are furthered by realism and undercut by consensus theory.

This essay has argued for greater reflectiveness and reflexiveness in theories of rhetoric and epistemology. An adequate theory of rhetoric must facilitate inquiry rather than stifling it. If argumentation is the study of people giving and assessing good reasons for actions and beliefs, it is better to study what makes a reason "good" and how people can be persuaded by arguments with which they initially disagree than to take a theoretical position denying the very ability of critics and arguers to defend any reasons as being better than any others. If we give up the notion of moving "closer to the truth" we must necessarily give up the notion of moving farther away, leaving the very idea of a rhetoric of inquiry in a precarious position.

Notes

1. Some examples of scholarship in the rhetoric of inquiry are Edmondson (1984), McCloskey (1985), and Nelson, Megill, and McCloskey (1987). Works on rhetoric and science are reviewed by Bokeno (1987), with emphasis on epistemological issues. Simons (1989) discusses the underlying epistemological issues of the rhetoric of inquiry in an essay on Burke.

2. For example, McCloskey (1985, 39–41 and elsewhere), in his critical work on argument practices of economists adds gratuitous statements of and defenses for relativism, although he is only arguing for pluralist methodology. Nelson, Megill, and McCloskey (1987, 5) at times want "rhetoric" to be synonymous with "sophistry." A related controversy is audience adherence: some see agreement as the only possible test of an argument's strength. This issue of argument validity is summarized in Cox and Willard (1982, xiii–xlvii).

3. Farrell (1982a, 430–31) includes himself in the group, Weimer says that "Knowledge is a matter of consensus" (1983, 1112), and Willard claims that "the term 'warranted consensus' is redundant" (statement at the First Wake Forest Conference on Argumentation, Winston-Salem, North Carolina, November 1982). The list could also include Brinton (1985), Jerry (1987), Carleton (1978), Hollinger (1985), and others who draw from Scott and Brummett.

4. For discussion of Rorty, see Gallagher (1984), Davenport (1987), and Munz (1987). On Derrida and Foucault, see Edwards (1986) and Hekman (1986). For a more general indictment of post-modernism, see Habermas (1987).

Part II

Form and Function in Assent
Descriptive Approaches

4

An Exploration of Form and Force in Rhetoric and Argumentation

James Jasinski

In *Modern Dogma and the Rhetoric of Assent* (1974), Wayne Booth describes two broad forms of social thought, or "sects," which constitute modern consciousness. The two forms of consciousness Booth discusses are the "scientismic" and the "irrationalist" (compare these with Apel's [1979] discussion of the "Western complementarity-system" of value-free science and prerational ethical decisions). These modernist sects, and the "dogmas" which they have produced, intimate important assumptions regarding the transformative, or assent-producing, capacity of rhetorical and argumentative practice. Despite surface differences in emphasis, rhetoric and argument scholars attend to the ways symbolic action produces transformations (change, assent, or most generally, movement and development) in assumptions, beliefs, practices, and affiliations. The dogmas produced by scientism and irrationalism explain this transformative process in different ways.

The dogmas of irrationalism conceive transformation or assent as the result of purely individual predilections of audiences. A change in belief or affiliation comes about because individual members of an audience *feel* like assenting to a rhetorical proposition. As Booth notes, for the irrationalist there can be no "good reasons," outside of an individual's affective condition, to warrant changing one's mind about anything. Assent, for the irrationalist, is a subjective achievement.

Those adhering to the dogmas of scientism understand argumentative transformation as emerging from self-evident, observable modes of proof that demonstrate the validity of proposed beliefs or practices. Perelman and Olbrechts-Tyteca describe this scientistic belief in self-evidence quite well: "Self-evidence is conceived both as a force to which every normal mind must yield and as a sign of the truth of that which imposes itself because it is self-evident" (1969, 3). The self-evident force of argumentative demonstration is completely objective; if the demonstration is not obscured by extraneous matters (interests, emotions), transformation and assent are guaranteed.

Like other critics of modernity (compare Bernstein 1983), Booth attempts to refute this mutually exclusive dichotomy. Booth returns to the Aristotelian tradition of rhetoric in his attempt to restore a rhetoric of assent: a mode of language practice that embodies justifiable grounds for rhetorical transformations. Like Booth's program, my project in this essay takes inspiration from Aristotle's original formulation of the rhetorical enterprise. Also like Booth, I find certain limitations in the traditional view of rhetoric, which necessitates further theoretical inquiry into the transformational force of rhetoric. Finally, like Booth, I attempt to account for assent or transformational force as well as outline a typology of the various symbolic manifestations transformational force might take.

In this essay I argue that a central principle for scholars interested in explaining how rhetoric and argumentation practices achieve transformational force is form. Specifically, I elaborate and extend Kenneth Burke's conception of form in order to reveal "inferencing" as the central feature of rhetorical and argumentative form. This sense of inferencing-as-form is then employed to (a) account for the transformational force of symbolic action and (b) develop a typology of inferential forms. This account and typology is the initial step in developing what might be called, in Burke's terminology, a grammar of argumentative form. In the final portion of the essay I relate this still inchoate grammar to central issues in contemporary rhetorical and argumentation theory.

I

Kenneth Burke's rather well-known definition of form maintains that "form is the creation of an appetite in the mind of the auditor, and the adequate satisfying of that appetite" ([1931] 1968, 32). Later in the same text, Burke asserts that "a work has form in so far as one part of it leads a reader to anticipate another part, to be gratified by the sequence" (124; on the "anticipatory nature of rhetoric," see

Hyde and Smith 1979). As the second passage suggests, Burke holds anticipation to be the operating or energizing principle of symbolic form. Form exists, for Burke, in those symbolic clusters that lead audiences to anticipate the direction and/or eventual culmination of a given symbolic practice. In symbolic form at large, cues are provided that encourage an audience to leap ahead—to anticipate—the unfolding of the total symbolic "text." Form is a kind of "deep structure" that, in Burke's initial view, should be understood as a relocating of Plato's universals from heaven into the human mind (and, we should add, into the symbolic practices which help constitute that mind). As the deep structure for symbolic action, form serves as the source for symbolic power or force in general. The instantiation of symbolic form does not result in the transmission of information; form gives birth to the transformational power of "eloquence" (see also Heath 1979).

Traditionally, the analysis of eloquence has been the province of rhetorical and argumentation theory. Burke's speculations on the nature of symbolic form at large provides rhetorical and argument scholars with an important insight: rhetorical and argumentative form is fundamentally a process of anticipation. We can understand more fully the anticipatory nature of form in rhetoric and argument, I suggest, by considering rhetorical anticipation to be a process of inference. Form in rhetoric and argumentation, in other words, is a process of inferencing (for background, see Brockreide and Ehninger 1960; Conley 1978, 1984; Ehninger 1977; Grice 1975; Gronbeck 1982; Leff and Hewes 1981; Searle 1969; Toulmin 1958).[1]

Taking Burke's observations on form as a point of departure, we can postulate that rhetorical and argumentative practices are based on an inferential deep structure. This inferential structure is the basic form of rhetoric and argumentation. An inferential structure, conceived within the scope of Burke's perspective on rhetoric, is not purely deductive in a logical sense. Inferencing, in the context of this discussion, implies only that there is some reconstructable pattern of anticipation and movement at work in rhetorical and argumentative practice. Additionally, based on the idea of a "formal" inferential deep structure, it can be argued that the force or power of rhetorical or argumentative discourse is predicated, at least in part, on the successful implementation of inferential form. Each of these points is elaborated below.

Important insights into the nature of inferencing have been provided recently by Leff and Hewes (1981). Their account of rhetorical inferencing is developed through a reinterpretation of Aristotle's description of topical argument and reasoning. Our understanding of topical argument has been hampered by, first, a failure to distinguish clearly two strains of topical theorizing that mark the rhetorical tradition and, second, a misreading of Aristotle's contribution to topical theory. In the classical tradition of rhetoric, two approaches to topical theory can be discovered. One approach can be labeled a "material" theory. Theories of this type understood topics to be a way of examining a subject in order to discover things to say. A second approach can be termed an "inferential" theory. Theories of this type understood topics to be a way of discovering connections, or "warrants," between argumentative premises (Leff 1983a). Aristotle's contribution to topical theory is misunderstood if it is read as a "material" theory. Leff and Hewes argue that reading Aristotle's *Rhetoric* as a contribution to "inferential" theory leads us in the direction of "a reconstruction of social reasoning." In addition to clarifying Aristotle's contribution to topical theory, Leff and Hewes's reconstruction of social reasoning identifies the central elements of inferential form.[2]

Leff and Hewes assert that "all arguments involve a movement from reason to conclusion and therefore must begin with what is known in order to resolve what is in doubt." As with the anticipatory nature of symbolic form at large, we are concerned with identifying the deep structure that makes argumentative or rhetorical "movement" possible. The structure of topical argument, as Leff and Hewes reconstruct Aristotelian theory, has three components. First, argumentative movement requires a "material base" that "furnish[es] the data on which arguments are constructed." Without a material base, "there would be no basis for the movement to the conclusion." Second, argumentative movement requires a claim or an end point that is to be achieved. Third, and most important, argumentative movement "require[s] a connection that links previously accepted propositions to the conclusion" (1981, 773–74). This connective element provides the basis for an "inferential leap" and, as such, is the critical component in the deep structure of inferential form.[3]

In Aristotelian theory, the connective elements of inferential form were termed *topoi* or topics. In the *Rhetoric*, Aristotle outlined two types of topic: the universal and the special (the *konoi topoi* and the *eide topoi*). While each has characteristics peculiar to its type, Leff and Hewes argue that all *topoi* have the same functional attributes. Specifically, all *topoi* must fulfill two functional requirements in order for the anticipatory or transformational capacity of form to be enacted. First, *topoi* must fulfill a "material criterion of acceptance." They must be believed or accepted as "true" (considered as a valid and correct statement about a particular person, place, or more general and abstract category of objects). Second, *topoi* must meet an "inferential criterion of connective potency." To fulfill this criterion, the topical proposition must, in general, "provide a sufficient reason to connect the datum or starting point to the conclusion" (1981, 775–76; compare Conley 1978). However, following Aristotle's original directive that rhetorical and argumentative discourse treats issues that are "contingent" and offer "alternative possibilities" (1954, 1357a5–a27), we need to avoid any temptation to establish necessary conditions for topical reasoning. The inferential criterion of topical reasoning and the capacity of form itself are predicated on the specifics of time, place, and person (that is, context of situation and interaction).[4]

Before proceeding to elaborate on the inferential nature of rhetorical and argumentative form, a digression to examine the potential restrictiveness of my account of form is in order. One significant argument against an enthymematic-like account of form typically holds that such accounts have a linguistic or propositional bias and hence cannot conceptualize the functional characteristics of "nondiscursive" phenomena like emotion (Willard 1981). An example from van Eemeren and Grootendorst's *Speech Acts in Argumentative Discussions* (1983) provides a way of considering this issue. They use as an example the case of showing someone (a jury for example) a set of fingerprints in order to support a criminal charge against some third party. As they describe the case, no linguistic communication transpires. Van Eemeren and Grootendorst conclude, however, that *"a form of argumentation underlies the convincing,* even if here the argumentation is not formulated aloud. . . . Showing the fingerprints is not, *in itself,* sufficient to convince the other person. He will only be convinced when he *links* [my emphasis] his observation with an interpretation corresponding to the argumentation just reconstructed"(49). The crucial point of the example, I believe, is the sense that a linking process of some sort is evident in nonlinguistic "argumentation" and that this linking process rests on a linguistically reconstructable deep structure (this seems to be the case in Willard's [1983a, 52–53] discussion of "nonverbal" arguments).

This deep structural linking process is, I contend, a manifestation of inferential form. A concept of form that is articulated through propositional examples does not entail that "the passions are reduced to being synonymous with the things said about them" (Willard 1981, 199). As I make clear below, the concept of form advanced here focuses on explaining how movement or transformation occurs symbolically; the fact that such an explanation eventually must be cast linguistically does not imply that an adequate account of the function of emotion in rhetoric and argumentation cannot be provided.

The central components of the deep structure of inferential form, and in particular the dual functions of the connective *topoi*, can be extended into the operations of ordinary language by recasting certain concepts into the terminology of language pragmatics. Such an extension works to identify the basic "grammatical" elements of argumentative form. Specifically, I propose treating the "material criterion" of topical reasoning as a claim to validity and the "inferential criterion" as a claim to legitimacy or appropriateness.[5] Embedded in the inferential form, or deep structure, of rhetorical and argumentative practices are two specific claims: that the material content of the argumentative topic is "valid" (true, correct) and that the performative function of the topic is "legitimate" (appropriate).

The legitimacy dimension of rhetorical form requires additional clarification. We can distinguish two distinct aspects of legitimacy that operate in any manifestation of form. First, a conventional or pragmatic sense of legitimacy can be identified. To be judged legitimate, inferential *topoi* must be considered as appropriate within the pragmatic linguistic context (the utterance sequence, episode, and encounter setting [see Frentz and Farrell 1976]). Second, a substantive or inferential sense of legitimacy can be located. To be considered legitimate, inferential *topoi* must be consonant with the actors' definition of situation, interests, and emotional attachments. It is this aspect of formal appeal that, I suspect, Burke had in mind when he argued that topics are a means of proclaiming substantial unity among people (1950, 56–57; see also Hochmuth [Nichols] 1952). Sharing topical substance (being "consubstantial") through rhetorical form actualizes the force of rhetorical and argumentative practice. (The various aspects, or—in a Burkeian sense—"grammar," of form are summarized in figure 1.)

When the claims to validity and legitimacy (pragmatic and inferential) are functionally intertwined within the composite deep structure, the inferential form of rhetoric and argumentation comes into being. At this point, we can speak of the potential force of inferential form. Actual force is realized only when the inferential

Grammar of Rhetorical and Argumentative Form

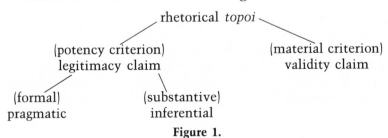

Figure 1.

form articulated in the symbolic practices of a social actor enters the concrete historical world populated by rhetorical audiences, marked by problems and exigencies (themselves constituted, to some degree, by discourse) and structured by institutions, traditional practices, and other constraints (see Bitzer 1968). Force is actualized when audiences participate in the form, when they "anticipate" or are "moved along" through the potential of form and are thereby transformed. In this process audiences attending to the symbolic act (and engaging the form) tacitly (if not overtly) pass judgment on the validity and legitimacy claims at the heart of the inferential form. The transformational force of rhetoric and argumentation is not a kind of compulsion that drives audiences to action or robs them of their autonomy as social agents (a Kantian fear of rhetorical practice regrettably shared, at least to some degree, by Habermas). Transformational force depends on the deep structure of inferential form and is actualized when audiences participate in the form by affirming the form's implicit validity and legitimacy claims (see Jasinski 1986).

Finally, we need to recognize—as Burke clearly does—that the potential of rhetorical form can lead to mystification as well as consubstantiality. In certain situations (which, regrettably, seem more like the norm), the force of form can be actualized through the artful suppression of validity and legitimacy claims. In a very simple sense, this situation occurs whenever the dogma of self-evidence is used to support an argumentative claim. In this case, the claim's force, which ultimately resides in an adjudicating audience, is distorted. By maintaining that a claim is self-evident (the typical strategy in ideographic argument [see McGee 1980]), advocates avoid having the audience reflectively engage the validity and legitimacy dimensions of the claim. The strategy of self-evidence suppresses the claims of validity and legitimacy thereby distorting, but by no means negating, the force of argument. Argumentative form is ambivalent; as form is inscribed in rhetorical and argumentative practices, the audience's ability to encounter an advocate's claims reflectively is enabled as well as constrained.

II

Given this account of form and force, the second task of this essay, introduced at the outset, is to develop a typology of inferential forms. The discussion extends upon Booth's (1974) attempt to describe the range of methods for producing assent through rhetorical practice. The six types of form described below represent major points of stasis on a continuum ranging from an abstract and highly impersonal "substance" to the uniquely personal "substance" of individual motive, personal authority, and human character.

Universal or General Forms

The inferential forms that constitute this first classification typically are broad, abstract patterns of reasoning. Examples include analogy, parallel case, generalization, and other abstract principles (see Gronbeck 1982, esp. 92–93; Brockreide and Ehninger 1960). The force of these inferential forms, as with all the rest, depends on securing audience participation in the unfolding of form. Such participation, as noted at the conclusion of the previous section, entails at the very least tacit judgments on the validity and legitimacy dimensions (claims) of the inferential form. A social actor wishing to manifest this form would need to construct a symbolic act so that an engaged audience would, first, determine the inferential form to be valid (that the discourse contained a "correct" analogy) and, second, would acknowledge the form to be legitimate (in the context of this policy question and/or in this particular argumentative exchange, an analogy between our city and city "z" is appropriate). It is very possible for an audience to engage two analogical forms and determine both to be valid yet, based on particular situation or interaction factors, reject a particular form as inappropriate. For example, engaging audiences through analogical form may be appropriate for issues of public policy (such as city services) but might be determined inappropriate for moral issues (such as birth control practices).

Special Forms

The inferential forms that constitute this second type are drawn from a society's fund of "social knowledge." Typically, they take the shape of statements about important values and beliefs adhered to by members of the society (see Leff and Hewes 1981, 777–79; Farrell 1976). Special forms achieve force by engaging audiences through claims to validity and legitimacy. Specifically, a social actor engaging an audience through a special form (for example, the value of "responsibility") would need, first, to construct a symbolic act in which the society's sense of responsibility is depicted. For example, a speaker could appeal to how our parents taught us the value of "being responsible" when we broke our neighbor's window or our sibling's toy. In this way, a speaker could establish an intersubjectively valid sense of responsibility. Second, the social actor relying on a special form needs to construct a symbolic act that situates the value in the context of an audience confronting a rhetorical exigence. When an audience is faced with a decision about whether or not they will penalize a corporation or politician for a potentially problematic act, an advocate can urge action based on the value of responsibility: those lacking in responsibility should be punished while those accepting responsibility should be commended. The decision is reached based on the appropriateness of the value as a way of organizing the diffuse conventional-pragmatic and substantive-inferential factors in the specific context.[6]

Tropes and figures of speech commonly are considered to be distinct from, if not antithetical to, argument. Increasing numbers of scholars are, however, exploring the "logic" and argumentative nature of tropes, especially metaphor. With respect to the typology of form being developed here, metaphor (and tropological inferencing in general) can be considered as a subtype of the larger category of "special forms." Suggesting this classification is not an assertion that no distinctions among metaphor and topical argument exist; as Leff notes, for example, we can uncover some clear differences in the realm of synchronic versus diachronic emphasis. The major point behind Leff's (1983b) recent inquiry, however, is to establish points of commonality between metaphor and argument. Form, considered as a process of inferential movement based on conditions of validity and legitimacy, establishes one point of common ground.[7]

For example, Jasinski (1987a) identifies a "feminization of liberty" metaphor in pre-Revolutionary American political symbolism. This metaphorical image—a feminine "vehicle" modifying the "tenor" liberty—appears in discursive and visual manifestations. In Leff's terms, the metaphor functions as an "imaginative inference" that moves auditors to see the world in a certain way and to act based on that perception. When liberty is feminized, the closing of the port of Boston *becomes*, is transformed into, rape. Such a transformation becomes the justification for violent resistance. (Visually, this idea of rape can be seen in Revere's print "The Able Doctor.") In terms of the conditions of validity and legitimacy, the feminization metaphor must, first, establish that the characterization of the feminine "vehicle" is satisfactory; that is, the qualities of femininity predicated to liberty must ring true for the rhetorical audience. Second, in order to actualize rhetorical force the perceptual structuring achieved by the metaphor must be deemed appropriate by the audience. For example, certain manifestations of the feminization of liberty metaphor could not be introduced in contemporary public discourse because of the inappropriate pattern of male/female relationships which the 1770s usage depicted. In colonial times, it appears that the feminine metaphor was inappropriate in a dynamic context; that is, when the focus of attention was on the *future* the feminine metaphor did not adequately structure perception. When the future was the focus the liberty tree metaphor, emphasizing growth, development, and endurance, appeared to be more appropriate.

Finally, recent research has uncovered a form that has certain characteristics of the universal and special forms. Osborn's investigation of archetypes reveals that there may be certain values, inscribed into *archetypal* metaphors, which do not seem to be society or culture bound in the same manner as typical special forms (see Osborn 1967, 1977). The values transcend temporal and social boundaries and approach a near-universal status. At the same time, archetypal images appear to function more like special forms of inference than like universal forms. Archetypal images depend upon a much stronger personal "acquaintance" (Farrell 1976) between social actors and the image's "organizing principle" (Burke 1950) than do abstract universal forms. As far as a typology is concerned, archetypal inferential forms can be considered a subtype of the special form.

Field-Dependent Forms

The inferential forms that constitute this third type are drawn from the practices, traditions, and convictions of particular discursive or symbolic domains. The idea of field-dependent warrants was popularized by Toulmin and has generated considerable scholarly attention. Despite conflicting interpretations, there appears to be a consensus that there are such things as specific "fields" of discursive or symbolic practice and that these fields typically have unique modes of argumentation. Field-dependent form is established, and force achieved, when a social actor engages a specialized audience through (a) the creation of a reasoning pattern or an appeal to a conviction that is considered valid within the field,[8] and (b) the application of the created pattern or appeal to a problem or issue for which, given the constraints of the field and problem, it is deemed legitimate or appropriate (see also Perelman and Olbrechts-Tyteca 1969, 465). For example, certain reasoning patterns may be judged suitable for certain field tasks (heuristic tasks) but may be inappropriate for other tasks (developing operational definitions).

Emotional Forms

The inferential forms that constitute this fourth type are drawn from and interact with the affective, emotional experiences of human beings. Typically, these forms take shape through the depiction of certain conditions (physical and/or psychological) that, when brought to the attention of an audience, induce an emotional response. This emotional response is the initial moment of a larger rhetorical transformation. Emotion can also enter rhetorical and argumentative practice in a nondiscursive manner (for example, graphic arts, music). In any event, if we attend to the functional nature of emotional experience in matters pertaining to rhetoric and argument an emotionally based inferential form can be discovered. Emotional form, like the others, ultimately is predicated on the claims of validity and legitimacy. Force is established through emotional form when (a) the symbolic depiction of the physical or psychological world is determined to be accurate by an audience and (b) the affective state necessary for the development of emotional form is judged appropriate given the accurate characterization of the physical and/or psychological world.

Just as the inducement of emotional experience, as the above account indicates, is inherently "reasonable" (reconstructable as well as justifiable), the completion of emotional form and the enactment of transformational force is reasonable as well. If a social actor's symbolic acts have brought about an emotional experience in an audience, and the audience members acknowledge this to be a valid experience (the audience agrees: "yes, I/we am/are angry"), it remains to be seen whether or not the emotional experience will be considered a legitimate basis for any particular action or belief. This second step in the unfolding of emotional form is the corollary to the initial moment described above. To reiterate: an accurate characterization of the physical and/or psychological world does not, in itself, induce emotional experience; the individual still determines whether the emotional state being recommended by another is appropriate (see Fortenbaugh 1974; Solomon 1973). To conclude the description of the second moment of emotional form: the social actor may bring the audience to the experience of anger, but that same audience can still reject the complete emotional form which sought to connect that anger to an endorsement of, for example, retribution in foreign policy.

Character and Authority Forms

The inferential forms that constitute this fifth type are drawn from and interact with our experience of identification and hierarchy (Burke 1950). Typically, these forms take shape through either appeals or images that depict the character and/or habits of a social actor *or* appeals and images that inform, or remind, the audience of the social actor's status within the social hierarchy. In the first case, through the enactment of form audiences come to identify themselves with a social actor and transcend the normal state of division. In the second case, through the enactment of form audiences come to see themselves as subordinate to another social actor. This realization, in turn, maintains the hierarchy that emerges from our being divided from each other. The key to inferential form in both cases is the social actor's ability to construct a symbolic act that establishes the validity of a particular identification (to use Burke's example: the politician that tells farmers "I grew up on a farm") or the characterization of a specific hierarchy (the junior faculty member reminding graduate students about work requirements in a seminar). Character and authority forms are fully developed, and force achieved, when the social actor is able to construct a symbolic act that also engages the audience's sense of legitimacy or appropriateness. The politician may appeal to mutual identification but such identification can be inappropriate when the subject at hand is foreign policy. The junior faculty member may engage graduate students attending a seminar in the academic hierarchy successfully but appeal to that hierarchy at a bar ("hey, buy me a beer") may be inappropriate.

Motivational Forms

The inferential forms that constitute this sixth and final type are drawn from and interact with the particular motives and interests that individual social actors may hold. Typically, these forms take shape through images and/or verbal appeals that present something (a policy, a specific course of action, a judgment, etc.) as in the audience's "best interest" or in their "self-interest." Motivational form is established, and force actualized, when a social actor engages an audience and (a) establishes that a specific item *is* in the audience's interest (the audience would agree: "yes, that is in my/our interest") while also (b) demonstrating that in this particular situational complex personal motive or self-interest is an appropriate basis for belief or conduct. In a capitalist society it is sometimes assumed that every situation calls for self-interested action (some would claim that this motive is fundamental to "human nature"). However, we all have encountered too many examples of unselfish behavior to allow such a generalization about our "human nature" to stand unchallenged. Like all forms that seek to engage us and thereby move us to another position, motivational forms must be infused with a sense of legitimacy or appropriateness in order to reach fruition.

III

Following leads suggested by Booth, this essay attempts to account for the assent-producing, or transformational, force of rhetoric and argumentation through the concept of form. The elements identified constitute essential components in an inchoate grammar of argumentative form: a systematic account of the principles upon which the rhetorical enterprise depends. While the account of form and force as well as the typology outlined above, like virtually any attempt to render a complex subject systematic, has its defects, there are two issues where the value of my discussion seems clearest. First, explication of the grammar of rhetoric and argumentative form enhances the "literacy" of rhetorical audiences. That is, a grammar of form contributes to the emergence of a "rhetorical literacy" (Jasinski 1988): an ability to read and adjudicate the nuanced transformations in argumentative practice. Second, if grammar describes the general principles of a structured, systematic practice, it might usefully be supplemented by an account of "syntax": a discussion of the critical factors that are implicated in the instantiation of rhetorical form. Two elements of rhetorical and argumentative syntax—power and time—are discussed below.

In his recent *Theory of Communicative Action*, Habermas (1984, 102–41) outlines a methodological perspective for the social sciences which he describes as "rational interpretation." A rational interpretation, Habermas argues, recognizes the inherent rationality of human action; to interpret an utterance *as* a reason implicates one in the rationality of action even if the overall soundness of the reason is not judged. There is, for Habermas, "a fundamental connection between understanding communicative actions and constructing rational interpretations" (1984, 116).

Rational interpretation is a perspective that allows the social scientist to uncover the inherent rationality (the "reasons" or validity claims) of human action. Rhetorical literacy, on the other hand, can be thought of as a practical competence which, when exercised by audiences, opens up the unfolding of rhetorical form so that the claims to validity, pragmatic legitimacy, and inferential legitimacy can be judged. The grammar of rhetorical and argumentative form described in the preceding pages has the potential to empower audiences by enabling them to be literate in the realm of rhetoric and argumentation. Based on an understanding of form, rhetorical literacy is a capacity to understand the logic and transformations of discourse and assess the claims being made in light of pressing circumstances, historical traditions, new possibilities, social interests, and personal motives.

Form, as I have described it here, is not simply a serial predication; form is an active process that comes into existence as advocates symbolically engage audiences. That engagement entails at least two related factors. First, rhetorical engagement through form introduces structure and, consequently, power in human affairs (as in the active sense of "forming"). Second, rhetorical form, in its potential to spread or extend through time, introduces temporality as a central factor in argumentation. Put simply, form enacts power while it unfolds through time.

The power of form is manifest as structure; power emerges as possibilities for thought, perception, or action are structured and thereby constrained through the formal engagement of advocate and audience (see Foucault 1983). Through processes of mystification and consubstantiation, form works to constitute power. In addition to studying how the suppression of validity and legitimacy claims establishes power as mystification, rhetoric and argument scholars might examine the structuring potential of each major category of form thereby probing how form contributes to a social type of consubstantial power.

For example, Jasinski (1987b) analyzes the use of the universal form of "analogy" in Andrew Jackson's public arguments regarding Indian affairs. In Jackson's acquiescence to the demand for Indian removal, he argued analogically comparing Indian relocation to the emigration of Europeans to America. In so doing, Jackson invited his audience to share a conceptual structure advocating a type of equality that, in obliterating all substantive differences between Indians and European immigrants, ultimately subjected the Indian tribes of the Old Southwest to domination. Further historical studies of this type, along with conceptual explorations of the formal categories, can further our knowledge of how form contributes to the establishment and enactment of power.

Finally, many formal models (for example, Searle's [1969] description of the constituent features of a "promise") cannot account for change because, generally, the models situate rhetorical and argumentative form outside time and history (Farrell 1982b). Although the entailments of logic may exist outside time, rhetorical and argumentative discourse rarely, if ever, moves outside time and history. Form is inherently temporal. It might be the narrow, yet highly complex, temporal frame of one speech (such as Lincoln's "Second Inaugural") or the shifting, contracting, or expanding frame of a social movement or a political campaign. In any event, the meaning, significance, and force of the rhetorical utterance are related to the temporal spread of form.

This insight can be used to guide a particular line of research. The central question would be: How do the six categories of form unfold and develop force over time and in specific contexts? For example, critical and theoretical inquiry could be directed toward ascertaining whether a form such as emotion requires a certain temporal frame in order to achieve force. Clearly, other research questions could be generated following this line of thought. In any case, the central point to emphasize is that the force of rhetoric and argumentation is achieved through the symbolic engagement of audiences via form. The engagement of audiences through form will be enabled and constrained by context and temporal factors. The force of rhetoric and argumentation can recede or accumulate over time as discourse moves from context to context and engages an evolving rhetorical audience.[9]

Notes

1. The position developed in this essay is an attempt to describe inferential form and force without retreating to formalism. As such, it seems consistent with Burke's Aristotelian emphasis on form as act (1945, 227–28).

2. Leff and Hewes do not claim to describe a deep structure of inferential form. They limit their discussion to arguments in "the realm of propositional discourse" (773). If the position they advance is a theory of social reasoning, however, we should be able to employ it to account for a variety of collective symbolic practices that appear to function as a type of social reasoning. My claim is that Leff and Hewes's formulation of topical argument can be used analogically to describe the elements of inferential form in rhetorical and argumentative practice at large.

3. As should be clear, Leff and Hewes's position, as well as my own, represents a reinterpretation of Aristotle's enthymeme. It must be recognized that conceptual approaches built on the enthymeme (or anything resembling it) have been seriously challenged. Major indictments of an enthymematic approach can be found in Jesse G. Delia (1970) and Charles A. Willard (1978). Each of these essays raises serious questions about traditional approaches to the enthymeme. However, the problem might be that our knowledge of the concept of enthymematic reasoning or thinking has been clouded by unnecessary interference from logic and philosophy. Delia, for example, implies that the enthymeme is only descriptive of that form of appeal described as *logos* and therefore cannot account for *ethos* and *pathos*. William Grimaldi, however, has provided evidence that *logos*, *ethos*, and *pathos* are all special *topoi* of enthymematic arguments. As such, enthymematic form (what is at issue here) can provide a plausible account of the effects of character and emotion in discourse (Grimaldi 1972).

Willard's major criticism of the enthymeme is that it leads to a conceptualization of argument as "a serial predication—a *thing*," which thereby leads to a neglect of situational and interactional issues. But this is an unnecessarily limited view of form. As Burke (1945) reminds us, there is an active dimension to the concept of form—as in "forming" something—which supplements a "thing-like" view of form (I return to this sense of form as an active process of structuring in the final section of the essay). As I hope to make clear later, a concept of inferential form as a rhetorical and argumentative deep structure is not incompatible with the need to consider situation and interaction elements in discourse analysis. An adequate conceptualization of inferential form will account for issues of situational legitimacy or appropriateness and will not necessarily "encourage the analysis of argument *in vacuo*" (Willard 1978, 123).

4. Leff and Hewes claim that "judgments about the use of a warranting premise [that is, judgments of connective potency] . . . rest upon the context" (779).

5. See Jurgen Habermas (1979, esp. 1–68; 1984, esp. 22–42, 273–337) for his general approach to discourse analysis that is a universal or formal pragmatics. My modification of Habermas's four-part claim structure is based on, first, the assumption that mutual intelligibility is not a problem in typical rhetorical or argumentative interactions (audiences recognize and take cognizance of the symbolic acts performed by social actors) and, second, a contention that validity and legitimacy are the principal elements of form (and thereby the source of transformational force) while "sincerity" or "truthfulness," despite being a powerful existential factor in argumentation, is only an adjunct to form. As Habermas acknowledges, sincerity or truthfulness ultimately "cannot be *grounded* [redeemed through discourse] but only *shown*" (1984, 41). I would add, speculatively, that sincerity or truthfulness has a greater role in shaping the unfolding of form and actualization of force as rhetorical and argumentative appeals spread through time. As the character of social actors is made known through other avenues besides specific symbolic acts, the force of the formal elements (validity and legitimacy) will be modified. I return to the issue of form and time later in the essay.

6. Clear distinctions between universal and special forms are hard to establish (witness commentators still debating this issue in Aristotle's *Rhetoric*; see Conley 1978). In my view, special forms typically assume a deductive shape. In the final analysis the distinction depends on emphasis: special forms emphasize validity and legitimacy potential of the *value* while universal forms emphasize the validity and legitimacy potential of the reasoning pattern.

7. Conley suggests that metaphor might be the "paradigm" for rhetorical practice (1984, 182); I am inclined to see metaphor as paradigmatic of the appropriateness condition of form. On the general relationship between metaphor and argument, see Leff (1983b) and Osborn and Ehninger (1962).

8. A scientist's appeal to "objectivity," if objectivity is used in a way specific to scientific practice, could constitute an appeal to conviction. Alan Gross has demonstrated how analogical patterns vary in different fields (Gross 1983).

9. The author wishes to thank David Zarefsky for advice and encouragement.

5

The Implied Arguer

Randall A. Lake

> Liminality, marginality, and structural inferiority are conditions in
> which are frequently generated myths, symbols, rituals, philosophi-
> cal systems, and works of art. These cultural forms provide [humans]
> with a set of templates or models which are, at one level, periodical
> reclassifications of reality and [humanity's] relationship to society,
> nature, and culture. But they are more than classifications, since
> they incite [humans] to actions as well as to thought.
> —Victor Turner (1969, 128–29)

Grounded in ethnographic fieldwork, the formative view of the nature of ritual held it to be nonrational, repetitive, largely physical
action associated with primitive tribal societies. Affiliated with
what Emile Durkheim ([1915] 1965, 52–57) called the "sacred" as
opposed to the "profane" sphere of life, ritual was said to concern
rules of appropriate conduct in the presence of sacred objects. Fundamentally religious, its rationale was said to lie in myth, wherein
archetypal characters perform the paradigmatic feats which ritual
subsequently enacts (Eliade [1957] 1959, [1958] 1965, [1963] 1968).
Its efficacy was attributed to magical invocations of supernatural
power. Its sociological function was to promote what Ernst Cassirer
([1944] 1975, 82–86, 101, 110; [1955–57] 1975–77, 175–99) called
the "solidarity of life," that is, group cohesiveness in the face of and
together with the cosmos. And its sociological effect was thought to
be profoundly conservative, preserving archaic tribal lifeways even
to the point of social atrophy.

More recent developments in the theory of ritual have burst these
limits. First to go was the notion that civilized societies have out-
grown ritual (Bocock 1974; Douglas [1970, 1973] 1982; Moore and
Myerhoff 1977). Others have argued that ritual is not irrational, is
not dependent on myth for its justification, is not dependent on

magic for its efficacy, is not restricted to the religious or "sacred" sphere, and may promote social change as readily as stability (Gay 1979, 40–49; Leach 1968–79, 13:520–26; Peacock 1975; see also Bocock 1974; Grainger 1974; Grimes 1982; Moore and Myerhoff 1977; Shaughnessy 1973). Other disciplines have appropriated the concept of ritual for their own purposes. It was extended by Freud ([1953–66] 1975a, [1953–66] 1975b; cf. Reik [1946] 1958) to include the neurotic, obsessive-compulsive personality, and by Erving Goffman (1967) to include virtually all human interaction.

However conceived, ritual may seem far afield from (even antithetical to) argumentation. At base, however, both are forms of human symbolic action, both physical and verbal. Ritual action (for example, dancing) ordinarily possesses a verbal component (for example, chanting) that often is addressed persuasively to the gods. Similarly, arguments (such as claims made at fundamentalist revivals regarding God's will) can be delivered ritualistically (repetitively, for incantatory purposes). In sum, both ritual and argumentation are, broadly speaking, rhetorical acts that invite assent.[1]

The following pages elaborate this relationship. First, I discuss concerns and concepts common to ritual and rhetoric. I argue that these two symbolic impulses merge in the phenomenon of the *persona*, that is, the implied actor that both argues for a claim and enacts a role, thereby inviting audiences to "be as I am." Second, I illustrate this common concern, examining a recurring "warrior" *persona* in contemporary Native American protest rhetoric. Indian activists typically implore their fellows to revitalize the traditional warrior role, thereby reviving tribal culture as well, while simultaneously embodying characteristic traits of the warrior. In short, activists both argue for and enact the warrior *persona*. Third, I examine the implications of the *persona* for three current issues in argumentation theory: (a) the nature of argumentation; (b) appropriate criteria for justified assent (Booth 1974); and (c) the relevance of argumentation theory to social praxis, and the desirability of critical advocacy. Initially, all arguments, as a form of rhetorical action, portray *personae*. Further, insofar as argumentation can be distinguished from other types of discourse, such as the scientific or the poetic, these distinctions will be manifest in the *persona* that each type portrays; that is, the implied *arguer* will be distinguishable, *qua* arguer, from other implied speakers. Second, the presence of *personae* means that all arguments invite assent on two levels simultaneously: discursively (with respect to their usually explicit claims) and presentationally (with respect to their usually implied *personae*). Consequently, any criteria of justified assent must contend with both levels, and with their interaction. Finally, the contemporary turn toward social advocacy among some critics and the opposition of others who champion a more "objective," "academic" stance illustrate the pervasive influence of *personae* in argumentation. For, in this debate, opposing critical *personae* as well as opposing claims compete for our adherence.

Ritual and Rhetorical Forms

The basis of the view I propose is the familiar distinction, or, more precisely, continuum, between instrumental and consummatory acts, that is, acts that are means to other ends and acts that are ends in themselves, respectively. The former require an audience that must be convinced to take subsequent action to achieve the desired end-state, while the latter do not depend on such subsequent acts for their efficacy and, therefore, could conceivably dispense with audiences altogether.

This continuum has figured prominently in theorizing about both rhetoric and ritual. The classical tradition treats rhetoric as instrumental (as deliberative, forensic, or epideictic discourse addressed to an audience for persuasive purposes), while ritual often has been opposed to "technical" or instrumental action and defined as "symbolic" or consummatory (action that does not perform a rational means-end function) (compare Solmsen 1954 and LaFontaine as cited in Elsbree 1982, 8). Hence, dancing around likenesses of wild beasts for purposes of ensuring a successful hunt would be a ritual act; scouting the migratory patterns of herds and sharpening one's spears would be a technical act; and instructing the tribe's warriors in hunting techniques would be a rhetorical act.

Fortunately, most rhetorical scholars have resisted these overly simple categories. As Burke ([1950] 1969, 19–46, 267–94) argues, in all symbolic action, no matter how consummatory, there is always a persuasive effect on an audience, if only oneself. Rather than a fundamental dichotomy in which instrumental, pragmatic, and primarily verbal rhetoric is contrasted with consummatory and largely formal ritual, most rhetorical scholars wisely have emphasized a continuum wherein rhetoric, too, can be consummatory to some degree (Berlo 1960, 17–18; Bennett 1977, 220–21; Gronbeck 1978, 268–73; Lake 1983, 139–40; Trent 1978, 284).

However, rhetorical scholars have been reluctant to grant that "primitive" ritual can be instrumental, on the grounds that ritual's efficacy is a function of magic, not persuasion (Burke [1950] 1969, 40–46; Scult 1979). In "primitive" societies, many rituals attempt to accomplish real feats in the world, for example, to heal the sick or inflict disease, ensure a successful hunt or harvest, and so on. True, success does not rely on the intercession of a human audience. Instead, ritual is "addressed" to supernatural power. Often termed *mana* by ethnographers, Codrington, who first observed the phenomenon in the beliefs of Pacific islanders, described it as "what works to effect everything which is beyond the ordinary power of [humans], outside the common processes of nature; it is present in the atmosphere of life, attaches itself to persons and to things, and is manifested by results which can only be ascribed to its operation" (1891, 118–19).

Something akin to *mana* has been identified in the beliefs of most "primitive" peoples throughout the world. The Sioux denote as *wakan* "everything that exhibits power, whether in action, as the winds and drifting clouds, or in passive endurance, as the boulder by the wayside" (LaFlesche 1925, 186). For the Iroquois, "the *orenda* power was different for each plant, animal, [human], or spirit, just as brains and muscles were different" (Underhill 1965, 21). Yet all things—animals, birds, plants, rocks, water, celestial bodies, meteorological phenomena—potentially have power. Thus, "all-pervading mysterious power" (LaFlesche 1925, 186) is, in the largest sense, "the animating principle of the universe" (Opler 1941, 205).

Ritual acts including songs, dance, and the construction of sacred medicine objects address and thereby invoke power. As Morris Opler observes of Apache practice: "The ritual details are important not because they cure in themselves but because once the proper procedure has been carried out the power . . . is expected to recognize its own songs and prayers and to honor its pledges to act at the individual's bidding" (1941, 207). The more automatic this invocation, the more ritual's efficacy is magical (as power is conceptualized more as mediating agent than as agency, ritual's efficacy becomes increasingly "prayerful," hence indirect). Nonetheless, I contend, it is always instrumental. Its efficacy may not depend on human mediation, may be more closely bound up in the performance of the ritual act itself, and thus may be more consummatory than other rhetorical forms, but is always mediated by power as addressee. To some degree, ritual always remains entreaty, as Susanne Langer observes: "No savage tries to induce a snowstorm in midsummer, nor prays for the ripening of fruits entirely out of season, as he [sic] certainly would if he considered his dance and prayer the physical causes of such events. He dances *with* the rain, he invites the elements to do their part, as they are thought to be somewhere about and merely irresponsive" ([1957] 1973, 158).

Furthermore, objections to ritual instrumentality presuppose a narrow conception of ritual dependent on magic, a conception, we have seen, that many scholars now reject. When one conceives of ritual more broadly as a form of symbolic action prevalent in industrial, secular, post-magical societies as well, the boundary between ritual and rhetoric blurs. No longer is one symbolic and the other technical, one consummatory and the other instrumental. Rather, both are symbolic and, I believe, can be instrumentally persuasive in moving an audience or consummatorily able to transform participants.

Paul Campbell (1972, esp. 244–50; see also Burke 1984, 179–215; Elsbree 1982) has analyzed most thoroughly the relationship between rhetoric and post-magical ritual. Treating both as dimensions of language, he contends that the essential difference between them is that (instrumental) rhetoric is discourse created by real speakers and addressed to real audiences, while (consummatory) ritual, being more poetic and dramatic, utilizes imaginary *personae* and appeals insofar as people "empathically inhabit," or engage in "the constitutive act of becoming," these fictitious beings. This distinction is only of degree, not kind, as there is no "pure" form of either ritual or rhetoric (P. Campbell 1972, 250; 1975).

Campbell's position has much to commend it. Yet, wherever symbolic action is concerned, distinctions based on the real versus the fictive are inherently troublesome. Rather than restrict *personae* to ritual, and then concede that all rhetoric is ritualistic to a degree, I prefer to view *personae* as the locus of interaction between rhetoric and ritual. That is, all speakers, however real, necessarily assume *personae* that not only consummate a role but also instrumentally invite audiences to participate, to "be as I am." The *persona*, I will argue, is both real and fictive, both persuasion and (even if implicit) enactment, both discursive and presentational (Langer [1957] 1973, esp. 79–102).

Intriguingly, the concept of the *persona* is well-established in both rhetorical and ritual theories. Originally it referred to the masks worn by Greek and Roman actors on the stage, then broadened to include the entire character or role played, then the actor, and then a whole range of related meanings (Elliott 1982, 19–32; Muller n.d.). So diverse has this range become that the term connotes, on the one hand, sheer artifice and, on the other, one's essential persona(!)lity. Contemporary laments over the carefully manufactured "images" of political figures (such as Ronald Reagan's "Teflon Presidency") attest to the former; yet, to Immanuel Kant, *persona* designated the moral essence of rational beings (Elliott 1982, 19).

In the abstract, the fundamental problematic underlying this range of meanings concerns the relationship between one's "self" and one's *persona*. How similar or dissimilar are they? Is a politician's image in the public eye merely a reflection of her character? Is the first-person "I" of a novel or poem a stand-in for the work's author? Or, on the contrary, are these imaginary, artfully constructed "persons" who exist only in the eye and ear?

These are hoary questions, made hoarier by certain seemingly ambiguous discursive forms. An autobiography, for example, may be nonfiction, but it remains literary, often written with a collaborator. To what extent is the "I" of such a work literally autobiographical?[2]

Literary, dramatic, and rhetorical theories (and Campbell is no exception) have tended to emphasize the dissimilarity between self and *persona*, which has come to mean "the imaginary, the fictive being implied by and imbedded in" discourse, "a being who has no necessary resemblance to the author."[3] In arguing that Marcus Garvey represented a "black Moses" for Harlem blacks in the 1920s, Ware and Linkugel (1982) do not mean that Garvey literally was an African reincarnation of the Jewish liberator but that he symbolically partook of the qualities represented by this preexistent archetypal figure.

Ritual, however, treats the relationship between self and *persona* somewhat differently. The use of masks has a long and vital history in "primitive" religious ritual, wherein the wearer becomes the figure represented by the mask, be this a god, spirit, animal, or ancestor (Eliade 1985, esp. 69–70; Elliott 1982, 22–23). To don a mask, it is important to understand, is not simply to *impersonate* the figure in the mask, in the sense of play-acting, but rather is to *personify* this figure, to be assimilated into its being and become transformed by it, and, thereby, "temporarily to incarnate cosmic reality" (Elliott 1982, 21). "Clearly this reverses our normal categories," Robert Elliott comments. "[I]nstead of the mask as a bogus front, hiding the real person behind it, . . . the mask mediates the highest reality of all" (1982, 21).

Thus, traditional rhetorical and ritual theories differ on the question: of one's *persona* and one's "self," which is more "real"? However, they share a tendency to emphasize that the two are starkly independent. Thus, the character Fletcher Christian in "Mutiny on the *Bounty*" is independent of the actor Clark Gable. Similarly, tribal totemic animals and the powers they possess are independent of the particular tribal shamans who may be transformed by them.

But this independence is only a half-truth. Although Gable is not Christian, nonetheless Gable's Christian is not Mel Gibson's Christian; both actors' performances inform our understanding of who the character "is." At the same time, it seems reasonable to assume that both Gable and Gibson are somewhat different for having played Christian. Similarly, tribal shamans are surely different for having assumed their ritual *personae* and, given the existence of some space for improvisation and creativity in ritual, one shaman's enactment of a *persona* need not be identical to another's and informs the tribe's understanding of what the totemic figure "is." In short, *personae* are never complete fabrications, uninformed by any real "self," and "selves" in turn are always shaped to a degree by the *personae* they portray.[4]

The human agent, therefore, is the locus of interaction between self and *personae*. In the language of social psychology, the agent— what George Herbert Mead ([1934] 1962, 1:135–226) calls the "self"—is forged in role-playing, the product of interaction between the individual "I" and the other-defined "me." In the language of ritual, the agent—what Victor Turner (1969, 94–95) calls a "liminal *persona*"—is forged in rites of passage. According to Van Gennep (1960, 11), all such rites, in which a neophyte is transformed from, say, a prepubescent child into an adult, consist of three phases: (1) the preliminal, or separation of the neophyte from his or her existing matrix of social roles and relationships; (2) the liminal (from the Latin "limen," meaning threshold) or marginal, the transitional condition in which the neophyte is suspended between and freed from the constraints of such matrices; and (3) the postliminal, or reintegration of the neophyte into a new matrix. In this passage, the agent is the product of interaction between the given biopsychological "self" and the ritual *persona*. The agent is both actual and transformed by the ideal, both "who she is" and "who she has become."[5]

A "person," in sum, is an agent in the process of being transformed by a vision of personhood (a *persona*) into a somewhat different person. This process of transformation is instrumental in the sense that all agents who witness the *persona* are its audience and are asked to assent to its legitimacy and accept it as "true." Yet, the process is consummatory in the sense that agents are invited to identify with and participate in the *persona*; the process's purpose is the creation of a new personality, a purpose accomplished simply by the process's culmination, that is, the enactment of the *persona*. Thus, *personae* are the loci of the twin human symbolizing activities commonly known as rhetoric and ritual. To the extent that all human "selves" are a mosaic produced in interaction with *personae*, human agents are, in a broad sense, perpetually liminal (in transition between selves), engaged constantly in these twin activities (and indeed, must be so engaged to be fully human).

The Warrior *Persona*

These relationships among rhetoric, ritual, and *personae* illuminate several important features of contemporary Native American discourse, particularly militant protest. Elsewhere I have examined the consummatory function in Indian activist rhetoric, demonstrating how the enactment of traditional tribal cultural practices also enacts militant demands and ritually recovers the past (Lake 1983). Here I want to focus on the *persona* that activists enact. Specifically, I argue that the "warrior" personifies culturally vital traits and roles and that, in enacting this *persona,* activists become the kind of people required to preserve traditional cultures, and thus precisely the kind of people they wish others to be.

One of the most striking features of native protest rhetoric, particularly in its most public phase from 1969 to 1973, was its reliance on the terminology of war (Frost 1974, 6). Militant literature was replete with militaristic references and allusions. The government presence at the siege of Wounded Knee, South Dakota, in March 1973, for example, was characterized in heavily militaristic terms:

Army material loans by the middle of March were staggering—over 130 M-16 rifles with 100,000 rounds of ammunition, 75 high-powered sniper rifles (M-14s, M-1s, and Springfields, all with scopes and ammunition); helmets, flak vests, signal flares, mine detectors, C-rations, jeeps, trucks, and maintenance technicians for the APCs (Armored Personnel Carriers) were all in possession of the Marshals and the FBI. The equipment, coupled with the manpower of the Marshals and the advice of the military, gave the government exactly what they wanted at Wounded Knee—a clandestine army ("Garden Plot" 1975, 7).

To the Indians, Wounded Knee was merely the most obvious case of military confrontation and oppression. Another, subtler example was the confrontation at the Alexian Brothers monastery in Gresham, Wisconsin, in January 1975, where, "as at Wounded Knee, there was really a war going on" ("Menominee Defense" 1976, 1; see also "Two Warriors Die" 1976). Indian-white confrontations involving the Seminoles in Oklahoma, the Sioux in South Dakota, the Iroquois in New York and Canada, and the Hoopa in California also have been characterized in these terms (see Chavers 1983; "Reign of Terror" 1975; "Economic History" 1977, 15; and "Hoopa Tribe" 1978, respectively).

Thus, militants allege, the role of the armed forces in Indian-white relations continues unchanged from the days of the cavalry. From the Garden Plot plan coordinating Army, National Guard, and local police in the suppression of domestic protest, and its "Cable Splicer" offspring covering four western states under the direction of the U.S. Sixth Army, to the CIA's "Operation CHAOS" (a domestic spying operation with undercover ties to local police forces), to government infiltration of AIM with paid informers, to rape, murder, and other vigilante actions that local police refuse to investigate, activists paint a black picture of armed violence and oppression ("Bringing Vietnam Home" 1975; "Anatomy of an Informer" 1975). The FBI and CIA, the Army, the National Guard, the U.S. Marshals, state police and Fish and Game wardens, county sheriffs, local police, white vigilantes, and Indian groups backed by the BIA police are viewed as partners in a concerted effort violently to crush the movement. "In the aftermath of Wounded Knee," an AIM pamphlet claims, "nearly 200 AIM members have been arrested. At least a dozen unsolved murders, knifings, shootings, suspicious accidents and suicides have claimed the lives of AIM members. A number of AIM women have been raped. And AIM members say Pedro Bissonette was assassinated by two Bureau of Indian Affairs (BIA) policemen on the Pine Ridge Reservation" ("Pine Ridge After Wounded Knee" n.d., n.p.).

Federal and state judiciaries are condemned as fellow-travelers in this violent campaign. Grand jury proceedings, militants argue, have become instruments of inquisition rather than investigation, while local courts have permitted and even encouraged unequal law enforcement; whites "use laws of the courtroom against us like they used diseased blankets and the Seventh Cavalry against our ancestors" ("A Statement from John Trudell" 1975; see also Native American Solidarity Committee n.d.).

Clearly, for contemporary militants, the "Indian Wars" never ended (*Voices* 1974, 89; Arkeketa 1973; "Book Reviews" 1978). Imprisoned activists are "prisoners of war" (*NASC News* n.d., 5; Peltier 1982, 20; Butler 1983). Crow Dog wrote from the Leavenworth penitentiary: "When they were taking me away to prison in handcuffs, I was thinking: 'Will they kill me like they killed Crazy Horse?'" ("Crow Dog From Prison" 1976). At Wounded Knee in 1973, militants refused the government's demand to disarm prior to negotiation in part because, at the original Wounded Knee in 1890, Big Foot's band had surrendered their arms just prior to being massacred by the 7th Cavalry (*Voices* 1974, 148). Moreover, while the bullets are very real, this "war" is not to be construed narrowly. Force of arms, activists allege, is only one way to destroy a culture; instruments of white society, including the educational system, organized religion, government, and science all constitute acts of war (Mohawk 1982; Maria and Mohawk 1977). Therefore, activists find themselves still engaged in a battle that "combines a struggle against colonialism with religious and political war" ("Pine Ridge After Wounded Knee" n.d., n.p.) in "an on-going conflict that we must continually address to maintain our individuality and our sovereignty" (*Voices* 1974, 97; see also "Let Us Act" 1983).

Perhaps unsurprisingly, militants frequently analogize their struggle to that of the Vietnamese.[6] The commitment of massive firepower to quell militant activities has been compared to the commitment made by the United States in Vietnam to avoid appearing like a "helpless giant"; the effort of authorities to apprehend alleged activist criminals has been compared to the Army's "search and destroy" missions; and the government's allegedly deliberate setting of grass fires at Wounded Knee has been compared to the Army's defoliation program in Vietnam ("Garden Plot" 1975, 7; *Voices* 1974, 77).

Activists see the Vietnamese as another native people, attached by farming to their land and way of life, fighting to keep both against a foreign, colonial, imperialist power (*Voices* 1974, 195–97; Keane 1983). This power engages in indiscriminate killing of women and children, resorts to provocation in order to justify massive counterattacks, and supports puppet governments, be they regimes in Saigon or BIA-backed tribal governments on the reservations (*Voices* 1974, 195–97). Supporters of native activism suggest that "[t]he peace movement grew out of the indignation of people over the illegitimate actions of the government and the military in Vietnam" and argue that "THE FUNDAMENTAL ISSUES INVOLVED IN THE NATIVE AMERICAN STRUGGLE ARE THE SAME" ("Who We Are" 1976; capitalization in original). The complexities of this analogy are contained within the slogan, "If you understand Vietnam, you can understand Wounded Knee."[7]

Military metaphors are a common contemporary *topos*, invoked, over the past two decades, in "wars" against a plethora of social ills (Stelzner 1977; Zarefsky 1977; Dolan 1986). In the context of Native American protest, use of this *topos* may serve several purposes. It may call upon nationalistic (tribal) ferver in the service of an urgent cause. Identification with the Indian wars of the previous century may appeal to Native Americans' feelings of independence, sovereign power, and injustice. Identification with the Vietnamese may play upon white America's disillusionment over that war while forging in Indians a sense of solidarity with other oppressed indigenous peoples across the globe. More fundamentally than these identifications, however, militaristic terminology evokes a warrior *persona* and calls upon the warrior's knowledge of supernatural power in the battle against white oppression.

The warrior role developed with tribal culture and thus is deeply and powerfully rooted. Tribal life was far from edenic; numerous folktales and oral histories attest to its dangers (F. Turner 1974, 30, 135). Importantly, a major source of danger is supernatural power, which is ambivalent. Neither good nor evil in itself, power works benefit or misfortune according to how it is used (Underhill 1965, 5; Park 1938, 87). Accordingly, the acquisition of power, which promises much benefit, is nonetheless also fraught with danger. Power, in short, is not benign. When acquired, "the individual suffers, and throughout his [sic] life he is constantly threatened not only with sickness but with death as well. He is endangered not only by his own acts, but also by either deliberate or thoughtless behavior of others" (Park 1938, 33; see also Castaneda 1974, 69). Because of power's capacity to turn on its user, it must be handled carefully. The ritual details must be observed scrupulously; should power objects be handled carelessly, songs or prayers recited incorrectly, power may turn against the offending individual.

Hence, both the natural and supernatural realms posed dangers in tribal life. Survival under such conditions demanded certain kinds of people and a certain style of life. The social role of the warrior responded to these demands. Courage and self-sacrifice were manifest in the provision of the physical necessities of life. The warrior was called upon to face the dangers of the hunt in providing food and the dangers of war in defending the tribe's security.[8] Courage and self-sacrifice were also manifest in the provision of the spiritual necessities of life. Despite its potent ambivalence, the warrior was expected to obtain a power and harness it for the benefit of the tribe. For example, in seeking a guiding vision (one method of acquiring power), it might be necessary to inflict self-torture, as in the Sun Dance of the Sioux (Erikson 1963, 114; Powers 1977, 95–100, 139–41).

Significantly, tribal society engaged white culture, and experienced its dangers, in both the natural and supernatural realms. The collapse of aboriginal cultures in the face of advanced technology has been well documented. Initially, the white race's inventions were unfathomable, seen as examples of the great power bestowed upon the race by the Great Spirit (F. Turner 1974, 247). There was power in the firearm and in the horse which, when introduced to the Plains tribes, was called "holy dog." There was power in the whispering wires of the telegraph and in the "iron horse." There was power in alcohol, which the Sioux still call *mni wakan* ("holy water") for its ability to produce effects first thought similar to dreams and visions (Lame Deer and Erdoes 1972, 77). And there was power in sheer numbers; the thousands of whites sweeping west were seen to indicate the high favor in which the Great Spirit (or the white God—Indians disagreed over whether the races shared the same deity) held his white children.

Further, throughout the course of white immigration and settlement, a dominant form of contact between the races was the Army fort and the traders that frequented it. Thus, contact with these strange new powers of the white race, together with the presence of the Army, demanded the services of the Indian warrior in the fullest sense: the warrior was called upon to do battle simultaneously with the U.S. Cavalry and the power of the white race's ways.

This warrior role is key to understanding much of the contemporary Native American activist movement. At Wounded Knee, young men painted themselves and prepared their personal "medicines" for battle, just as they had done during the occupation of the national BIA headquarters the previous November (Weiss 1975, 9). Such practices are emblematic of militant efforts to reconstitute traditional "warrior societies" among Indians ("Bellecourt Explains" 1973; Flanders 1983; "Opening Statements" 1974; "Great Lakes" 1975; *Akwesasne Notes* 1983, 1). "Warrior society" to activists designates

the men and women of the nation who have dedicated themselves to give everything that they have to the people. A warrior should be the first one to go hungry or the last one to eat. He should be the first one to give away his mocassins [*sic*] and the last one to get new ones. . . . He is ready to defend his family in time of war—to hold off any enemy, and is perfectly willing to sacrifice himself to the good of his tribe and his people. That's what a warrior society is to Indian people, and that's what we envision ourselves as, what we idealistically try to be. (*Voices* 1974, 61–62; see also "'When in the Course'" 1973)

The warrior is a *persona*, a character to be enacted, and not only a congeries of virtues to be espoused. As Kills Straight contends, AIM is "a new warrior class of this century, bound by the bond of the drum, who vote with their bodies instead of their mouths" (Kills Straight 1973). This *persona* places preeminent value on the virtues of selflessness and courage. Moreover, it fuses the militaristic connotations of a warrior in the profane world with the metaphysical connotations of a warrior in the sacred world, thereby staging a battle with both natural and supernatural dimensions. The warrior, therefore, is a *persona* of power; in enacting the role called forth by their militaristic terminology, Indian activists may enlist the supernatural in their "war" with whites.[9] Grace Black Elk, for example, warns:

And they even stopped the food and they even stopped our fuel, but now the Great Spirit's gonna punish them by stopping most of the fuel, so they're running short on fuel. And pretty soon . . . there's gonna be starvation coming to the white people. And since we've already been in poverty we know what to do to get by. . . . And then the electricity, that's where our sacred eagle comes in, he controls the weather, and he's gonna see to it that pretty soon there won't be any electricity for the white people. . . . And one of these days they're gonna realize how they hurted us. They're gonna be hurt by it too. (*Voices* 1974, 239)

Implications

This essay has argued that rhetoric and ritual are fundamentally related symbolic processes whose cooperative workings are best seen in the phenomenon of the *persona*. The *persona* is not simply a rhetorical or dramatic device, a mode of ethical proof or catharsis in the classical sense, much less equivalent to an explicit, discursive argument that one should behave a certain way. Nor is it purely a ritual phenomenon whose power can be an artifact of magic. The *persona* instrumentally invites, "Be as I am," and is consummated in each and every person who accepts the invitation and gives the *persona* life, both rhetor and audience. And the more one makes one's "self" over in the image of the *persona*, the more perfectly has this instrumental purpose been consummated.

This perspective casts new light on certain fundamental issues in contemporary argumentation theory. In this section, I wish to discuss the answers which this perspective suggests to three fundamental, related questions: (1) What is argument? (2) When is assent justified? and (3) Can (and should) argumentation theory address issues of power and domination and thereby be a force for change in the world?

WHAT IS ARGUMENT? To this point, I have said little about "argument" per se, using this term synonymously with "rhetoric" in a rather off-handed way. My view of *personae* accounts for this usage.

The most traditional conception of argument holds it to be a discursive, relatively discrete inferential form in which claims are adduced from evidence and supporting reasons. Neo-Aristotelians hold that argument is a subset of rhetoric whose paradigmatic form is the enthymeme (which is itself, they contend, derived from the demonstrative scientific syllogism) and which appeals primarily to *logos* rather than *ethos* or *pathos* (Thompson 1975). As the scope of contemporary rhetorical theory has expanded beyond discourse to include the study of film, music, cartoons, and icons (to name but a few), even scholars who suspect that the distinctions between the classical modes of proof may be suspiciously arbitrary tend to restrict argument to the discursive realm of relatively explicit reason-giving.

Such formal distinctions, however, should be viewed as provisional at best, and often misguided. Argumentative discourse often is more instrumental (that is, addressed to an audience for purposes of gaining assent to an explicit claim) and perhaps more "rational," than, say, poetic discourse or sculpture that has no obvious "message" for others and whose very existence seems to consummate the rhetor's (or artist's) purpose. However, argument in its purest traditional form (the syllogism of formal logic) is also argument at its most ritualistic, that is, a repetitive form whose validity is not dependent upon its instrumental effects, but is consummated solely in the arrangement of its constituent elements. In brief, the syllogism is simultaneously instrumental and consummatory, rhetorical and ritualistic.

Given the framework outlined previously, then, we should expect syllogisms to exhibit a *persona*. Indeed they do. Syllogisms invite assent to an explicitly stated claim, but they also invite participation in an enacted *persona*, and the means by which the former is accomplished is key to understanding the latter. Syllogisms not only *invite* assent, but in a sense *compel* it, through "demonstration," or, the formally valid arrangement of constituent terms. Both arguer and audience are immaterial to demonstration; a valid syllogism is eternally True, no matter who says it and no matter whether any audience agrees with it (this is either the syllogism's great virtue or vice, of course, depending on one's predilections). Yet, this formal arrangement of constituent elements is itself a psychological inducement to assent and action (Burke [1953] 1968, 124). How? One explanation, I suggest, is that syllogistic *form* enacts "logic," and thereby invites assent to and participation in the *persona* that is Reason itself—pure, immaterial, and immutable. Admittedly, to speak of a wholly disembodied *persona* may seem paradoxical. But a *persona* it is, nonetheless. Syllogisms ritually incarnate eternal Truth.

If the quintessential argumentative form portrays a *persona*, then it is not unreasonable to expect, *a fortiori*, all arguments to do so. In fact, these *personae* will be easier to identify because, being more embodied, they will seem more like characters and less like abstract essences. As one moves from formal logic to practical argumentation, one also moves from immutable Reason to historically conditioned and contextually variable "good reasons" (Wallace 1963; Fisher 1978, 1980; Perelman and Olbrechts-Tyteca [1969] 1971; Toulmin [1958] 1974). This means that arguers (and audiences)—or "good reasoners"—not just arguments, again have a role in argumentation.

In this circumstance, both real and implied arguers will be present. To an extent, the latter will be shaped by the *ethoi* of the former. In addition, implied arguers will portray their real counterparts *as people who make arguments*—that is, as "clear-headed," "sensible," "right-thinking," and "reasonable." And this portrayal is the implied arguer's (or *persona's*) admittedly implicit, nondiscursive "argument."

Finally, it should be noted, other symbolic forms may enact, and thereby invite participation in, *personae* of a different character. The *persona* of a painter or poet, for example, as portrayed in her works, may be that of the "inspired genius" or the "tortured recluse" but is less likely to be that of the "reasonable person." So argumentation is not the rational part of rhetoric as a whole, but its *persona* is more "reasonable," just as other types of symbolic action may be differentiated on the presentational level. Nonetheless, all such acts enact *personae* of *some* kind and thereby both rhetorically seek assent to and ritualistically invite participation in a "claim." Argument is no exception.

When Is Assent Justified? In the history of argumentation theory, criteria of justified assent have ranged from the precise validity rules of formal logic to the more expansive standards of "practical reasoning," discussed above, to the even more flexible (too flexible to be useful, some have argued: see Rowland 1987; Warnick 1987) measures of the "narrative paradigm" (Fisher 1987). In today's world, flexible criteria of some kind seem self-evidently necessary; what constitutes a "sound" argument depends on a number of situationally variable factors.

This essay will not examine these criteria on their own normative terms; instead, I want to observe that all such norms are of restricted utility in that they function only as measures of the soundness of an argument's discursive claim. However, this essay has contended, arguments seek assent not only to the claim stated but also to the claim enacted. Therefore, no matter what criteria one favors at the discursive level (and assuming that one is not a radical skeptic who rejects even the possibility of such a thing), the presence of *personae* in argument suggests two additional questions to be posed at the presentational level. First, does the *enacted* claim warrant assent? Is the *persona* "sound," that is, does it portray a type of person with traits we ought value, a type that deserves emulation? Second, are the stated claim and the enacted claim mutually reinforcing? Are *persona* and discursive argument consistent? If either question is answered in the negative, greater skepticism probably is warranted, as Karlyn Kohrs Campbell's (1972) harsh critique of Richard Nixon's 1969 "Vietnamization" address suggests: Nixon argues explicitly that the public must be told the "truth" about the war in order to unify the nation, yet the *persona* that he enacts is of a man who will misrepresent the truth in order to divide the nation and stifle dissent.

I make no attempt to specify criteria by which to answer these two questions, because any such criteria inevitably must be flexible; the "soundness" of a *persona*, too, depends on a number of situational factors. Just as some audiences at some times will find good reasons to adhere to a discursive claim, while others will not, so will some find reason to celebrate and enact a *persona*, while others will not.

The warrior *persona* is illustrative. As the intersection of the rhetorical and ritualistic impulses, the warrior *persona* is both an argument for and the embodiment of a set of ideal Native American attributes. In a process not unlike that outlined by Edwin Black (1970), this *persona* characterizes what its audience *should be*, while simultaneously equipping that audience to transform itself according to the characterization. Thus, this *persona* is instrumental, seeking adherence, asking witnesses to assent to the desirability of the embodied attributes; it is also consummatory, inviting identification and participation, asking witnesses to adopt those attributes. Further, this particular *persona* encompasses both the natural and supernatural; the warrior, that is, is a *persona* of power. As a result, it can transform witnesses, ritually accomplishing its own purposes.

However, this *persona* is not uniformly appealing. The warpaint and feathers worn by many activists, for example, ritually invoke the societally laudable warrior role for many Indians, whose culture is rich with such ritual possibilities; yet these same items seem comic and incongruous to most white audiences because whites have been conditioned, by film, literature, and so on, to evaluate the Indian warrior decidedly less positively, and because white culture recognizes fewer (or at least different) ritual possibilities (Lake 1983, 127–29).

Similarly, activist rhetoric appeals more to some Native Americans than others. For the Indian audience is not homogeneous; the warrior *persona* celebrates the proud, independent, and self-reliant tribalist who has survived for thousands of years on this earth, at the expense of the militarily vanquished progressivist determined to assimilate into the melting pot of American society. Both characterizations, while oversimplified, are partially borne out by the historical record and claim adherents among Indians (for an interesting analysis of these characterizations in the anthropological literature, see Bruner 1986). The militants who seek restoration of traditional tribal culture dismiss the more assimilationist progressives as "apples" (red outside but white inside) or "Uncle Tomahawks." Therefore, traditionalist Indians, and militant Indians who desire to be traditional, identify with this *persona* more strongly than do progressivists, who have given up at least some of the traditional world-view that makes the warrior role compelling.

This point can be made in another way. As Victor Turner argues in this essay's prefatory quotation, conditions of liminality and marginality (that is, transitional and "in-between" states) often generate rituals that found new models of life and move individuals, not simply to assent to the models but to act them into existence. Modern Native Americans exemplify this liminal condition, existing on the margins of American society, caught literally in-between the traditional tribal matrix and white technocratic culture. And militant Indians must surely sense this condition most acutely, having experienced the full force of the latter and, as a result, sought restoration of the former.[10] If so, the activists' militarist terminology and other actions that form the warrior *persona* may be a contemporary ritual born of the moment but deeply rooted in a traditional symbolic frame. And the contemporary ritual would speak most powerfully to those who value the tradition and wish to see the two as one. For enactment of the warrior role *is* this very synthesis.

It is also important to keep such variability in perspective. The warrior *persona* elicits assent from a broad spectrum of Indians. Further, in the 1960s and 1970s, many white youths were attracted to the quasi-tribalistic communal lifestyle of the "counter-culture," a subculture that was rich in its own ritual possibilities and identified strongly with the "Indian way of life," to the point of adopting Indian dress and even certain religious, ritual practices. Even Americans who subscribe wholly to the technocratic values of our age may be moved to assent to the native warrior *persona* at least to the degree that militant appropriation of the Vietnam experience rings true. Indeed, the great strength of the warrior *persona* is that its enactment is accessible to a wide range of otherwise diverse individuals. As Janet McCloud (1977) has observed, a warrior can be "a man, or a woman, an elder or a youth"; a warrior "may feel desperate enough to take up arms" or become a doctor fighting disease or a lawyer fighting injustices; a warrior might become a teacher "combatting ignorance" or a "brother in prison trying to pry open the iron doors"; a warrior might be "a medicine man fighting against the death pattern that plagues our people and striving to revive the life-instincts."

In sum, the ritual and rhetorical impulses are universal because the impulse to symbolize is universal. And if human personality is the product of interaction between self and *personae*, all humans potentially may be induced to assent to a *persona* to some degree. The degree, however, is variable, dependent on at least two factors: (1) the extent to which one's cultural worldview values the ideal attributes embodied by the *persona* in question; and (2) the relative value that one's cultural worldview attaches to rhetorical or ritual action. The warrior *persona*, for example, offers variable bases of assent, from (weakly) adherence to (moderately) participation to (strongly) magical transformation.

Can (Should) Argumentation Theory Address Praxis? One of the most prominent trends in recent rhetorical theorizing concerns what Philip Wander (1983, 1984) dubbed the "ideological turn" in criticism. Proponents contend that critics, as observers of events, cannot stand outside the social milieus they observe, and, as interpreters of events, necessarily must be partisan. Indeed, the argument continues, the critical task should be the partisan effort to demystify the workings of power and ideological domination in society.

While this argument easily can be (and often is) made from the perspective of so-called critical theory, a similar case can be built upon less Marxist moorings. All statements about language, being themselves couched in language, are reflexive. Therefore, all theories of argument are themselves arguments, just as all theories of criticism are themselves critiques and, more generally, all theories of rhetoric are themselves rhetorical; all, to some degree, are perspectives that seek adherence, not Truths that compel. And, according to the position articulated in this essay, adherence is invited on both discursive and presentational levels.

Therefore, in the debate over activist criticism, each side not only states a case discursively but also enacts one. Just as formalistic theories of argument enact the *persona* of unquestionable Reason or Truth, so opponents of an activist stance embody a critical *persona* that coolly, dispassionately, and objectively hands down conclusive judgments from a neutral (and usually privileged) position "above the fray." On the other hand, just as theories of practical reasoning exhibit as much concern for arguers as arguments, so those sympathetic to ideological criticism embody an impassioned, activist critical *persona*, one that has a stake in the events she analyzes and is committed to a vision of the good life (this *persona* is discernible, I submit, in Fisher's [1987, 69–73] narrative critique of Jonathan Shell's *The Fate of the Earth*). Burke, too, emphasizes the interdependence of arguers and arguments when he quips, "you cannot have ideas without persons or persons without ideas" ([1945] 1969, 512).

Moreover, different theories of argument, and their companion critical *personae*, possess, in some measure, different "political" implications. Formalist theories are more supportive of elitist, conservative programs; defense of "technical reason" produces real-world consequences somewhat at odds with theories of "public knowledge" (Farrell 1976, 1978b; Carleton 1978; Farrell and Goodnight 1981; Fisher 1987; Goodnight 1982; cf. Lake and Keough 1985).

In short, not only arguments but also theories of argumentation portray *personae* that invite participation. One implication is that critics cannot avoid advocacy and its attendant tangible consequences. This implication does not mean, however, that proponents of activist criticism have won an unqualified victory. On the discursive level, the insistence by formalist theories upon comparatively determinate, conclusive rules of validity is a needed reminder that just any reason need not be a good reason, no matter what the political stakes. Conversely, practical theories rightly point out, probable truths need not be invalid; "good reasons" can be good enough.

An analogous condition arises at the presentational level. The competing *personae* described above are mutually correcting. The formalist *persona* extols the virtues of objectivity and accuracy to the neglect of committedness and involvement, while the practical *persona* embodies activism and concern for the human condition but at the expense of measured, independent judgment. Each *persona* enacts a critical but incomplete character of admirable but by themselves inadequate traits.

Therefore, the best balanced academic criticism may be that which conforms to accepted tests of argumentative soundness, when its advocacy is explicit, clarifying its own assumptions, values, and point of view, and when, as a result, it self-consciously enacts the *persona* of the reasonable advocate. On its face, such a middle course argues its best case for whatever claim it makes, while acknowledging this claim's necessary partisanship and limitations. In so arguing, this middle course equips its audience to test its "good reasons" as best they are able, thereby showing concern for arguers as well as arguments. In so equipping its audience, it both implicitly argues that criticism should balance concerns of social Justice and rational Truth and enacts the *persona* able to do so.

This view is admittedly imprecise; some may find its emphasis on traditional reason conservative or even reactionary, while others may see its subjectivity as excessively relativistic. The middle ground is always, by definition, guilty of such uncertainty. Nonetheless, the *persona* of the reasonable advocate seems appropriate both because uncertainty is appropriate in the face of morally untidy, politically charged issues and because this *persona* reflexively enacts the views of this essay. If all theories of argument are themselves arguments, then so is this one. And if all arguments both state and enact and should be judged on both levels, then so should this one. The *persona* of the "reasonable advocate" seems to enact most appropriately my explicit view that argumentation theory can and should conjoin Reason (the rhetorical, discursive, instrumental argument) and the Advocate (the ritualistic, presentational, consummatory implied arguer) in the concept of the *persona*.

The next turn of this reflexive wheel, of course, would judge whether the *persona* enacted in this essay is consistent with my discursive claim about the *persona* of the "reasonable advocate." By my own precepts, I would not be able objectively to judge this matter, nor did I desire to do so; here, too, uncertainty is appropriate. Nonetheless, it is hoped that this essay has illustrated sufficiently some implications of expanding argumentation beyond a concern for arguments to include the role of the implied arguer.

Notes

1. Rhetorical scholars have shown increasing interest in ritual, in the related concepts of myth and archetype and in the works of authors such as Cassirer, Eliade, Geertz, Jung, Turner, and Van Gennep. In addition to works previously cited, see: Geertz (1973); Jung [1966] 1977a, [1966] 1977b; V. Turner 1974, 1980; Van Gennep 1960. Dominating this literature have been studies in social movements (Cathcart 1978; Lake 1983), film criticism (Solomon 1983; Rushing 1985), and political communication (Bennett 1977, 1980, 1981; Farrell 1978a; Klumpp and Hollihan 1979; Weaver 1982; see also Balthrop 1984; Corcoran 1983; Hoban 1980).

In some essays, scholars have applied well-developed anthropological models to contemporary communication phenomena, discovering specific ritual forms. In this vein, Richard B. Gregg and Gerard A. Hauser (1973) explored the similarities between Kwakiutl potlatch ceremonies and President Nixon's 1970 address announcing the invasion of Cambodia; similarly, David A. Frank (1981) analyzed rites of passage in the Israeli peace movement, while Janet Hocker Rushing and Thomas S. Frentz (1980) discovered them in a Vietnam War film.

In other studies, the notion of "ritual" is used only loosely, to denote recurrent rhetorical strategies in recurrent situations. For example, Leo Finkelstein, Jr. (1981), called inaugural addresses a "calendrical rite"; Judith S. Trent (1978) termed the emergence of presidential candidates "ritualistic"; and Ellen Reid Gold (1978) examined the "ritual" of self-defense in the 1976 campaign (more generally, see also Gronbeck 1978).

Thus, sometimes the "ritualistic" is equated with the "symbolic" and contrasted with the "practical" uses of language; in others a ritual seems synonymous with a genre; and in still others it uniquely signifies little or nothing. As Edmund Leach has commented, "even among those who have specialized in this field there is the widest possible disagreement as to how the word ritual should be used and how the performance of ritual should be understood" (1968, 13:526; see also Goody 1977).

2. The "I" of literature is never identical with the author, if only because, even in autobiography, the author must select some details for inclusion and exclude others (Elliott 1982, 58). A rhetorical criticism that illustrates this point, albeit without employing the concept of *persona* per se, is Thomas Benson's (1974) study of Malcolm X.

3. P. Campbell 1972, 391. Other scholars have discussed *persona* from a literary point of view, including Wayne C. Booth (1961, esp. 169–270), Leo Spitzer (1946), and George T. Wright (1960, 1–59). Representative rhetorical studies that employ this concept include Ernest G. Bormann's (1973) study of the Eagleton affair; Phyllis M. Japp's (1985) examination of the abolition-ist-feminist rhetoric of Angelina Grimke; David S. Kaufer's (1979) comparison of Nixon and Kennedy; Walter G. Kirkpatrick's (1981) critique of Bolingbroke; Berel Lang's (1975) examination of space, time, and philosophical style; Christine Oravec's (1981) study of John Muir's rhetoric of preservationism; David L. Rarick et al.'s (1977) critique of Jimmy Carter's 1976 presidential campaign; John W. Rathbun's (1969) analysis of historical criticism; Thomas O. Sloane's (1965) study of Donne; and Ann Vasaly's (1985) examination of Cicero's *Pro Roscio Amerino*.

For somewhat different applications of this concept, see Edwin Black (1970) and Philip Wander (1984).

4. For example, when a court forbade actor Clayton Moore to wear the mask of the Lone Ranger, Moore protested: "When I put on the mask I become the Lone Ranger" (Elliott 1982, 23). Similarly, singer Annie Lennox of the rock group Eurythmics recently objected to media commentary on her "image," contending: "It's not something that I possess, it is something that is me. An expression of me and expression of Eurythmics. . . . for me, personally, it is just an extension of myself. So I find it very odd when people say to me, 'Oh, your new image is this or that.' I don't understand it" (Van Matre 1986).

5. For a somewhat different view of the *persona* from a psychoanalytic point of view, see C. G. Jung's "The Persona as a Segment of the Collective Psyche" ([1966] 1977b, 156–62). For a somewhat different discussion of the "self" as the center of opposing forces, see Henry W. Johnstone, Jr.'s (1970) discussion of the "problem of the self."

6. Erik Erikson (1968, 319) foresaw the possibility that "continued American action in Vietnam" might promote "a world-wide identification of colored people with the naked heroism of the Vietcong revolutionaries."

7. D.C. Wounded Knee Defense Committee 1975, 1. Native activists identify not only with the Vietnamese but also with other indigenous people across the globe. For but two of dozens of examples, see "Mapuches Continue Their Struggle" (1975) and J. C. Rojas (1976).

8. The former, of course, was not a vital concern for the planting tribes. The virtue of self-sacrifice is also evident in the give-away, which helped equalize wealth within the tribe and maintain the poor, while recreating the original give-away of the Great Spirit (Erikson 1963, 140; see also Gregg and Hauser's [1973, 176–77] discussion of the Kwakiutl potlatch ceremony).

9. See, for example, Warren K. Moorehead's (1914, 179) discussion of medicine bags and Ghost Shirts. Opler's (1941, 248–49) description of the en-

counter between Apache shamans and witches, a contest characterized in terms of warfare, is most appropos, revealing the interpenetration of these two forms of battle. Of course, the supernatural need not be real; it is sufficient that it be a hypothesized resource of the *persona*.

10. The activist movement originally was primarily an urban phenomenon; AIM, for example, was founded in 1968 in Minneapolis (and called Concerned Indian Americans or CIA) to monitor alleged police harassment. In recent years, the movement has de-centered and faded into traditional reservation life (Ross and Most 1976; cf. Stumbo 1986).

6

Metaphor and Presence in Argument

Charles Kauffman and Donn W. Parson

The debate over strategic policy occasioned by the Reagan Administration's defense buildup during the 1980s illustrates well the difficulty in formulating arguments that can forge a consensus on public policy. The shrillness of Administration cries for increases in strategic forces was matched by equally piercing pleas from the freeze movement for unilateral disarmament (Caldicott 1986). Each side preached its dogma, not so much to convert the innocent as to create a record of having tried. When the opposition, predictably, ignored the arguments, each could charge the other with unreason, which, after all, seemed to be the point. Productive argument in the public sphere requires an element of risk; if argument is to be at all functional, advocates must be prepared to be influenced themselves while they attempt to persuade others. The retreat of both positions into orthodoxy has all the characteristics of an intellectual siege and enacts the problem in contemporary rhetoric described by Wayne Booth in *Modern Dogma and the Rhetoric of Assent* (1974). It is noteworthy that in spite of the recognized urgency of the nuclear weapons debate, neither side is willing to advance beyond its wall of discourse. This reluctance is a sign of the misgivings still associated with an art than can change minds without leaving a mark.

If argument is to function as a vehicle of assent, that is, as an instrument to forge the informed agreements necessary for public policy, it must encourage the intellectual risk-taking that is a necessary part of the process of mutual influence. In Booth's words, "the rules of good discourse ... can no longer be confined to logical prose—we must take in the proofs of personal appeal and commitment, of art and myth and ritual" (1974, 203). In particular, we believe that concepts of presence and metaphor offer a way to understand the shortcomings of modern rhetoric and a possible way to its rehabilitation.

Presence

Throughout *The New Rhetoric* (1969), Chaim Perelman and L. Olbrechts-Tyteca insist on the centrality of "presence" to argument. Presence, they claim, is an "essential factor to argumentation" because, "through verbal magic alone," a rhetor can "enhance the value of some of the elements of which one has actually been made conscious" (1969, 116–17). Presence is a quality arguments possess to varying degrees, endowing them with a sense of urgency. Arguments that lack presence lose this sense of urgency; indeed, they are more likely to be taken as truisms than arguments.[1] Therefore, rhetors can evoke presence to heighten our awareness of a controversy or deliberately suppress it to conceal disagreement. Nevertheless, presence is among the most powerful assets of argument and would seem prerequisite to a rhetoric of assent.

The relationship between presence and assent is easier to understand if we construct a scale, after Edwin Black (1965), to chart the relationship between degrees of presence and audience attention and audience effects. As presence increases, one should observe corresponding increases in audience attention, for urgency should create attention, and in audience effects (arguments with greater presence should be more persuasive). It might even be argued that presence may attract audiences by making an argument "available" to people by demonstrating its importance to them. On the other hand, as presence decreases, audience attention and audience effects should show corresponding declines. At the extremes, arguments with very high levels of presence should resemble arguments almost lacking in presence. Presence is an ephemeral quality; just as the repetition of a peculiar sensation numbs sense organs so does an argument exhaust its ability to excite the imagination. Thus, an argument with perfect presence would, having persuaded everyone, lose its quality of presence as it achieved universal assent. An argument completely without presence, in one sense, would produce another sort of universal agreement: if no one gave it heed, the argument would succeed perfectly in maintaining the existing orders of things.

Here is the relationship between presence and assent. Arguments with greater presence invite participation in a controversy and encourage the intellectual risk taking necessary to overcome dogma and produce assent (Karon 1976, 106–08). Arguments lacking in presence serve, by contrast, to maintain the presumptions upon which dogma is based. Insofar as these arguments discourage participation, they act as barriers to assent. At the same time, by repeating dogma, arguments lacking presence thus reinforce it. This relationship is the reason for much of the profitless controversy that surrounds the debate on strategic weapons. Each side repeats its arguments without engaging the other; as positions calcify, productive argument becomes increasingly difficult to attain.

While insisting on the importance of presence, Perelman and Olbrechts-Tyteca have little to say about the means by which arguments acquire presence. In their discussion of the techniques for producing presence, Perelman and Olbrechts-Tyteca mention repetition, evocation of detail, the use of the present tense, definite pronouns, synecdoche, and amplification. Presence is associated, as one would expect, with the "presentational" aspects of argument. It is surprising that Perelman and Olbrechts-Tyteca do not discuss metaphor as a source of presence because elsewhere they comment on the ability of metaphor to seize the imagination. We believe that metaphor, which borrows from argumentation and poetic, is a primary vehicle for both the evocation and suppression of presence in discourse.

If presence is to be found in the intersection of the poetic and the rational, then it makes sense to look for it in conjunction with metaphor. Metaphor in argument draws conclusions and attracts attention through the juxtaposition of ideas. We believe that metaphor can be a powerful tool to induce or hinder assent because of its ability to make the abstract concrete and the concrete abstract. That is, metaphor has the capacity to command attention to new ideas, paving the way to assent. On the other hand, by making the extraordinary seem routine, metaphor can hide the power of ideas behind a screen of orthodoxy. Metaphor thus has the capacity to evoke presence or suppress it. We shall now attempt to describe and account for these processes.

Metaphor and Presence

Aristotle was only the first to comment on the close, formal relationship between metaphor and the traditional techniques of argumentation. In the *Poetics* (1977), Aristotle uses metaphors drawn from argumentation to describe the operation of metaphor: "Metaphor by proportion occurs when the second term [b] is related to the first [a] in the same ways as the fourth [d] to the third [c]; then the poet may use the second [b] in lieu of the fourth [d] or vice versa" (1457b 16–20). Furthermore, Aristotle (1954) argued that metaphor, in addition to its ability to adorn language, had a unique ability to convey insight: "it is from metaphor that we can best get hold of something fresh" (1410b 14). In approaching Aristotle, Ricoeur posits the superiority of the metaphor over a simile in creating the fresh, for the metaphor was more elegant, the simile longer and less attractive; "simile explicitly displays the moment of resemblance that operates implicitly in metaphor" (Ricoeur 1977, 27). Thus, for Aristotle, metaphor was a process by which meaning was transferred, analogically, from one term to another in order to animate elegantly and clarify ideas. Modern argumentation theorists, however, have not been sanguine about metaphor or its cousin, argument by analogy. When they discuss metaphor at all, which is seldom, it is with reservation about its probative value, and they consider it a weak form of argument. Russell Windes and Arthur Hastings (1965) summarize the conventional attitude: "The strength of the analogy—its quality of abstraction—is also its weakness. Any situation is so complex that many abstractions can be made from it" (183, 184). Although theorists such as George Campbell have defended the rationality of metaphorical argument, with the rise of empiricism metaphor has been more often distrusted as a form of argument.

This distrust of metaphor and argument by analogy has obscured the basis for constructing a modern rhetoric of assent. Any rhetoric of assent necessarily involves the search for fruitful metaphors that can form the basis for agreements conducive to argument. Susanne Langer (1957) argues, "Metaphor is our most striking evidence of *abstractive seeing*, of the power of human minds to use presentational symbols. Every new experience, or new idea about things, evokes first of all some metaphorical expression" (141, emphasis in original). Langer distinguishes two types of symbolic forms—the discursive and the presentational. Discursive form comprises language with "permanent units of meaning which are combinable into larger units"; it is governed by rules of grammar and syntax, encoded into phrases, sentences, and larger units; its "meanings given through language are successively understood and gathered into a whole by the process called discourse" (89). Presentational forms by contrast are forms of symbolism that are understood "only through the meaning of the whole, through their relations within the total structure." Forms such as music, art, and poetry typify the presentational. Meaning is conveyed in all symbol use; its understanding in discursive form is successive but in presentational form it is "grasped in one act of vision" (89, 86). Because metaphor is a linguistic creation, it shares in the resources of discursive form. The particular power of metaphor arises from its fusion of forms; discursive and presentational inducements to assent are presented simultaneously, and in this process of reinforcing one another, they create repetitive form, yet another level of symbolic inducement. This *dynamis* lies at the heart of Parke Burgess's (1985) discussion of "The Dialectic of Substance." Similarly, Ernst Cassirer (1946) sees metaphor as the possible link between Langer's symbolic forms; in Cassirer's terms it is the "intellectual link between language and myth." The power of metaphor may lie in the bridging of symbolic forms. Rather than simply combining categories, metaphor may transcend to create a new category; "it is not only a transition to another category, but actually the creation of the category itself" (84, 88).

Modern approaches to metaphor commonly treat it as an aspect of cognition and, despite the many prevailing theories, underlying most of them is a fundamental rational principle that makes metaphor, if not argument, at least argument-like. The principle is this: in order for metaphor to function as a comparison, the grounds on which the comparison is based have to be "available" to audiences. One must recognize essential similarities between the things compared and conclude that the two ideas are, in some respects, consubstantial.

This decision, even though rooted in the varied experiences of each person, is not less rational because it is framed experientially rather than empirically. Consubstantiality is not rooted in surface appearances but is, instead, constitutional in nature and is to be found in the essential constituents and properties of ideas. Hence, the success of metaphor is based on abstraction, which reveals essentials that fuse to form new meanings.

This process is capable of replication and verification. Metaphors redeem themselves heuristically through a sort of consensual validation. We do not mean to substitute one empirical test for another by suggesting that a "valid" metaphor is one that works for the greatest number of people. People will, of course, differ in their evaluations of the pertinent similarities between the ideas compared. Even so, the basis upon which the comparison rests can be described and people can deliberate about the adequacy of the comparisons (Osborn 1963).

Common to most modern theories of metaphor is the idea that metaphor is, at least partially, a rational instrument of cognition that makes possible insights and understanding that might otherwise be lost. And each of these approaches recognizes the power of metaphor to organize thought and experience. As Michael Osborn (1982) concludes, "once we adopt and commit to such ruling metaphors as time is a flowing river or language is a series of discrete meaning containers, or love is a battle between the sexes . . . these images become available as fundamental premises for the reasoning process" (12). It is the ability of metaphor to develop these fundamental premises that makes it central to the problem of assent.

Metaphor is usually described as an instrument to seize the imagination and enable it to apprehend something new. However, just as metaphor animates the imagination, it also numbs it. It is commonplace that language is made up of "faded" or "dead" metaphors, words whose metaphorical origins have long been forgotten. And there are metaphors that, with overuse, become trite, as has happened, for example, to the phrase "ship of state." Lakoff and Johnson (1980, 10–13) have argued that language is made up of terms whose metaphorical referents have become lost over time. These same authors have noted the power of faded metaphors to accustom people to the routines of life. Kenneth Burke (1965) goes so far as to argue that faded metaphor produces an "orientation" that acts, in effect, as a trained incapacity insofar as it directs the attention in particular directions but not others. Those metaphors that are variously described as "homely," "hackneyed," or "dead" play a strategic role in shaping thought. Familiar metaphors accustom us to points of view that serve as the basis of our reasoning, habituating the mind to particular points of view and helping to perpetuate the status quo. We think the importance of these metaphors has been underestimated in everyday argument. While routine metaphors are often criticized on aesthetic grounds, these metaphors provide important symbolic reassurance about the continuity and stability of reality. And metaphor does this reassuring without preaching, hiding its point of view in the routine and mundane.

We would add two points to these observations. First, faded metaphors, because they cloak themselves in obscurity, deliberately avoid the quality of presence. Because the urgency of presence is absent, faded metaphors are thus powerful conservators of dogma, giving substantial presumption to the way things are and placing the burden of proof on those who would depart from the existing order. While presence becomes a key to gaining assent, faded metaphors act as powerful barriers to assent; that is, they encourage uncritical acceptance of dogma. Second, the suppression of presence is not necessarily a sign of rhetorical incompetence or the lack of imagination. Instead, it can be an effective technique to reinforce the status quo.

An Extended Example

The Reagan administration came to Washington in 1981 promising to restore American military power to its position of preeminence and close the "window of vulnerability" opened by the Carter administration. For years, debates about nuclear policy had centered on who was ahead in the arms race. Less prominently featured in all of these debates were more fundamental questions about how new weapons, once built, would be used. While the debates about weapons procurement played on the front pages (with acrimonious debates about the B-1 and MX), the arguments about their uses were left to more specialized literature, where they seldom came under public scrutiny. Even when these debates came to public attention, they were often difficult to understand.

Consider the following statement by Dr. Keith Payne (1984), a specialist in strategic studies: "The objective of [U.S. nuclear targeting policy] has been to provide the United States with escalation control, that is, the military potential to threaten escalation of any level along the spectrum of violence—thereby providing the opponent with a powerful disincentive to engage in any level of conflict" (85). The jargon of strategic planners is, admittedly, rather dense but the discourse should not be taken simply as doublespeak or its subspecies, "nukespeak" (Hilgartner, Bell, and O'Connor 1982). Nor should the passage be taken as mere academic argument, divorced from real world applications. Arkin and Fieldhouse (1985) note that the NATO nuclear operations plan has incorporated similar ideas into the plan for the defense of Europe: "the 'flexible response' doctrine [is] designed to respond appropriately to any level of potential attack and . . . pose the risk of escalation to higher levels of conflict" (86, ellipses in original). Payne's words have been influential in shaping defense policy in the Reagan administration and have important consequences for citizens of the United States, Europe, and the Soviet Union. Nevertheless, Payne's rhetoric distances itself not only from its subject but also from its audience. It is an example, we think, of discourse that suppresses assent and can be analyzed to discover the techniques by which it separates itself from its audiences.

The metaphors of the passage are designed to remove the discussion from the realm of ordinary experience and to make the meaning accessible to a very narrow linguistic community. While the metaphors themselves are common, their meanings, in context, are sufficiently obscure so that there is little danger that the public will intrude on the realm of experts. "Escalation control," a metaphor from the shopping mall, has a long history in strategic planning (the word "escalator" was originally a trademark for a moving stairway). The "escalation" metaphor was deliberately adopted by Herman Kahn (1965, 3–51) to describe and predict the levels of violence likely to arise at any particular stage of conflict. The metaphor promotes the view that planners can control the conduct of war by choosing policies that culminate in particular levels of violence. The escalator is a useful metaphor because it leaves the impression that planners control both the decision to employ violence and the nature and extent of the violence that will ensue. When the appropriate level of violence has been achieved, the conflict is managed by simply stepping off the escalation ladder at a given floor.[2] The metaphor is obscure but subtle; it implies that policy choices about levels of violence remain even in the midst of nuclear war. And in this way, the metaphor extends the doctrine of "warfighting," the idea that the United States should prepare to fight and win a nuclear war.[3] By the 1980s, the escalation ladder had become part of the routine vocabulary of strategic studies, and its metaphorical origins (along with Kahn's discussion of the metaphor's limits) had been forgotten. Forgotten as well were some conceptual problems inherent in the metaphor. While escalators and ladders allow movement up or down, Kahn's model predicts escalation but not "de-escalation": he limits the model to the process by which threats and force are used in international conflict. Kahn argues that the model does not apply to the processes by which threats are defused and violence eliminated.

In the discussion of escalation, Payne refers to the range of destruction caused by nuclear weapons as "the spectrum of violence," a metaphor that dissociates violence from its physical effects. Metaphorically, levels of violence, like light refracted through a prism, are arranged in orderly, predictable wavelengths, like the bands of a rainbow. The metaphor reinforces the notion that particular sorts of violence can be chosen rationally, produced and controlled by strategic planners. The escalation and spectrum metaphors support one another nicely: escalation predicts discrete levels of violence while the spectrum explains the relationship among the levels. The metaphors work well together because each links the abstract to the abstract. An escalation ladder evokes no more specific imagery than does a spectrum of violence. The extent to which these metaphors hinder thought is revealed by a simple change in Payne's phrase. Suppose that Payne had referred to the "specter of violence" (specter and spectrum share the same Latin root, *specere*, "to look"). The small change in diction replaces the imagery of optical physics with the imagery of death. This simple shift in terms makes the distancing effect of the spectrum metaphor all the more evident.

Finally, Payne's description of nuclear war in terms of "opponents" in "conflict" creates the impression that the United States and the Soviet Union are participants in a contest. But the metaphor dampens even that feeble association by depersonalizing the players; they are faceless opponents, markers on a game board whose movements have no significance beyond the game. On the other hand, the notion that nuclear war is a kind of game contributes to the distancing effect of the previous metaphors by surrounding the discussion with an aura of unreality.

The point to stress is that presence and metaphor are not simply tools to make an argument vivacious; rather they are the means by which discourse selects audiences and makes itself available to them. Suppression of presence is a strategy to distance argument from broad public audiences and to speak instead to a narrow elite. In effect, the strategy removes discourse from the public realm even when the discourse is ostensibly public. Meanwhile the discourse simultaneously reaffirms orthodox principles, venturing no new ideas. Nor is this technique reserved to one side of the debate about nuclear weapons. As J. Michael Hogan (1987) has demonstrated, the discourse of disarmament advocates such as Jonathan Shell and Helen Caldicott rely on similar techniques to rally their followers while avoiding argument. Given such techniques on both sides of the issue, the possibility exists that there may become more nuclear discourse designed to suppress presence than discourse designed to create presence.

It is useful, strategically, for advocates to evoke presence selectively in argument, to emphasize some qualities while drawing attention away from others. In its discussions of nuclear strategy, for example, the Reagan administration attempted selectively to engage the audience. In order to generate support for weapons procurement, descriptions of the shortcomings of U.S. strategic forces were vivid: Reagan bemoaned our aging B-52s, our "antique" Titan missiles, and the lack of a ballistic missile defense, which left the United States "naked." Meanwhile, Reagan depicted the Soviet Union as an "Evil Empire" led by "monsters." General Gordon Fornell (1985), testifying in favor of deployment of the "Peacekeeper" (and it is noteworthy that those who testify in its favor refer to it by that name), uses presence to heighten the need for a new missile: "The present U.S. ICBM force consists of Titan IIs, Minuteman IIs, and Minuteman IIIs. The most modern of these was designed with 1960s technology" (3788). New weapons systems are described in terms that are both curative and preventive; the names correct the ills implicit in the former terms.

At the same time, however, debates about the uses and effects of nuclear weapons take place in arcane terms that distance them from the public and foreclose public discussion. The quotation from Keith Payne is a good example of the process. Discussion of nuclear strategy in terms of countervalue, countercity, counterforce, and counterleadership attacks conceals more than it reveals. General Fornell's (1985) testimony on the necessity for the "Peacekeeper" continues: "The current Soviet ICBM force of 1,398 missiles, of which over 800 are SS-17, SS-18, and SS-19 ICBMs, represents a dangerous countermilitary asymmetry which must be corrected in the near term" (3788). Amplifying General Fornell's remarks, General Davis (1985) explained: "What I need are prompt, accurate weapons that can hold valuable hardened targets at risk—missile silos, hardened control facilities, and so forth. Right now, I can't do that job very well. . . . Our current deficiency in prompt, hard-target capacity is highly destabilizing, coercive, and is a weakness in our overall fabric of deterrence. One hundred Peacekeeper missiles with 1000 weapons will help redress this imbalance" (3750).

As we move from the need for new weapons to discussion of their deployment, the distancing effect becomes evident. We are invited to consider the need for the "Peacekeeper," but it is much more difficult to apprehend the circumstances surrounding its use. Much the same case can be made about President Reagan's strategic defense initiative (SDI). Having proposed SDI, Reagan left all technical issues to the experts and refused, publicly, to discuss even the most elementary aspects of the system. In the second campaign debate against Walter Mondale, Reagan (1984) criticized his opponent for referring to the strategic defense initiative as "Star Wars" and continued, "But when you keep Star Warring it, I never suggested where the weapons should be and what kind, I'm not a scientist. . . . And suddenly, somebody says: oh it's got to be up there in the Star Wars and so forth. I don't know what it would be but if we can come up with one, I think the world will be better off." Reagan's words reinforce the common assumption that strategic policy is beyond the ken of ordinary citizens and best left to the scientific and technical elite. While the need for weapons systems is created by metaphors that evoke a high degree of presence, discussions about the technology, its uses and effects, take place in terms that remove the public far from the discussion. Former Secretary of Defense, Robert McNamara (Scheer 1983) commented, "the potential victims have not been brought into the debate yet. I mean the average person. The average intelligent person knows practically nothing about nuclear war—the danger of it, the risk of it, the potential effect of it, the change in the factors affecting risk" (219).

The suppression of presence and its selective evocation act as powerful barriers to assent by concealing from audiences the basic assumptions and core values that could serve as the basis for argument and a change in perspective. If nothing else, the strategy removes discussion from the public sphere, a tactic used by strategic planners of all persuasions to retain control of the debate. Michael Wright (1985), editor of the *New York Times* "Week in Review" section wrote: "a former national security official in the Carter administration said, 'From start to finish of [the 1984 Presidential campaign], the [national security] community set the parameters of the debate, whether the subject was arms control or the need for a new manned strategic bomber like the B-1.' With the impatience with outsiders that seems endemic to the trade, the analyst added: 'These questions are too complicated for either politicians or the public. They need help' " (59).

Lacking expertise, the public has left the discussion to the experts even though many of the most important issues about nuclear weapons are not scientific and technical but are, instead, political and ethical. Kosta Tsipis (1983), a physicist and director of MIT's Program in Science and Technology for International Security argued, "The minutia of technology do not count much when it comes to deciding whether or not a given weapon system should be deployed. . . . the irony is that the public is not always aware what the relevant information is, nor that the information is in fact readily available, and so delegates its decision making to the experts" (291).

Awareness is a precondition for assent. A rhetoric of assent, instead of concealing controversy beneath faded metaphors as a device to maintain a favored position, must draw attention to the bases of controversy. Kenneth Burke's (1965, 69–124) insight into the value of "perspective by incongruity" offers guidance here. Most disagreements, Burke (1965, 85) notes, are rooted in the differences in the fundamental premises that serve as the basis for argument. Metaphor, by drawing its premises from two rival orientations and juxtaposing them directly, invites such perspective because it achieves its effects through the urgency engendered by the direct clash of rival ideas. This urgency is central to Perelman and Olbrecht-Tyteca's concept of presence. The clash of imagery creates presence and the puzzle presented by the conflicting ideas invites transcendence. The systematic questioning of the premises upon which argument systems are built offers the best opportunity to develop a rhetoric of assent and include a much broader public audience in the shaping of our nuclear weapons policies.

Notes

1. ". . . deliberate suppression of presence is an equally noteworthy phenomenon, deserving of detailed study" (*New Rhetoric,* 118).

2. Kahn is aware of the problem of rationality and answers objections with the argument:

> . . . researchers who study these problems do not really assume that decision-makers are wholly rational, but rather that they are not totally irrational—which is quite different from the assumption of rationality.
>
> There is also likely to be, at least in the American case, a premium on cool conduct, a pattern of expectations built up to influence decision-makers in times of nuclear crisis. As courageous behavior, whatever personal fears may be felt, is expected from a soldier as part of his professional standard, so coolness and rationality already have been established as part of the expectations the public has of its crisis leaders in the nuclear age. (*On Escalation*, 220–21)

3. One of the objects of the escalation ladder metaphor is to prove that tactics are still relevant in the nuclear age and to overcome the notion that "'war is unthinkable' or 'impossible'". Hence, Kahn devotes chapter X of *On Escalation* to a discussion of "War-Fighting."

7

Arguments in Fiction

Michael Weiler

In *Modern Dogma and the Rhetoric of Assent,* Wayne Booth finds in the rhetorical tradition an answer to the debilitating dogmatism of the modern age. For Booth, rhetoric offers a life-affirming alternative to the moral aridity of positivist science on the one hand and the moral imperialism of romantic irrationalism on the other. To serve this function, rhetoric must be a means of discovering and communicating good reasons. It must be the process by which human beings in society achieve justified consensus on questions of action and belief (Booth 1974).

Booth believes that rhetoric generates knowledge, the kind of knowledge that helps us to judge when we should change our minds, especially about value questions (Booth 1974, 12). Rhetoric, because it is constitutive of good reasons, tells us when we are in the presence of truths worthy of our collective assent. This assent will be grounded neither on self-evident conclusions from empirically secure premises nor on blind faith, though faith and empirical observation will be elements of it. Justified social consensus, in Booth's view, must rest on the inherently human process of communal reasoning which the classical rhetorical tradition encompasses. This process operates not in the realm of philosophic logic but of probabilistic, contingent judgment, and it involves not the imposition of the views of a speaker on a passive audience but the active participation of members of a community in a mutual search for truth.[1]

Modern Dogma and the Rhetoric of Assent is about how to recognize good reasons when we see them, but it is also about where to look. One place of particular interest to the author of *The Rhetoric of Fiction* is the fictional narrative. "Every kind of argument," Booth (1974, 181) observes, "that anyone could ever use in real life might be used in a narrative work." Booth looks at narrative argument in two senses; both the argument that a narrative *as a whole* communicates, and the arguments that various rhetorical conventions *in* the narrative communicate (Booth 1961, 415–17). In both cases he attempts to assess under what conditions narrative arguments constitute good reasons for accepting the "truths" that the narrative presents.

In this essay, I will focus on one of the rhetorical conventions in fictional narratives that authors use to communicate arguments; namely, arguments themselves. Though Booth and others have analyzed the arguments that novels and the rhetorical conventions within them communicate, little has been said about what is being argued when an author chooses to have the characters make formal arguments or engage in arguments with each other. When literary critics talk of a novel's arguments, they are referring usually to argument messages as translated from nonargumentative forms. In other words, though critics are accustomed to describing the arguments presented by the use of metaphor, allegory, metonymy, etc., they have had less to say about what is being communicated by the use of argument forms as such.[2] This essay addresses that question.

By "argument form" I mean nothing more complicated than the common sense usage of the term. When Polonius says to Laertes "This above all: to thine own self be true . . . ," he is giving advice. But when he adds, "and it must follow as the night the day, thou canst not then be false to any man" (Shakespeare, 1.3: 78–80), he has presented an argument in two related senses. He has made a causal claim that is controversial, and he has given a reason for being true to oneself. Controversial claims made for the purpose of influencing action and belief are formal arguments in the sense in which I am using the term. Undoubtedly, there are hard cases in which it is difficult to distinguish such arguments from other kinds of statements, but I think they can be avoided. I am looking for statements in fiction that most thoughtful observers would agree are in the form of arguments.

My objective is to explore the range of possibilities for the use of argument forms in fiction. I will describe this range across two continua: from relatively simple to relatively complex argument forms, and from relatively explicit to relatively implicit argument messages. In the first section of the essay, I will discuss arguments of unrejoined advocates, or what Daniel O'Keefe (1982, 3–4) has called statements of the Argument I type. These are arguments that individuals "make," in the absence of an interlocutor (although, perhaps in the presence of an audience). The second section will address statements of the Argument II variety, arguments offered by speakers who are "having an argument" with someone else.

These categories are formal. They are not meant to rule out the possibility that arguments in the Argument I category might be presented as responses to counterarguments of a real or imagined interlocutor temporarily removed from the scene, or as preemptive answers to the arguments of a future opponent. Nor should we ignore the possibility that in Argument II situations, a speaker might proceed as if the interlocutor was not there at all. Because my concerns are with the formal use of arguments, however, these categories are a useful way of marking the movement from the simple to the complex ends of the formal argument continuum.

My second continuum is concerned with the content of argument meanings. It is bounded at one end by arguments with messages that are relatively explicit, and on the other by arguments with relatively implicit messages, those that invite, and indeed, require considerable interpretation. I argue that these two continua are roughly parallel. That is, I believe that the most complex argument forms tend to require the greatest degree of interpretive ingenuity from the critic who would appreciate fully what they mean. My selection of examples cannot "prove" this claim, of course. Even if they appear to redeem my judgment, it always can be objected that I deliberately have chosen simple arguments with explicit messages or complex arguments with obscure ones and ignored all counterexamples. Therefore, I offer this analytical scheme as simply one way of approaching the question of the relationship between argument form and argument content. With additional refinement, it may prove fruitful.

I have sought my argument examples in well-known novels employing easily identifiable narrative forms. Thus, I have avoided works for which the very term "novel" may be problematic (as, for example, Thomas Pynchon's *Gravity's Rainbow* or even the fictional works of Virginia Woolf). This method of selection has the virtue of reducing the variables in my analysis to two: the novel's point of view, and the argument type. Beyond making the topic more manageable, this reduction allows me to suggest tentatively (though not to investigate systematically) ways in which novels and their arguments as a *formal* combination may reflect and contribute to ideological tendencies of a particular historical period. In other words, it opens the way for a more comprehensive analysis of the political linkages between the novel as a textual form and the historical circumstances in which it has flourished (see Watt 1957).

Arguments of Unrejoined Advocates

In George Eliot's *Daniel Deronda*, we find the following:

A human life, I think, should be well rooted in some spot of native land, where it may get the love of tender kinship for the face of the earth, for the labors men go forth to, for the sounds and accents that haunt it, for whatever will give that early home an unmistakable difference amid the future of widening knowledge: a spot where the definiteness of early memories may be inwrought with affection, and kindly acquaintance with all neighbors, even to the dogs and donkeys, may spread not by sentimental effort and reflection, but as a sweet habit of the blood. (Eliot, 19–20)

Why is such "rootedness" important? Eliot completes her argument by justifying her recommendations for early childhood with the observation that

At five years old, mortals are not prepared to be citizens of the world, to be stimulated by abstract nouns, to soar above preference into impartiality; and that prejudice in favor of milk with which we blindly begin, is a type of the way body and soul get nourished for a time. The best introduction to astronomy is to think of the nightly heavens as a little lot of stars belonging to one's homestead. (20)

This passage is an example of the simplest and most explicit type of fictional argument, a series of claims that are evidently nothing more or less than what they say. Here, the author and narrator are, for all appearances, the same person. The argument is a commentary on the story to follow, a statement of values forming an interpretive background to the experiences of the novel's characters, in the immediate case, those of Gwendolen Harleth.

We could summarize the message of this narrator/author's argument in various ways, but because of its explicitness, these summaries would amount to little more than restatements. Our example illustrates not just impersonal narration but a form of narration seemingly external to the story itself, a comment on but not an integral part of the narrative. Nevertheless, Eliot's argument is clearly germane to the theme of the novel; the importance of familial history as an anchor in the uncertain and rootless world of nineteenth-century Western societies (Booth 1961, 214–15, 262–64).

From here, we can move to a more complicated case: a narrator who is neither author nor character. The point of view of this narrator is frequently that of a contemporary of the novel's characters, but evidently unconnected with them personally. He/she shares their historical milieu but not their lives.

In *The Man Without Qualities*, Robert Musil's narrator makes the following claims about the psychology of capitalists in pre—World War I Europe:

And it must not be thought that the presidents, chairmen of boards of directors, governors, directors, or managers of banks, concerns, mines, and shipping companies were at heart the bad men that they are often represented as being. Apart from their very highly developed family sense, the inner reason of their life is money; and it is a kind of reason with very strong teeth and a hearty digestion. They were all convinced that the world would be much better if it were simply left to the free play of supply and demand. . . . But the world being what it is . . . they made thoroughly sound use of the advantages to the public welfare offered by customs negotiations backed up by armed force or by using the military against strikers. But it is along this road that business leads to philosophy (for it is only criminals who presume to damage other people nowadays without the aid of philosophy). (Musil [1953] 1980, 226–27)

We have a choice here of accepting these arguments as the serious observations of an unintentionally satirical narrator, or as the deliberately sarcastic comments of the author himself. From the former point of view, our narrator is an unwitting representative of the delusions of his age; from the latter, a "playful" (Lukacs 1964b, 98–134) but not entirely reliable (Booth 1961, 211–15) reporter of people and circumstances.

In either case, however, we cannot take the argument entirely at face value. We can interpret its meaning only through its relationship to the author's point of view. In the case of Eliot, the descriptions in *Daniel Deronda* of people, places, and events create a richly illustrative context for the arguments she presents, but we can reach a reasonably clear understanding of what she is arguing without such illustrations. In *The Man Without Qualities*, however, we must read at least far enough to realize that Musil and his narrator are not identical. The narrator's arguments reveal the author's truths, but do not tell them. To the explicit message of the argument we must add our understanding of its tone, or we will miss its full substance.

In many novels, narrators are also characters. Sometimes such characters are omniscient, but more often their vision is limited or at least slanted in ways that complicate the task of interpreting their arguments. Umberto Eco's *The Name of the Rose* exemplifies several of these complications. The narrator is Adso of Melk, a Benedictine monk in the fourteenth century. The events of his story are set around 1327, but he tells it from a standpoint several decades removed. He is eighty years old, reporting events that occurred in his youth.

Adso's narrative begins with an argument:

In the beginning was the Word and the Word was with God. This was beginning with God and the duty of every faithful monk would be to repeat every day with chanting humility the one never-changing event whose incontrovertible truth can be asserted. But we see now through a glass darkly, and the truth, before it is revealed to all, face to face, we see in fragments (alas, how illegible) in the error of the world, so we must spell out its faithful signals even when they seem obscure to us and as if amalgamated with a will wholly bent on evil. (Eco 1983, 11)

This argument operates at several levels of meaning. First, it is self-justificatory. Adso is about to tell a worldly and at times embarrassing (for him) story. To explain why a pious monk should devote himself to such a task, he must argue that in the error of the world, the truth is revealed. He does not promise that such truth will emerge obviously or completely, but in a world of sin and sinners there is no place else to look.

Adso's argument is self-justificatory in a second sense. His story includes his own experiences as well as those of others. He must explain those thoughts and actions of his own that are open to criticism. At the most obvious level of meaning (above), his argument describes in general terms the problem of separating truth from error. In this context, the problem is one of impersonal judgment, of philosophical interpretation. But knowing what is true is also a personal, moral problem, as it was for Adso when, as a young man, he tried and occasionally failed to negotiate the narrow path of virtue through an undergrowth of sin. It is hard to know what is right when the truth can be glimpsed only in fragments and through a glass darkly. We cannot blame Adso too much for his occasional moral lapses.

At a third level of meaning, Adso's argument is a theory of language expressed allegorically by way of the doctrine of original sin. In the beginning was the Word. The period before the Fall was a time of linguistic purity when the truth could be asserted unambiguously, completely, and repeatedly. Once language became the property of human beings, however, it began its slide toward corruption, a situation where words are not things but merely stand for them. Meanings are never fixed or clear; they are always open to interpretation. "Illegibility" is one way to summarize these qualities of language. The word on paper has a certain fixity. But the meanings of words constantly elude us. It is as if we cannot quite make them out, however hard we try to read what they say.

Eco the author is, of course, Eco (1976) the semiotician, and knowing this fact influences a critic to hear linguistic theories coming out of his narrator's mouth. Adso's argument is not, however, the only hint that moves a reader toward this interpretation. *The Name of the Rose* begins with an explanation of the author's(?) difficulties in locating a reliable version of Adso's narrative, and therefore his decision to write his own. As we read this narrative-before-the-narrative, we find our credulity heavily taxed, and when we are told that the author found most of his few direct quotations from Adso's original manuscript he cites in a work entitled *On the Use of Mirrors in the Game of Chess,* our doubts begin to turn to certainties (Eco 1983, 1–5). But what is Eco's game?

One answer is that this novel is a kind of a treatise on the characteristics of language that uses narrative mode as illustrative device. Such an interpretation takes us far afield from the relatively explicit argument messages we found in Eliot. If it is true, however, as I have argued, that the level of complexity of narrative forms corresponds in some way to the level of complexity of argument meanings, then with Eco's choice of a narrator/advocate, we should expect to find arguments open to several interpretations ranging from the obvious to the obscure.

Narrators are fruitful sources of unrejoined arguments. However, characters who are not narrators make them as well. In such cases, a central interpretive question is how the arguments a character presents relate to the argument of the novel as a whole, to the views of the author.

Joseph Conrad's *The Secret Agent* is a story of terrorism and its reasons. Mr. Vladimir, an official in the German embassy in London, has commissioned a rootless socialist zealot, Verloc, to carry out a terrorist act. The question is what the act should be. Mr. Vladimir explains that in order for terrorism "to have any influence on public opinion . . . [it] must be purely destructive . . . and only that." It must "go beyond the intention of vengeance." Such "senseless destruction" is necessary because if terrorism is directed toward some rational objective (for instance, the U.S. Marine headquarters in Lebanon), then it can be understood as the violent manifestation of the political aspirations of some oppressed group. "But," Mr. Vladimir asks, "what is one to say to an act of destructive ferocity so absurd as to be incomprehensible, inexplicable, almost unthinkable; in fact, mad?" He concludes, "madness alone is truly terrifying" (Conrad [1907] 1982, 35–36).

It is decided that the astronomical observatory at Greenwich will be Verloc's target. This is as close as Mr. Vladimir can get to a direct attack on the idea of rationality itself. "It would really be telling," he says, "if one could throw a bomb into pure mathematics." That not being possible, he suggests "having a go at astronomy" (36–37).

Mr. Vladimir's arguments about the nature and effects of terrorism are not Conrad's. Indeed, the argument of the novel as a whole is that terrorism is futile. Mr. Vladimir, in fact, is no devotee of revolutionary upheaval. His goal is to repress socialist movements in Europe. He hopes that the terrorism he sponsors in England will force the British government to crack down on socialist activity. He expects a little anarchism to lead in the end to a healthy dose of authoritarianism.

Verloc, on the other hand, is a pathetic character, unaware of Mr. Vladimir's duplicity. He has come to socialism as a hoped-for escape from his mundane existence. He is the unwitting agent through which the movement he represents is corrupted. Conrad appears to be arguing that this corruption is inevitable. In other novels, he has expressed powerfully what for him is a central human truth: the loftier the project, the more likely that human venality, myopia, and malice will undermine it (see Watt 1979). Together, the characters of *The Secret Agent* vividly exemplify these traits.

The choice of Mr. Vladimir to plan terrorist strategy and through his arguments to convince others to carry it out is one way Conrad communicates his views about terrorism and human nature. Mr. Vladimir turns terrorism against itself by recruiting manipulable and incompetent agents, and by convincing them to carry out acts that will deprive their movement of political legitimacy. His doctrine of senseless destruction is the embodiment of what Conrad suggests every terrorist movement always becomes: irrational, counterproductive of its goals, and dominated by corrupt leaders.

This brief survey of the arguments of unrejoined advocates in novels has emphasized two concerns: the messages of the arguments, both explicit and implicit, and the formal status of arguers, whether as authors, narrators, or characters. I have suggested that changes in the latter category are related in roughly parallel fashion to changes in the former. Certainly, the treatment has been far from exhaustive. I have neglected many possibilities of narrative form. Moreover, I have ignored cases where the unrejoined status of an advocate is in doubt, for instance, in novels where a character appears to be arguing with himself (Burke 1973, 103–04) or with a physically absent but dramatically present interlocutor (Booth 1961, 155). The examples I have discussed, however, have illustrated a number of important analytical issues for the critic of argument in fiction. This essay's final section is a discussion of a case where two characters argue with each other in front of a third. We will find that this dialogic argument raises additional questions as regards the relationship between argument form and argument meanings.

Arguments between Characters

Dialogic argument is a rhetorical form with its own definitional problems. Is any adversarial dialogue an argument? If so, then even a wife and husband having a "fight" amounts to an argument. Viewed in this way, the range of such arguments becomes uncomfortably (for analytical purposes) broad. If we wish to narrow it, however, where do we draw the line? Does a dialogue have to meet Platonic standards to qualify as argument? As in the case of unrejoined arguments, we are without precise definitional criteria. Again, therefore, it is best to avoid borderline cases, and instead to focus on situations where two or more characters respond and counter-respond to each other's statements in a relatively organized way. In other words, they observe certain rules such as taking turns, avoiding physical violence, and acknowledging the preceding statements of their opponents as they speak (see Weiler 1985, 277–88).

These criteria define a rhetorical convention of considerably greater formal complexity than the unrejoined arguments we have discussed. It should not be surprising, then, if the formal characteristics of dialogic arguments turn out as well to have greater analytical significance than in the previous cases. I will argue that the presence of the dialogic form of argument in fiction, in addition to the presence of any particular dialogic argument, can be an integral part of the message of the novel as a whole. Indeed, form can become substance in the sense that it places the novel's argument in a particular context of meaning. I will use a dialogic argument from Thomas Mann's *The Magic Mountain* to illustrate these relationships.

I have chosen Mann because he is a writer who attempted to select rhetorical conventions that corresponded to his subject matter. Mann sought "a perfect consistency to content and form." For him, the aim of every literary production was "always and consistently to *be* that of which it speaks" (Mann [1953] 1969b, 723).

How can an argument be what it speaks? Surely, various dialogic arguments can "speak" radically different messages. Yet their forms are similar. A resolution of this paradox requires us to consider the meaning of Mann's novel as a whole, and then to return to the question of the role that dialogic argument plays in its rhetoric.

The Magic Mountain was written partially before, but mostly after, World War I and published finally in 1924. It was begun as a satire on prevailing methods of treating tuberculosis, but with the intervening catastrophe of the Great War, it became a much larger work that addressed, among other things, the possibilities of rational political thought and action, and the future of the human race.

The theme of the novel is the inevitable dialectical tension between the democratic humanism of the capitalist age and the romantic authoritarianism that constitutes its antithesis. For Mann, the grounding of democratic liberal thought in the bourgeois capitalist system prevented it from becoming anything but an ideological straightjacket for truly liberating human impulses. The romantic counterstatement, however, based as it was in traditional sources of authority, and denying as it did the potentialities of individual human accomplishment, could serve no more positive purpose than as part of a dialectical process aimed at the eventual transcendence of both ideologies. Thus, a culturally and spiritually deprived democratic liberalism might give way at some future time to a democratic socialism.

The shape of the future, however, was not Mann's literary concern. In the tradition of the realistic novel, his task was to capture human existence as it was, in all of its complexity and contradictions (Lukacs 1964c, 47–97). This claim may sound paradoxical in view of the "unrealistic" scenes in which many of Mann's novels are set. His "Joseph" novels occur in biblical Egypt, *The Holy Sinner* takes place in medieval Europe, and the events of *The Magic Mountain*, though contemporary, are set in the other-worldly atmosphere of an Alpine tuberculosis sanitarium where patients lose track of time as lived "down below." As Georg Lukacs (1964c, 82–83) has noted, however, when Mann dealt with a distorted sense of time, he treated it *as distorted*. Indeed, the novel is full of narrator's comments on this topic. Mann's goal was not to present this distortion as real, but to compare it to reality, and in so doing, to reveal the nature of that reality all the more clearly.

Mann's aim was to mirror his own time at the most basic level. He sought to capture the essence of the bourgeois age, and this meant finding a way to express the tendencies and dynamic of that age rather than simply describing its people and places in scrupulous detail (Lukacs 1964a, 32). For Mann, expressing the bourgeois principle was as much a matter of the form of that expression as of its content; indeed, he sought a "perfect consistency" of the two.

If the nature of contemporary society could be understood best in dialectical terms, then dialectical forms should pervade the story of that society. If the essence of democratic liberalism was deliberative decision-making according to definite rules, then this form of action would be appropriate to a narrative written in and of the democratic liberal period. These considerations, I believe, are what led Mann to use the dialogic argument form in *The Magic Mountain*, and in other novels as well (Mann [1948] 1966, 111–25). Regardless of his intentions, this form is, in my view, supremely appropriate to the meaning of this narrative.

When arguments occur in *The Magic Mountain*, they involve Settembrini, an Italian academic who presses the case of humanistic rationalism. Settembrini, like the other residents of the sanitarium, has tuberculosis, but he refuses to succumb to the seductive atmosphere of the place. He constantly intrudes down-to-earth (literally) ideas and attitudes from the outside. He does not allow the timeless quality of the scene to deprive him of his philosophical bearings. His creed is democratic liberalism, and he affirms proudly that "our Western heritage is reason—reason, analysis, action, progress: these and not the slothful bed of Monkish tradition" (Mann [1927] 1969a, 377).

Settembrini's frequent opponent is Naphta, in fact a Catholic monk, who replies, "Monkish tradition! As if we did not owe to the monks the culture of all Europe. . . . But the labor of these religious was neither an end in itself—that is to say, it was not a narcotic, nor was its purpose to further the progress of the world, or to reap commercial advantage." Here, Naphta critiques the individualistic excesses of liberal capitalism, a system that encourages the obsessive pursuit of material gain, claiming all the while that naked self-interest, when universalized, serves the general welfare. The tradition of religious authority, on the other hand, is the foundation of culture. "What I am calling your attention to," concludes Naphta, "is nothing less than the distinction between the utilitarian and the human" (1969a, 377).

Settembrini will not accept this polarity. He considers his own philosophy the embodiment of "the human." "Ah! I see that you are still dividing the world up into opposing factions," he responds shortly (1969a, 377). Settembrini, as representative of the hegemonic ideology of his time, is naturally anxious to encompass all desirable positions (see Gramsci 1971, 241). His strategy is to deny contradictions, arguing instead that the attractive values of the old social order can be preserved within the new, even in the absence of their institutional supports.

Naphta will have none of it. Bourgeois capitalism by its very nature has corrupted these values. A choice between the old and new is inevitable. "I grieve to have incurred your displeasure," he taunts. "Yet," he adds, "it is needful to make distinctions, and to preserve the conception of the *Homo Dei*, free from contaminating constituents" (Mann 1969a, 377).

No one wins this argument in the conventional sense. It is a dialectic that points the way to transcendence and synthesis, though these are not realized in the novel. Instead, the arguments are simply interrupted at some point before a clear winner emerges. Both protagonist and antagonist are partially blind; neither of their political philosophies can stand careful scrutiny. Settembrini's failure as advocate is the most profound, however. He speaks for the world as it is. His inability to rationalize that world in terms of his ideology, to resolve its contradictions, suggests that these contradictions will one day become decisive. His idealism, though seemingly admirable at first, soon becomes merely pathetic. His pious platitudes cannot rescue his ideology from Naphta's subversive demagoguery (Lukacs 1964a, 38).

The argument thus described is performed for a third character, Hans Castorp. He is the main character of the novel, a charmingly naive young engineering student who comes to the sanitarium to visit his sick cousin and is forced to stay when he too is diagnosed with tuberculosis. Mann narrates from Castorp's point of view, reporting the youth's reactions to the arguments he has witnessed.

Though Castorp listens attentively, he never seems very impressed by what he hears. He is open-minded but detached. His lack of commitment to pre-formed ideas makes him particularly vulnerable to his surroundings. He finds himself sinking ever deeper into a world where degeneration and death are the norm, and hope is lost because the need for it ceases to be felt. In such a world, deliberative discussions have no place.

Young Castorp is "saved" at the last moment, however, by the arrival of World War I. In Mann's final scene, we see him trudging through the muck of the battlefield, perhaps to survive, perhaps not. "Farewell to Hans Castorp," Mann (1969a, 716) bids, "whether he lives or dies." We are told that though his "prospects are poor, . . . Out of this universal feast of death, out of this extremity of fever, kindling the rain-washed sky to a fiery glow, may it be that Love one day shall mount."

Thus, the prospects of mankind. We know from Mann's diaries (1982, 23–25) that he hoped the end of the war would bring a form of socialism that could rescue the idea of "the human" from its bourgeois definition and propel it powerfully into a new postwar world. His later novels, in many ways, tell the story of his progressive disillusionment as the socialist stirrings of postwar Germany gave way to a brutal Fascist reality.

In *The Magic Mountain*, we have an especially rich example of a work that argues as much by form as substance. The apparent substance of the arguments that Settembrini and Naphta present is fully intelligible only if we ask why they are presented dialogically, as a case of two characters having an argument. As we appreciate the whole context of their verbal battle, its lack of closure, its audience, and its dialectical character, we can begin to interpret the meaning of the argument structure as a whole, and how that structure relates to the meaning of the novel. This section of the chapter has been an exercise in this kind of interpretation.

Conclusion

We have moved from relatively simple argument forms and relatively straightforward argument meanings, to complex forms and meanings that require considerable interpretation. Along this path, we have surveyed various narrative modes and authorial points of view. In the case of Eliot, we analyzed an argument "on its own," almost as if it stood outside the novel. The argument's formal simplicity and explicitness allowed this approach. The argument could have appeared as easily in an essay as in a novel, or so it seemed.

As our examples became more complex, however, the relationship of the argument's meaning to the meaning of the novel as a whole became a more important issue. In other words, it became clear that the arguments of these later examples meant more than they said. In the case of Musil, this larger meaning could be discovered only by considering the author's point of view. In the case of Eco, both the author's point of view and the multiple levels of meaning in the novel had to be considered. In the case of Conrad, the meaning of the argument could be appraised only in the context of the novel's argument. Finally, in the case of Mann, the larger meaning could be approached only by realizing that the form of the argument was as important a clue to its meaning as was its substance.

These examples have by no means exhausted the critical questions we may wish to ask as we consider the role of arguments in fiction. If the novel form is an expression of bourgeois ideology then what role do arguments within novels play in clarifying these reflections? Is the dialogic form of argument particularly appropriate to bourgeois fiction as Mann's work suggests? If so, is this because we find embodied within it the liberal capitalist ideal of the "market place of ideas," so often defined in polar terms as a case of presenting "both sides of the story."

These and other questions remain to be examined. They are beyond the scope of this survey. What does seem clear, however, is that arguments in fiction are important formal and substantive constituents of many novels and must be accounted for in any fully rounded reading. And because deliberative argument is so much a part of the ideological assumptions of the capitalist age, its presence in the literature of that age may be an important clue to the ideological significance of works of fiction. In this sense, arguments in fiction are not simply arguments of authors or characters but of all of us. As such, they should interest all students of argument.

Notes

1. A growing number of political philosophers have joined with rhetoricians in recent years to promote classical conceptions of rhetoric and politics, especially those of Aristotle. On the political side, see Crick 1982; MacIntyre 1984; Beiner 1983; and Sullivan 1982. For a rhetorical emphasis, see Booth 1974, 143–45; Leff also comments on this classical turn. See Leff 1985, 362–72.

2. Booth's *The Rhetoric of Fiction* (1961) is the definitive treatment of how fiction argues, but it does not emphasis formal arguments as a way of arguing. Zahava Karl McKeon (1982) systematically applies Aristotlian rhetorical concepts to literary criticism but looks primarily at arguments of rather than arguments in novels. Chaim Perelman and L. Olbrechts-Tyteca's *The New Rhetoric: A Treatise on Argumentation* (1971), an exhaustive survey of argument forms, uses fictional arguments as examples but does not isolate arguments in fiction as a category. Many critics discuss the rhetoric of various literary figures and tropes. See, for example, Lodge 1977.

Part III

Form and Function in Assent
Field Studies

8

Purpose, Argument Evaluation, and the Crisis in the Public Sphere

Robert C. Rowland

There is wide agreement that we live in a time of epistemic crisis, a crisis that seems to deny the very possibility of rational resolution of disputes within the public sphere. For instance, in *Modern Dogma and the Rhetoric of Assent* Wayne Booth first notes that "Attacks on reason and thought abound" (1974, ix) and later concludes that "We are a society groping for meaningful affirmation, for intellectually respectable assent. The old faiths seem shattered" (1974, 200). The conclusion that currently public argument has little capacity to resolve problems, especially value-related issues, is hardly unique. For example, Goodnight argues both that "the public sphere is being steadily eroded" and that the very realm of public knowledge itself "may be disappearing" (1982, 223–25). Farrell and Goodnight echo this finding in their conclusion that the communication practices in the Three Mile Island accident illustrate a decline in "the practical art of rhetoric" (1981, 299). And Willard argues that "epistemic relativity" in the public sphere is a hard fact that cannot be avoided. The result is what he calls the "balkanization of knowledge" (1983b, 7), a situation in which the "guarantors of ordinary knowledge claims" no longer relate to public knowledge or tests of argument but relate merely to "explicit and implicit tapestries of power" (1983b, 9).

The foregoing should make it clear that the traditional tie between argumentation and both decision-making and pedagogy is under attack. Since the Greeks, the study of argument has been justified as a means of improving public and personal decision-making. For example, even Willard admits that "the dream of optimum decision-making has been the discipline's organizing thread unifying its historical preoccupations with critical thinking, rationality and deliberation" (1983b, 2). However, if there is no link between argument and rational choice-making then the traditional rationale for the study of argument obviously is destroyed. Here, the crucial question relates to whether it is possible to evaluate accurately the quality or strength of arguments. A number of recent theorists have answered this question in the negative.

Willard and others have argued for the value of description and against evaluation as the end of argument criticism. According to Willard, the ultimate goal of argument criticism should be not to identify the truth, but to create doubt about all orthodoxies (1982a, 47). Willard rejects evaluation as an aim of argumentation because he believes that evaluative standards depend upon field theory (1982a, 3) and that there can be no ultimate guarantee that the standards of a particular field are correct (1983a, 112; 1982a, 31–33). In addition, he claims that intrafield argument evaluation is pointless because the result can be only to reaffirm the dogma within a field (1983a, 11; 1982a, 13). While intrafield evaluation is useless, interfield evaluation is impossible. According to Willard, there are no justifiable field-invariant standards for argument evaluation (1982a, 9, 31–32; 1983a, 70–71). In fact, the very search for such standards leads to an infinite regress. A skeptic can always shrug his or her shoulders and ask for the justification behind a proposed standard (Willard 1982b, 27–28; Weimer 1979, 4–6). Consequently, any attempt at interfield evaluation inevitably ends with the application of one field's criteria to a different field. However, the use of one field's standards in another field serves no purpose. No activity has the right to take an "imperialistic stance" toward another field (Willard 1982a, 32). The ultimate conclusion is that because the critic can identify no ultimate guarantor for knowledge, argument evaluation should be rejected. Willard is not alone. Although Hample is unwilling to go quite so far, he also doubts whether appropriate standards for evaluation can be developed and instead refers to evaluation as no more than a "knack" (1981, 886). Booth has made a number of similar points. He has attacked the value of composition texts that teach traditional rules of ordinary logic (1974, 88), questioned whether the application of rules of logic or argument can be useful apart from social discourse (1974, 149), and argued for an expansion of "the rules for good discourse" to cover more than "logical prose" because "we must take in the proofs of personal appeal and commitment, of art and myth and ritual" (1974, 203).

The historical tie between argumentation and pedagogy and decision-making would seem to be threatened. If evaluation is not useful or if art and other nondiscursive forms are accepted as "good discourse" apart from explicit or enthymematic reasoning, the unique functions of argument are undercut.

Despite the apparently growing consensus concerning the limited epistemic merit of argumentation, I want to defend the position that the study and practice of argumentation, via traditional standards for evaluating ordinary logic, has much to offer both argument pedagogy and critical decision-making, even in the area of value argument. While I agree with Willard that evaluation is a difficult process and that there are no objective standards for evaluation, this conclusion, does not, I suggest, deny the need for evaluation; it merely says that good evaluative criticism is difficult to produce (see Rowland 1985). In short, I want to defend the utterly traditional (and now quite controversial) view that argument criticism is linked to both rationality and effective problem-solving, and at the same time explain how such a view is consistent with our understanding of the public sphere.

In order to develop this position, I will first attempt to show how three approaches to the problems of the public sphere—dialectic, audience centered, and field theory—are inadequate, by themselves, to resolve the difficulties afflicting public argumentation. I will then argue that there is an important role to be played by argument evaluation based on traditional tests of informal logic. In the final section I will consider the implications that a purpose-centered view of evaluation has for argumentation theory and the public sphere.

Potential Solutions to the Crisis in the Public Sphere

The discussion of the crisis in the public sphere largely has focused on means of recreating a "public" or adding efficacy to "social knowledge." Booth has characterized our attempts in this regard as aimed at constructing "rhetorics of a kind of assent that cannot be dismissed as 'mere faith'" (1974, xi). Our attempts to create a new "rhetoric of assent" that avoid the problems associated with the study of informal logic in argumentation have taken three primary forms. Some scholars, notably Booth himself, have argued that valid social knowledge is created through the rhetorical interaction of people in a community. Others, focusing on the relationship between process and knowledge generation, have developed a dialectical definition of justifiable knowledge claims. And finally, Willard has argued that field theory (which he calls "epistemics") provides a first step toward resolving the crisis in public argument. While each of these approaches has much to offer, unfortunately none of them provides a fully adequate means of identifying or creating public knowledge.

The first approach to the crisis in the public sphere defines knowledge based on the agreement of a rhetorical community. The most important statement of a community-oriented standard for validation of knowledge claims is found in Booth's discussion of a "rhetoric of assent." Booth begins with the assumption that "there really is a difference between good reasons and bad" (1974, xiv) and rejects doubt in favor of a "process of systematic assent" (1974, 104), in which "the way we establish values is the way we establish anything: by earning communal validation through trying them out on other men" (1974, 146). The answer, therefore, to the problems in the public sphere is to "build new rhetorical communities," for if we do not "every institution we care about will die" (1974, 150).

In his "rhetoric of assent" Booth taps into a long tradition in argumentation theory. Beginning with Aristotle, who treated the views of the people as both containing a measure of knowledge and as the proper place to begin any discussion, various theorists have endorsed audience-centered standards for defining rational argument. Farrell, for example, writes: "not even the potential soundness of a rhetorical argument may be surmised until an audience has either acted or has been rendered capable of acting" (1977, 143). Fisher makes essentially the same point when he applies Farrell's work on social knowledge to the logic of good reasons: "Reasons are thought to be good when they are expressed by persons who have ethos" (1981, 116). Zarefsky defends a similar position (1981, 88). Aside from Booth, the most important proponent of an audience-based test of good reasoning is Perelman who has argued that the reaction of a purely rational "universal" audience is the best test of an argument's worth (Perelman and Olbrechts-Tyteca 1969, 31–33; also see Ray 1978, 361–75).

The view that good reasons can be identified based on the response of a rational audience is important, but not fully adequate. Clearly, it makes sense as Booth says to "grant some degree of credence to whatever qualified men and women agree on" (1974, 101), but the proviso that Booth adds at the end of this statement illustrates the basic problem with exclusive reliance on such a standard: "unless one has specific and stronger reasons to disbelieve." The basic problem is that the idea of using a universal audience or a rhetorical community to define rationality for a society is tautological. Ray writes of the universal audience: "When we say that the universal audience is always a correct standard because it is the standard of all rational people, we are simply uttering a tautology by saying that what is rational for all people is rational for all people" (1978, 374).

Booth begins *Modern Dogma and the Rhetoric of Assent* by discussing the irrationality of both the administration and the student protesters in an incident at the University of Chicago. Yet, clearly these two groups operated in what one would expect to be a highly rational rhetorical community, a major research university. Booth faces this problem by limiting his rhetoric of assent to any "thoroughly qualified—human being" (1974, 110). Booth notes: "The fact that one or a million voters have been persuaded is never in itself adequate reason for concluding that they are right. In rhetorical inquiry we must always take into account both the reasons and the voters' qualifications" (1974, 119). Here, Booth comes very close to simply restating a principle of informal logic that on factual questions the views of experts should be given precedence. Interpreted in this way, the "rhetoric of assent" has little that is new to offer. Later, he defends the value of rhetorical interchange "for man only when those engaged in it fully respect the rules and the steps of inquiry" (1974, 138).

Booth and the other advocates of an audience-centered approach to reconstituting the "public" (Booth 1974, 149) are clearly correct that one useful means of supporting any conclusion is to look at what other rational people say about that conclusion. Ultimately, however, this view does not resolve the crisis in the public sphere. For this view to be useful, we need criteria for distinguishing the truly "rational" rhetorical community from such apparently rational groups as the University of Chicago. And if we can identify those criteria, it would seem that they, rather than the agreement of the community, are the real standards for rational consensus. In order for a rational audience to identify good reasons they must have some standard defining a good reason. It is that standard that is at issue here.

In addition, there is no certainty that all the members of a rational audience would necessarily identify the same evidence and reasoning as reasonable. When the National Academy of Science discusses scientific problems, there is no guarantee that its decisions will be unanimous. In fact, controversy is prevalent even in science (Rescher 1977, 110–24). Similarly, there are instances when the Supreme Court splits five to four. Yet, surely the Supreme Court and the National Academy of Science come as close as is possible in our society to purely rational decision-making bodies. If the members of these organizations often differ on what constitutes a good reason, the value of an idealized rational audience as an evaluative standard must be questioned.

A second possible means for solving the crisis in the public sphere lies in the dialectical process. According to the proponents of this view, good arguments win out in free and open debate against weak arguments. Hardwig develops a dialectical definition of rationality when he argues that dialogue is "the final court of rational appeal" and the only means of attaining rationality (1973, 171). Weimer makes a similar point when he argues that "criticism is the essence of rationality" (1979, 48). Weimer's position is somewhat similar to that of Rescher, who treats formal debate as the paradigm case of a rational activity (1977, 40). Rescher also argues that the highest form of human rationality—science—can best be described as a form of disputation among advocates (1977, 110–11).

The position that dialectic is the best means for testing argument quality is quite appealing because it seems to provide an objective means of identifying good reasons. Good reasons win out in debate against bad reasons. Moreover, this view would seem to suggest that all we need do is open up the public sphere to free discussion and the result will be a new societal consensus.

Despite its appeal, however, the dialectical standard is not adequate. Initially, there is no guarantee that any individual dialectical encounter will end with the discovery of truth. One only need read the *Congressional Record* to understand that the best reasons and arguments for a position are not always presented. Nor do the strongest reasons always win out in Congressional debate. The basic problem is that the dialectical process is not itself a standard for evaluating arguments. Rather dialectic is the mechanism through which standards are applied. Unless argument evaluation is to be purely idiosyncratic, there must be some general standard for evaluation that can be applied within the dialectic. A theorist who advocates debate or dialectic as the test of rationality may have identified the best process for testing rational arguments, but he or she has not identified the standards used to test those arguments. This explains why Rescher in addition to advocating dialectic identifies a number of tests for adequate scientific reasoning. In his view, formal debate is the best means of applying those tests.

There is also reason to doubt whether a dialectical standard could be extended to resolve the problems of the public sphere. There is no lack of competing voices in discussion of issues of public concern. If anything, the problem is that there are so many inconsistent views of any issue that the public has a hard time deciding to whom they should listen. Are the Contras freedom fighters, fascists, soldiers of fortune, or something else altogether? There are "experts" defending each view. We have tried the dialectical standard in the public sphere and it has led us to the current situation.

In an essay at the Wake Forest Conference on Argumentation in 1983, Charles Arthur Willard develops a third answer to the problem of knowledge justification. Willard argues that the best approach to the problem may be to rely on field theory or the study of "epistemics" (as opposed to epistemology). Willard believes that "the public sphere" must "recognize the facts of relativity" among fields, because "The retreat [to a particular field] shuts off debate, or leaves it at a standstill, since it demands from the public a passive acquiescence to field authority" (1983b, 20). Thus, "field theory is a useful basis for understanding the groundrules and—likely—a good starting point for a full dress philosophy of the public sphere" (1983b, 20). The first part of this philosophy, in Willard's view, will be a principle of attention, which "enjoins us to listen to the fields for whom discourse is an open option and suggests that we are not obligated to attend to fields which succeed by virtue of 'closure'" (1983b, 20–21). Through the application of such standards we can begin to develop traditions that eventually will let us solve the problem of the public sphere; "We needn't decide whether a field is right—only whether its argument practices are fair enough to merit our attention" (21).

As always, Willard's views are clearly argued and interesting. His focus on the relationship between field practices and power is particularly insightful. However, his approach to "epistemics" does not resolve the problems facing the public sphere and it is frankly inconsistent with his attack on argument evaluation. In a sense, Willard's claims for epistemics are similar to the plan for ending the Vietnam war proposed by the then Senator from Vermont, George Aiken, who suggested that we should declare victory and simply get out. Similarly, Willard claims that reliance on epistemics can resolve the problems of the public sphere, when in fact the theory explicitly states that no such solution is possible. If Willard is right that the ultimate guarantor of any field is "power" then there is no possibility of attaining a "rational" consensus. There are no ultimate standards, and disagreement among fields is inevitable. In recognizing the inevitability of disagreement among fields, Willard no more resolves the crisis in the public sphere than George Aiken's peace plan would have brought victory to the U.S. forces in Vietnam.

In addition, Willard wants to have his cake and eat it too. While labeling relativity as inevitable, Willard also endorses the application of what is obviously a field invariant "moral" standard for argument, the principle of attention. When Willard says that we should not listen to fields like cost-benefit analysis because they are closed to outside reasoning, he is isolating a universal standard that can be applied to all argument. If he is right about the principle of attention, then it would seem that he must be wrong about relativity and also about the impossibility of justifying argument evaluation, at least in some situations.

Each of the three approaches I have discussed has merit. It makes sense for an arguer to begin with the accepted beliefs in a society. There is also reason to prefer argumentative positions that are tested in a dialectical process. Finally, procedural norms and evaluative standards do vary by field, and the principle of attention is a useful device (although inconsistent with Willard's other work) for identifying fields that rely on argumentative closure. At the same time, none of the three standards I have discussed is fully adequate. At one level all of them depend upon the existence of a set of general field invariant standards for distinguishing strong and weak arguments. In the next section, I will argue that despite the attacks of Willard, Hample, Booth, and others, ordinary logic can provide us with justifiable field invariant evaluative standards. These standards in turn can be tied to the traditional pedagogical functions of argument, teaching critical thinking and improving decision-making.

Shared Purpose and Argument Evaluation

Before an adequate set of evaluative standards can be developed, however, the argument critic needs to confront one final problem, the infinite regress that Willard and Weimer see behind all attempts at evaluation. I suggest that the infinite regress facing justificationist epistemologies can be avoided only by rejecting justificationism itself (see Weimer 1979, 1–19). One avoids the infinite regress by recognizing that no ultimate standard can be identified and instead grounding a theory of argument evaluation in pragmatic utility. The critic does not attempt to justify the evaluative standards as a form of knowledge but uses them because they serve his or her needs. Rescher writes: "there is certainly no better way of justifying a method—any method—than by establishing that 'it works' with respect to the specific tasks held in view" (1977, 96–97). The infinite regress, in which a skeptic continually asks how we know a claim to be true, can be avoided only by shifting to a pragmatic standard.

If Rescher is right that standards for evaluating argument can be justified pragmatically, then the proper place to begin the search for such standards is with the purpose served by argument. Although people argue for a variety of reasons, the general purpose of all argument is to solve problems. People build arguments as a means of discovering the solution to a problem or in order to convince others that they already have discovered the answer to the problem. Thus general standards for evaluating argument should reflect those characteristics that make it more likely that an argument will solve a problem. While nearly all argument serves the general purpose of solving a problem, it also serves any number of specific purposes that influence its character. People argue to solve problems in the sciences, the law, and many other activities. Thus, all argument shares certain similarities, because of its general problem-solving function, but there are also important differences among arguments, because of the specific purposes served by argument in different areas. I have argued elsewhere (Rowland 1981 and 1982) that shared purpose is the force that energizes the various fields of argument. It is their problem-solving purpose that leads a group of arguers to choose a subject area, a particular argumentative form, a mode of resolution, and all of the other argumentative characteristics that come to define the field.

Therefore, two sets of standards can be derived from an analysis of argumentative purpose: general field invariant standards for testing whether argument fulfills its problem-solving function and field dependent criteria for evaluating whether the argument solves the specific problem in a given field. The field dependent standards have received a great deal of consideration, but, perhaps because of this concern with field theory, there has been little emphasis on field invariant standards.

Before considering those field invariant standards, however, it is important to note that there are no universally applicable standards for argument evaluation. The field invariant standards I will describe are useful "rule of thumb" criteria for evaluating arguments. They are not universally applicable. Rather, they are general evaluative criteria that a critic can presume to be useful, absent strong counter arguments. Rescher makes a similar point in his discussion of criteria for evaluating scientific theories. He identifies simplicity, uniformity, and the weight of evidence as standards for choosing among theories (1977, 39–41). Rescher admits that these standards are not perfect but claims that other things being equal they are useful (1977, 115). A theory that is backed by the weight of evidence may be proved not to be useful, but it is more likely to be correct than its competitors, which are not supported by the best evidence.

There are three sets of field invariant standards that can aid the critic in evaluating arguments: tests of evidence, tests of formal coherence, and comparisons to expert knowledge (see Wenzel 1982; O'Keefe 1985). The most valuable standards are rule of thumb criteria for evaluating evidence such as might be found in an informal logic text. The value of such general criteria for evaluating evidence is difficult to dispute. For example, while a biased or incompetent source can produce useful testimony, it is clearly rational to prefer the unbiased expert. Similarly, there are undoubtedly instances in which it is perfectly rational to reason from atypical examples to general conclusions, but as a rule arguments for which there are many examples can be considered superior to those supported by a single instance.

The second set of invariant standards relates to the formal coherence of arguments. Here, I do not mean form in the sense of syllogistic logic, but a more general test of argument organization. There are two specific formal standards that are useful. First, there is strong reason to prefer an argument that is consistent to one that is not. Willard is clearly correct that consistent arguments may be wrong and inconsistent arguments correct, but this in no way denies the value of consistency as a rule of thumb standard for argument evaluation. For example, proponents of handgun control argue against state laws banning handguns because the citizens of a state that had banned handguns could circumvent the law by buying guns in another state. However, they also argue that a Federal law banning handguns would be obeyed by all law-abiding citizens. These two positions are apparently inconsistent. If law-abiding citizens would obey a Federal law banning handguns they would obey a state law as well. The identification of this inconsistency is important. From it a critic might conclude either that the handgun lobby's arguments for a Federal gun law are weaker than had been thought or that compliance with such a law is less certain than the handgun lobby claims.

As the previous example indicates, arguments built on inconsistent assumptions are likely to break down or lose their generalizability. This view is shared by nearly all informal logicians. For example, Geach writes: "if we tolerate inconsistency in the thoughts we harbour and pass on to others, some of those thoughts will be false—will be at odds with the way things are in the world" (1976, 6). Ironically, even Willard defends a variant of the consistency principle. He argues that "when a field borrows concepts from another field, it takes on the conceptual implications of the borrowed idea" (1982a, 32–33). Here, Willard is really saying that to be consistent an arguer who borrows a concept should be held responsible for the assumptions upon which the concept is built. Willard's principle of conceptual borrowing is merely one aspect of the larger principle that arguments should be consistent.

The second standard fitting within the category of formal coherence is that, all other points being equal, an argumentative position in which counterarguments are refuted is preferable to one in which the counterarguments are not confronted. Refutative adequacy is not an absolute standard. An arguer can be right although unable to refute the arguments of the other side. However, when an arguer explicitly considers and refutes counterarguments or when a critic tests the refutative adequacy of an argument this adds argumentative weight to the position. By testing the refutative adequacy of a position, the critic can gain an idea as to how well the position holds up against criticism.

One useful way to apply this standard involves fallacy systems often found in texts on informal logic. The application of fallacies such as ad hominem, begging the question, red herring, and so forth has great appeal. The use of a fallacy system gives the student a set of stock questions that can be asked about any argument. On the other hand, fallacy systems are notoriously difficult to apply and justify. In some situations a personal attack is justifiable, as in a case where someone's integrity is at issue. And one person's red herring may be another's reasonable objection. Consequently, it makes the most sense to use the fallacy systems as a memory aid to jog the mind of the critic in order to get at the refutative quality of the argument. We should use fallacy systems to try and create counterarguments that we can then test using the refutative standard. Through this application, we can get the worth out of fallacies but largely avoid the problems associated with them.

The third presumptive standard relates to expert knowledge.[1] As a general rule, the critic should grant a presumption to the accepted beliefs of the experts in the subject area of an argument. If someone argues that money supply is not related to inflation, the critic could evaluate the claim by noting that most economists disagree. Again this standard is not absolute. An arguer could build a strong case that the expert consensus is wrong. However, absent argument to the contrary, the critic has no real option but to accept the views of the consensus of experts. The critic rarely possesses the requisite expertise to evaluate personally the substance of an argument. It is certainly more rational to accept the opinion of the consensus of experts, rather than that of the minority of experts or the general public. The critic of argument is not concerned with what is accepted as a social truth but with what is the closest approximation of the facts (and is therefore the best solution to the problem under consideration). And on questions of fact, an expert audience is likely to be much more knowledgeable than is the general public. Here, it should be noted that on some questions, especially questions of value, there is no expert audience. In a dispute between environmentalists on the one hand and oil company executives on the other about drilling for oil in Alaska, there are experts who could be consulted on the value of the oil lands or the ecology of the oil field area, but there are no special experts on the proper relation between environmental protection and economic development. There are no special experts on this subject, because in a sense we are all the experts. On most questions of value all people can function as experts and there is no privileged group that should be granted a special presumption.

In addition to the general standards I have identified, argument quality can be evaluated based on field dependent standards. These field dependent standards are drawn from the specific purposes of the field in which the argument occurs and may be either substituted for or applied along with invariant standards. For example, legal rules for evaluating witnesses largely are consistent with the more general rules of evidence that I have described. In other instances, the field dependent standards may directly contradict the field invariant standards. The polygraph is banned in some legal settings, despite the high degree of accuracy which a trained operator can obtain, because it does not fill the needs of the law. As a rule, if there is a conflict between the general purpose of all argument and the specific purpose of the field, it is the specific purpose and therefore the field dependent standards that take precedence.

At this point, it is finally possible to answer the question: Under what circumstances can an argument be said to be justified? The ultimate standard for evaluating any argument is whether the argument works, that is, whether it serves its function. General rule of thumb standards and more specific field dependent standards are both derived from this principle.

This conclusion illuminates the earlier discussion of audience centered, dialectical, and field theory answers to the problem of rational justification. In general, it makes sense to begin any discussion with the views of rational actors in an area, to test those views dialectically, and to appreciate the requirements of the particular field, but these individual tests are important precisely because they are linked to the general problem-solving function of argument. However, as soon as argument criticism is viewed from a pragmatic perspective the place of the dialectical, audience-centered, and field-oriented approaches becomes obvious as partial tests of argumentative function. The great value of a purpose-centered view of argument evaluation is that it integrates each of these theories into a coherent system that also tests consistency and evidence quality.

Implications

A purpose-centered view of argument evaluation has a number of important implications for a theory of argumentation. First, a purposive view of informal logic provides the critic with useful tools for evaluating arguments. It is useful to discover that former President Reagan often used atypical examples when building a case. It is useful to know that the pro-gun control lobby uses inconsistent arguments. These evaluative standards are needed if the rational problem-solving function of argument is to be fulfilled. As Rescher writes: "A means for appraisal and evaluation is a fundamental precondition of rational controversy" (1977, 43). General field invariant and specific field dependent standards answer this need.

A second implication is that the process for evaluating an argument is reflexive; it can be held up to standards for evaluating argument quality. A good critique should be consistent, refute opposing arguments, meet appropriate evidence standards, and so on. Consequently, the critic must be ready to justify the standards he or she applies in a specific case. Moreover, the critique itself can be evaluated based on those standards. For example, Hardwig's essay on dialogue as the means of rational deliberation apparently is built on an enormous inconsistency. Hardwig develops the case for dialogue as the method of reason in an essay that is not a dialogue.

While the argument critic can presume the value of field invariant standards, he or she must be prepared to defend them if attacked. By contrast, the critic applies field dependent criteria by first building a case for the priority of a given field. Some argumentative disputes can be considered from the perspective of several fields. The evolution-creation controversy might be considered from the perspective of science, the law, or politics. The critic can identify the proper field for evaluating the dispute, by isolating the purpose unifying arguers in the area. If the creationists and evolutionists argue in order to find out how humans actually came into the world, then their goal is knowledge and the scientific field provides the appropriate standards for analysis. If their goal is to identify the proper role of the state in establishing public school curricula, then the dispute occurs within the competitive field of politics and standards drawn from it would be most appropriate. In other words, the critic builds a case for the priority of a set of field dependent evaluative standards by showing that the argument to be judged serves the same purpose as does the field.

Third, the view that both field invariant and field dependent standards for argument evaluation are derived from shared purpose helps explain the process by which standards for evaluation develop. All critical standards are consensual, whether they take the form of explicit rules, as in the law, or generally accepted guidelines. While the standards are consensual, they are not arbitrary. Rather, the standards have developed through an evolutionary process in which those criteria that work are retained and improved while those that do not work are discarded. Rescher writes of this process in science: "Moreover they [evaluative standards] are themselves evolved, through an historic process of retaining what works and abandoning what doesn't" (1977, 102). Both field dependent and field invariant standards evolve over time in order to fulfill better the problem-solving purpose of argumentation.

Finally, the standards that I have described are an essential part of any project for reclaiming the public sphere. Initially, the inherently probabilistic nature of evaluation should make it clear that we will never achieve the kind of perfectly warranted consensus that some theorists seem to desire. Some of the writing on the public sphere seems to long for a time when all citizens will participate in reasoned discussion of complex issues that will then be resolved by consensus or through dialectic. Clearly, this vision is a fantasy. Not only is the evaluative process inherently fraught with difficulty, but the world itself is too complicated a place for such a vision to be realized. Consider for a moment how a rational citizenry would go about evaluating an issue such as nuclear power. To decide rationally whether nuclear power should be supported one would have to consider all aspects of the various technologies involved in mining, processing, and transporting nuclear fuel, the nuclear power generation process itself, waste disposal, economic issues relating to uranium costs, availability of other fuels, and so forth, as well as safety and geo-political issues. On each of these questions there are experts who say that nuclear power should be supported or should be eliminated. In addition, the issue is itself complicated and, as Three Mile Island demonstrated, important information may be lacking, so it simply may not be possible to answer some questions relating to nuclear power at all. Moreover, the average citizen is not in a position to weigh the evidence on many of the technical issues. He or she inevitably will have to trust one side or the other's experts. Finally, the nuclear power issue involves questions of value for which there are no answers. How much money is it worth to avoid strip mining for coal? How many lives is cheap electricity for a region worth?

Clearly, then, the dream of a perfectly rational, re-energized public sphere is unattainable. Difficulties of the type I have described have led some to throw up their hands and say that evaluation as a pedagogical aim of argumentation is valueless. The proper conclusion, however, is that while evaluation is difficult and does not always lead to successful solutions to problems, there is no alternative. The standards I have described are not perfect and they are difficult to apply, but they can tell us important things. During the investigation of the space shuttle *Challenger* explosion, it quickly became clear that government bureaucrats had ignored the warnings of the experts on the booster rocket (the engineers for Morton Thiokol), had reasoned from an inadequate sample of previous cold weather launches, and had not considered the competing arguments for why this launch could be different from previous launches. If the NASA bureaucrats had applied something like the invariant standards I have described they might not have made the disastrous decision to launch the *Challenger* on that cold January morning.

Argument evaluation using general rule of thumb standards will never return us to "golden age" of public deliberation for which some critics seem to long. For one thing that golden age probably never existed. However, the application of such standards can aid people evaluate questions of policy (or any other question for that matter).

Against the value of such standards someone might argue that the most important conflicts in the public sphere are over values and that it is widely believed that questions of value cannot be rationally decided (see Booth 1974, 7). For instance, someone might use the example cited earlier of a conflict over oil production in Alaska between the oil companies and the environmentalists to argue that application of standards of informal logic would achieve little.

I certainly agree that a basic conflict between two inconsistent values cannot be decided through argument evaluation procedures. It was David Hume who first demonstrated that we cannot derive an "ought" from an "is." However, the difficulty of creating standards for judging value conflict does not mean that field invariant standards have no worth on value-related issues. In the Alaskan oil example, for instance, it would make sense initially to check the factual statements of each side. Perhaps oil drilling need not destroy the ecosystem. Alternatively, it may be that there are other wilderness areas containing the same species that could be protected instead of the oil fields. On the other hand, the reasons for drilling in the area may be suspect. Are the geological reports sound? Do we have adequate technology to drill in the area? Are other oil reserves more accessible? The point is that while one cannot derive an ought from an is, oftentimes factual questions are at the heart of value conflicts. Second, evaluative standards could be used to test whether there is some way around the value conflict. Are there means of drilling for oil that would avoid or minimize the ecological destruction? Finally, if the public can agree on the purpose of an activity, then the standards I have described become relevant even on issues that are directly value related. Standards of informal logic could not be used to decide whether the environment or economic development is more important in oil exploration. However, once the purpose of the particular argument has been determined (to protect the environment, to create economic growth, or perhaps a combination of the two), then the standards can be used to test particular means to those ends. Even on questions of value, standards of informal logic derived from the general and specific purposes served by argument can be quite useful.

In sum, argument evaluation is an essential aspect of argumentation as a discipline. While there are no universal standards that can be applied to evaluate objectively all argument, application of rule of thumb standards drawn from the general problem-solving purpose of argument and field dependent standards derived from the specific purposes of argument in a specific field give the critic useful if flawed tools for argument evaluation. Such a method of evaluation is needed if rational discourse is to continue.

Notes

1. The concept of expert knowledge is somewhat similar to Farrell's view of technical knowledge. See Farrell 1976. The relationship between technical and public argument is developed in Goodnight 1982.

9

The Problem of the Public Sphere

Three Diagnoses

Charles Arthur Willard

The question before us is, "When, if ever, is assent justified?" Modernity's answer is that assent is justified when it comports with the prevailing consensus in a relevant expert community. Postmodernism's answer changes *justified* from an adjective to a verb, making the question seem to betray a false consciousness. Thus Foucault denounces the illusion of critique. Critique, he says, is compromised by the power formations in which it is hermetically sealed; it only takes us from one canonical *oeuvre* to another. *Justified* is *inevitability*'s mask. So the postmodern answer is the modernist's answer in determinist drag: "Unfortunately, assent is always justified (legitimized)."

Many people have qualms about both answers. Conceding that modernity is not so bad that it allows only a choice between conformity and anomie, one is still left with a relativized world. Though postmodernists may stop short of Foucault's pessimism, they find it hard to value the human disciplines except as points of leverage against one another. And both answers seem extravagant: modernity does not oblige us to value every consensus equally; postmodern skepticism need not become (as Lyotard might say) an epistemological paranoia. One can't help but think that the question of when assent is justified is not meant to provoke evangelism or a wholesale endorsement or dismissal of modernity.

The question seems to invoke the sort of postmodern stance in which the questioner expects to deplore the answer but to be able to do something about it. The question thus asks, "What are the grounds of a sound consensus?" "How do we know a trustworthy consensus when we see one?" Or "Is efficacious critique possible?" So put, the question fixes our attention on the practices that yield claims and buttress institutions. At least since Rousseau and Tocqueville, and certainly since Dewey, this question has been thought to epitomize the problem of the public sphere.

In this essay, I consider two prominent diagnoses of the problem of the public sphere, the *epistemological* and *pedagogical*.[1] The former suggests that the public sphere is withering for the want of a commensurating discourse; the latter operationalizes the needed discourse in terms of argument techniques. Neither diagnosis is satisfactory: the epistemological view is largely irrelevant to the problem of the public sphere and the pedagogical diagnosis is exaggerated. Both diagnoses are inferior to what might be called the *epistemic* diagnosis. "Epistemic" here means nonepistemological (critical or social scientific) views of knowledge. I argue elsewhere (1987b) that these approaches are coalescing to such a degree that a new discipline, "Epistemics," is forming. Here I consider two aspects of the epistemic diagnosis of the problem of the public sphere: the relativity dividing the elite decision-maker from the expert (the former's dependence upon and incomprehension of the latter) and the relativity that divides experts.

This focus is compulsory in a short essay, but it runs the risk of inflating the importance of relativity. This risk is more than conjectural, for often relativity is discussed as if it is an isolated phenomenon. The problem of the public sphere, I argue (1989b), is a complex of problems: the proliferation and growth of literatures, the closure and alienation caused by commensurating discourses, political competition among authorities, and the long-term effects of misunderstandings or spurious agreements. These problems are as important as and synergistic with relativity. And they are aggravated by the postmodern vocabulary for idealizing public life: authenticity, community, and commensurability—three goals that muddle our thinking about public life and that give the literature on relativity its eschatological tone. Relativity arises in contexts created by our ways of speaking about it—modes of expression colored by epistemology that are sometimes as harmful as the differences themselves. The problem of the public sphere, in other words, is a family of problems—two parts of which are the focus of this essay.

The Epistemological Diagnosis

Epistemology proper searches for a privileged overarching discourse commensurable with and capable of arbitrating among all particular discourses.[2] It stems from a philosophical impulse to find universally valid veridical and judgmental principles. The universality requirement is idiomatic to Kant's philosophy: many disputes can be solved by *an* overarching discourse (one that transcends two local positions but not all others), but a solution that transcends only two positions is merely a third position. If it is not demonstrably a universal, its only merit is its local success. Those who hold that human knowledge is (or can be) a universal unity are dissatisfied with merely local solutions.

The twentieth century has not been kind to universalists. The epistemological ideal entered this century intact and robust, but it is now common to underscore the fragmentation of knowledge. Something once thought to be monolithic has been rent asunder, scattered, subdivided into sovereign domains. The casualty is an ideal not a polity, but political terms reflect knowledge's historic associations with statist images (captured in Toulmin's expression, "cities of truth"). Knowledge seen as a single, impersonal, universal system now seems to be a doubtful prospect.

The Euclidian symmetry and logical precision of Cartesianism surrendered to projective geometries. Paradoxes persisted in the systems that wedded mathematics to logic. Frege's axioms, the *Principia Mathematica*'s consistency proofs, and Hilbert's *Grundelagen der Geometrie* seemed to authorize progressively less certainty after Godel. If mathematics starts from undecidable formulas or cannot prove its own consistency, it inspires no epistemological confidence. The reduction from substantive sentence to logical equation to mathematical equation is unjustified in principle. Similarly, the Vienna Circle's proposal that physics might be a commensurating discourse underwent revision at the hands of Bohr and Heisenberg. The Copenhagen Interpretation did not destroy positivism, but it fueled doubts that physics might be a privileged arbiter and buttressed the relativist's case with such ideas as perspectivity (the importance of the observer's stance and viewpoint) and systematicity (the idea that flawless systems might be incommensurable). And Tractarian reductionism, the hope that an arbiter might inhere in the structure of natural languages, gradually succumbed to the conception of language games in Wittgenstein's *Investigations*.

Still, the *Tractatus* is not without influence—especially when epistemologists attack epistemological relativists. Thus Davidson (1973–74) holds that incommensurability is an incoherent idea. To describe an incommensurability requires possession of a sufficiently overarching language to cast the dispute in common terms. If this is possible, the incommensurability is spurious.

This position is, I think, irrelevant to the differences that in fact divide people. But as an epistemic proposition—a claim about ordinary discourse—Davidson's position has merit, for it implies that differences among public positions may admit of local solutions. These two points are worth considering more fully. The first claim turns on the difference between epistemological and epistemic relativity; the second implies that relativists should take care not to exaggerate relativity.

Epistemic versus Epistemological Relativity

The epistemic position is this: there are cases in which sincere arguers, proceeding correctly with the approved methods of their discourse domains, make incompatible knowledge claims that cannot be adjudicated by commonly accepted methods. *Contra* Davidson, the fact that we can describe a dispute does not mean that we can referee it or bring the disputants to a higher synthesis—*not* because they are bullheaded or mistaken but because they are proceeding competently within their fields. Thus there can be nontrivial differences across discourse domains vis-à-vis the things taken as knowledge and the veridical/judgmental procedures that yield them.

Among the cases field theorists have discussed have been the pro- and anti- positions vis-à-vis abortion, creationism, nuclear power, arms control, cost-benefit analysis, military discourse, and various moral issues. Pro-nuclear power technologists hold themselves accountable only to the special assumptions and veridical standards of nuclear engineering (Goodnight 1982). Faced with external critique, they claim special privilege by virtue of their status as field experts and by retreating into the shell of the field's special assumptions (Collingridge and Reeve 1986).

Cost-benefit analysts are protected likewise when they refuse to be at risk to arguments not couched in the language of fiscal costs and benefits—a tactic that ensures immunity from moral critique (Willard 1982b). Formalization makes it impossible to express ideas that do not fit the scheme. Thus environmentalists are prevented from expressing the things they care most about when they try to adapt to the discourse of costs and benefits (Socolow 1976). And in airline safety, cost-benefit analysis dictates the industry-wide belief that a zero defect system is too costly; the loss of a certain number of lives is inevitable. This is not mystical thinking a la *Fate Is the Hunter* but a financial tradeoff between safety and cost. Why are airliners lined with fabrics and plastics that emit toxic fumes when burned? Why are passengers not given shoulder harnesses? Why are redundant systems in some planes bunched together so that damage to one system threatens the integrity of all? In each case, safety costs may outweigh the value of lost lives. Thus arises an explicit philosophy of tolerance for an unspecified but low death rate. In the face of criticism, the cost-benefit analyst takes refuge behind the ledger: the costs of safety must be weighed against its advantages *in the same language.*

Conviction not deviousness causes such retreats. Challenged, one goes to ground—that is, to one's field—for proof. One confronts the enemy with the facts—and assumes that any refutation must follow the procedures of one's own field. One assumes this stance not from a fear of criticism but because one is right; the interlocutor is wrong. Thus the creationists do not insist on the admissibility of personal revelation as epistemic evidence out of malice or because of the argumentative advantages it yields but because they think it is true.

Argument fields are going concerns because people believe in them. They vie for political power because their actors believe that their facts bear upon public issues. Their authoritative claims assume the validity and cogency of the judgmental and veridical standards, traditions, and practices that license them. And these in turn are authorized by the faith and trust field actors place in them. So the retreat to one's field is the logical outcome of sincere arguers making true claims.

Thus we have one component of the epistemic diagnosis of the problem of the public sphere. Sovereign domains that left alone might go their own ways are brought into political competition by the press of events. They thus compete for political power and demand that the public acquiesce to their pronouncements, but they acknowledge no legitimate competing interests or parties to the social contract. The retreat to the field when challenged is a respectable epistemic move made by sincere advocates making true claims. In the face of competing claims, there exists no public philosophy capable of arbitrating or resolving the disputes. This situation is not what the epistemologist might call the want of a commensurating discourse. Cost-benefit analysis *is* a universal adjudicating discourse. It is, the epistemic analyst says, a problem of fitting discourses and methods to problems. Because they are dependent on authority, as we shall see, public decision-makers have no principled way of arbitrating among hegemonic discourses.

This illustration perhaps suffices to show the difference between the epistemological and epistemic diagnoses (and between Epistemics and Epistemology as intellectual fields). Thus I turn to the second point about Davidson's position, that it is utilizable as a distinctively epistemic claim.

Relativity becomes apparent in communication. Its effects depend on the disputants' knowledge of communication. O'Keefe (1988) predicts systematic differences in communication among people who see the purpose of communication as (1) making one's thoughts known to others (expressives), (2) following public recipes (conventionals), and (3) defining selves, roles, and situations so as to make cooperative action possible (rhetoricals).

Relativists make their cases more hyperbolic than necessary when they use an expressive view of communication (*A* and *B* are said to have incommensurable positions as if their positions were immutable expressions of their private points of view). When positions *are* expressive, Davidson's belief that to be able to describe differences is to be able to resolve them is obviously mistaken—witness the abortion dispute, which seems to have more than its share of such positions. These expressive positions may explain why both sides of the dispute often seem dogmatic and shrill. But positions are not solely expressive. To think that they are is to underestimate the conventional and rhetorical resources for changing people's positions. Conventional positions may be overarched by other conventions. Cost-benefit analysis thus resolves value disputes in the law. It is so widely used in this way that it may be the prototypical public language. In such cases, Davidson's reasoning succeeds. And rhetorical communication gives still another twist to the commensurationist position, albeit one Davidson might not like. Davidson seems to see disputes as obdurate realities to be more or less correctly mirrored by a descriptive language. But disputants can sometimes reach agreements if they can redefine their roles or definitions of situation. In such cases, the aim of public discourse is not to achieve identity of private beliefs but to create working agreements that make cooperative action possible. The Palestine Liberation Organization, for example, has achieved diplomatic breakthroughs by conceding that Israel has a right to exist, even if its members privately disagree. And we have seen Western nations attach enormous importance to Yassar Arafat's public renunciation of terrorism. Expressive communicators might see this stance as naïveté, but public commitments often entail social contracts that are binding regardless of one's private thoughts. Public stances may permit further cooperative endeavors and inhibit certain actions. By redefining their roles and definitions, social actors may create an agreement that bypasses their differences. But if the Israelis see Arafat's stance solely in expressive terms (that is, Arafat is either telling the truth or lying), they may not be able to capitalize on the diplomatic opportunities licensed by Arafat's public commitment.

So relativists must take care not to exaggerate the incommensurabilities or de facto differences that divide people. Some differences—the ones that do not depend on intransigent repetition of expressive positions—may be open to compromise if their proponents are imaginative or skillful.

Of course not all differences are solvable. Some disputes do not turn exclusively on the dogmatism of proponents; not all pro- and anti-abortion advocates are expressive; one can take either side without making logical mistakes; and no one has found a commensurating discourse or working agreement that resolves or bypasses the dispute.

In sum, the epistemological diagnosis of the problem of the public sphere is that public discourse has fragmented; the center has not held. The search for a public philosophy is a search for common commensurating ground, a universal arbiter. The epistemic critique of this diagnosis is that, while local commensuration may succeed (for example, Davidson's position can be adapted to local dispute resolutions), the language of epistemology is a poor guide to thinking about the balkanization of knowledge and thus about the intellectual content of the public sphere.

The Pedagogical Diagnosis

For Aristotle, the problem of the public sphere is a simple one. Ordinary folks are morally deficient. They lack practical wisdom, the acquired states of capacity (*hexes*) for feeling, thinking, and acting rightly. They are slaves of passion—their decisions little more than blind lunges at narrow self-interest, their reflective lives suffocated by a swinish pursuit of pleasure and self-gratification.

The clarity of Aristotle's problem and the logic of his solution are artifacts of an odd doctrine. The *Rhetoric* holds that truth has a natural tendency to triumph over its opposite when advocates of equal skill present both sides of an issue. The aim of pedagogy is to equip advocates to assist truth in its natural course, to impart deliberative excellences and facts of legislation. The result is *phronesis*, practical wisdom—a package of habits, skills, and acquired states of capacity that join to create a predisposition for truth.

This teleology is hard to take seriously even on Aristotle's reasoning. He distinguishes opinion (*doxa*) from proof (*pistis*) and knowledge (*sophia*) and relaxes his epistemological standards to create standards of prudential conduct, presumably because *doxa* is an imperfect mirror of nature (Rorty 1979). He says that rhetoric deals with contingent affairs, ones dependent on human action and open to revision. So how can truth's telos dominate human contingencies? In Aristotle's system, logic is a better mirror of nature than *doxa*, but the materials of practical and rhetorical syllogisms are still probabilities and matters of choice. So why should we not suppose that Aristotle's twin pictures of human contingency and of the depravities of ordinary people (the "depraved character of the audience" is a recurring theme in the *Rhetoric*) are as or more powerful than truth's telos? And what is the causal connection? How, that is, do contingent, opinion-based affairs nudge the truth? Even inside Aristotle's system, then, the proposal that truth tends to triumph over falsity is a dubious move.

Why bother with so flimsy a claim? Aristotle's system does not preclude a utilitarian (or checks and balances) rationale for public debate. But perhaps Aristotle feels obliged to confront the fatalism in popular Greek thought. Truth's telos is a rationale for believing in the efficacy of human effort. Rhetoric may assist truth in its natural course—from which the *Rhetoric* infers that we have only ourselves to blame when events turn out badly. This inference may be why truth's telos is still used (for example, Smith and Hunsaker 1972). The idea that truth needs only a nudge from right-minded persuaders is a more earnest portrait than utility: it depicts a Frank Capra world where the right prevails because human action matters. It is an implicit answer to Foucault's grim vision.

Foucault's view of Sisphyean critique emasculated by system telos is not all that different from Hellenic fatalism: the mirage of criticism hermetically sealed in an authoritative literature seems much like the architecture of Oedipus' fate. Indeed the following might be a commentary on Sophocles: "[T]here is no freedom in Foucault's world because his language forms a seamless web, a cage far more airtight than anything Weber ever dreamed of, into which no life can break. The mystery is why so many of today's intellectuals seem to want to choke in there with him. The answer, I suspect, is that Foucault offers a generation of refugees from the 1960s a world-historical alibi for the sense of passivity and helplessness that gripped so many of us in the 1970s" (Berman 1982, 34–35). Perhaps Oedipus' story served similar purposes. Perhaps truth's telos is merely Sophocles' fate with a happy face. And the persistence of truth's telos in our own time may stem from a similar predicament as Foucault rubs our noses in the inefficacy of critique. Literatures cannot replace gods without keeping some of the trappings.

Truth's telos is idiosyncratic to Aristotle's or Foucault's positions and likely is seen as a minority view except among Aristotelians and Foucaldians. Outside these positions, truth's telos can only be a loose metaphor, like epistemological phlogiston, or a rationalizing myth. If truths inhere in prevailing consensuses, if they are constituted rhetorically in the practices of disciplines and professions, then argument pedagogy will justify itself as affecting pragmatic conditions. Efficacy will be bracketed or taken for granted.

Disentangled from teleology, the rationale for argument pedagogy shifts ground to the techniques of democracy. Packaged by Dewey, a concern for the unity of reason and practice dominates Argumentation's concern for deliberative rationality and the reflective skills of citizens. The dream of optimum decision-making, a belief in the possibilities of political rationality, has been the discipline's organizing thread unifying its historical preoccupations with critical thinking, rationality, and deliberation.

This pragmatism has a Hobbesian bias embodied in a tendency to frame the discipline's organizing questions on the horizon of technique. Logic, Carnap says, is Reason's toolbox. To build arguments is to manipulate the materials of belief—to bolt premises together and to nail down conclusions. To scrutinize arguments, we disassemble them, break them down to their component parts to reveal their structure. Argumentation's pedagogy, in other words, is a group of procedures and techniques packaged in a therapeutic language: logical and procedural errors are the malady, elementary skills pedagogy the remedy. Thus Argumentation, like the Informal Logic and Critical Thinking movements, sees itself as a practical discipline seeking the unity of Reason and Praxis in a language of therapy.

This posture can become as flamboyant as the postmodernists', for it involves a rhetoric of democratic enfranchisement whose effect is to give its advocates custody of democracy's most basic values. It uses Aristotle's "depraved character of the audience" as a rationale for skills pedagogy. Thus the need for informed citizens skilled in the deliberative arts is thought to authorize pedagogy in argument, critical thinking, and informal logic. The rhetoric, in sum, is premised on the belief that the public sphere is withering for the want of a skilled citizenry.

There ought to be two constraints on this claim. First, a skilled citizenry may not defeat epistemic relativity. I argue (1989b) that the dynamics of mass democracy differ from the processes by which organizations function. Better citizens may improve the tone and content of popular politics, but epistemic relativity befuddles even elites. A fully committed and competent electorate may not resolve the substantive differences that divide society. The complete success of the critical thinking movement might only enhance the scope of collective befuddlement. And second, argument and critical thinking skills are best suited to correcting mistakes. The rationale for correcting mistakes is much like Russell's theory of descriptions, which held that philosophical problems are traceable to flawed expressions.

Translated to ordinary discourse, this doctrine implies an oversimple picture: beneath the disagreement, find the mistake; fix the mistake and solve the dispute. This view is to some extent plausible, for the incompetence and intransigence we see in life *are* sometimes traceable to fallacies, contradictions, procedural flaws, and misunderstandings. Perhaps many public problems can be solved, or compromises reached, or the most intemperate voices muted, by correcting expressions. But public actors are also divided by substantive differences that do not depend on mistakes. Arguers proceeding competently with the methods of their respective fields may disagree about issues in the public agenda. A citizenry fully equipped with fallacy theory, consistency checks, and Dewey's problem-solving sequence may still find itself beset with epistemic problems.

So it is one thing to defend deliberative skills pedagogy as a kind of consumerism and another to equate the problem of the public sphere with the want of deliberative skills. The plausibility of the former is not a rationale for the latter if the problem of the public sphere has elements that cannot be remedied by improvements in the public's skills. Epistemic relativity is one such element. I now turn to the most virulent strain of this relativity.

The Problem of Authority

Consider the problem of authority—the fact that decision-making in most human endeavors is dependent on expert testimony. This dependence has been thought to be a crisis at least since the 1930s when the Beards decried the cult of the expert, and a thoroughly modernist crisis at least since Bernstein and Habermas (and in Argumentation, Cox and Goodnight) have diagnosed the problem of public discourse as the want of unity between Reason and Praxis. This ideal unity is the very heart of Argumentation's pedagogical rationale.

The unity of Reason and Praxis, unfortunately, is more a slogan than a proposal. Goodnight (this volume), for instance, wants to revive the art of deliberative rhetoric that, Atlantis-like, has sunk beneath specialism, expertise, and authority. He underscores the tendency of expert authority to dilute skepticism and coopt critique. The *point* of invoking authority is to transform inquiry into action, to let deliberation yield policies and decisions. But what is it about the lost deliberative art that will amend or diminish the public sphere's dependence on experts? One wonders, in other words, about the concrete particulars behind the slogan.

Modernity can as easily lay claim to the unity of Reason and Praxis as its critics. Technologized, specialized, and expert discourses *are* unities of reason and practice—ones better suited to special problems than the discourses that preceded them. They are, to adapt Stephen Jay Gould's expression, "splendid local adaptations." The rifts between these discourses are symptoms of their problem-adaptedness and local successes. Cardinal Newman's dream of a university community speaking a common language enabled by a shared religion has been replaced not only by discourses in different niches but also by multiple ecologies.

So the postmodern critique, whatever its disaffection with our reliance on authority, must accommodate to the fact that expertise is indispensable. In a complex, specialized world, the nonexpert's deference to authority is presumptively rational (Stich and Nisbett 1984)—routinely the prudentially, morally, and legally preferred course (Willard 1989a). Given the numbers and enormity of technical literatures, and the complexities within them, we accept expert testimony in lieu of inspecting evidence for ourselves. We believe in evolution "not because we have in mind the evidence and experience it would take to envision the process and grasp it in a fully rational way, but because we trust biologists" (Haskell 1984, xi). The courts that have condemned creation science *qua* science have done so on the authority of scientific testimony. They could not have acted otherwise because jurists are not qualified to examine the fossil record for themselves; they should not have acted otherwise because their procedures in consulting appropriate authority comport with our standards of "rational argumentation."

Imagine that I am a city councilman. I am a demographically typical civic leader—in business or the professions, college educated, relatively prosperous. In the languages of two-step flow theory and political theory, I am an opinion leader and an elite. The city council is considering a university's request to build a recombinate DNA laboratory inside the city limits. As a civic booster, I favor new construction. But the commonweal includes public safety, and it is an open question whether the proposed laboratory poses public health hazards. (I am loosely glossing press accounts of the case in Cambridge, Massachusetts.)

How do I assess the benefits and risks? I am untutored in molecular biology—and likely to remain so, for I am a typical public actor whose deliberations span multiple subject matters. Next week I will need knowledge of economics, business, sociology, and engineering. This breadth distinguishes public from disciplinary agendas and ensures my continuing dependence upon experts. Thus, because predictions of benefits and risks depend upon technical and specialized knowledge and intuitions, I will turn to experts.

The experts present me with a mess. The pro-experts paint a picture of scientific necessity, of the possibility of dramatic breakthroughs in vital areas including cancer research. The anti-experts paint a doomsday scenario: cancers crossed with virulent viruses—malignancies as contageous as the common cold—escape by unforeseen routes into the general population. I am confronting two kinds of relativity—the dispute between the experts and the gulf of incomprehension that divides me from both camps. The former relativity puts me in the position of adjudicating among competing experts; the latter ensures my incompetence.

My incomprehension is not an epistemological relativity, for it is beside the point to say that I might *in principle* acquire the needed expertise. My ineptness is a pragmatic fact. Nor is my position improved much by popular science writing. My handicap need not stem from *total* incomprehension. If I am a political elite, I am presumably conversant with the language of general intellectual discourse. I can read essays in the *Atlantic, New York Times Magazine,* and *Omni.* At a higher level, I can read trade paperbacks dealing with the quantum domain and biotechnology. (At a higher level, there is the general discourse of academics—in the sense that any reasonably educated academic can read *The Structure of Scientific Revolutions* or *The Mismeasure of Man;* and at a still higher level there is the generally readable book whose conclusions are comprehensible but whose reasoning and evidence are fuzzy to the nonspecialist, for example, *Philosophy and the Mirror of Nature.*) But even if I am conversant with the contents of half a dozen popular books on quantum physics, no one would think that I am on equal epistemic footing with Bohr, Heisenberg, and Pauli. No one, in fact, would think that I am ready to become a student of quantum physics.

Reading a hundred more popular books on biotechnology will not improve my position. Given the limits of general writing, there are only so many slogans, metaphors, and images appropriate both to the general audience and to the specialized knowledge. Popular science writing will prepare me only for the mode of testimony I am likely to receive. Though I am a political elite, I am a general public to the experts. The experts will frame their testimony in a language fitted to my capacities. They will adopt slogans, metaphors, and images that, though misleading (that is, not fully accurate representations of the scientific facts), may come close enough to get their ideas across. They will put me, in other words, in the position of choosing among authorities. If I am lucky, there will be ten Nobel laureates on one side and only a few on the other. I cannot evaluate an expert's virtuosity, but I can acquiesce to the expert community's evaluations. Or I can align my thinking with the prevailing expert consensus. And, of course, in addition to acquiescing to authority, I can seize upon the slogans or metaphors that catch my fancy. But no matter how much popular science writing I read, I cannot adjudicate the differences among the experts: some of these disputes are open questions among them.

So expert discourses have coopted the public sphere for a very good reason. Decision-making is fueled by facts; facts come wrapped in authority. Hobbes foresaw this predicament in *Leviathan*, though he thought it a simple difference between accepting a position on its merits versus accepting it because of its advocate's merits. Early fallacy theorists followed suit. But field theory puts a different face on the matter. The field theorist holds that we assess a claim's meaning and merit by the niche it occupies in an intellectual ecology and by its fit with the judgmental/veridical apparatus of its relevant field. Our judgment of its substantive merits, therefore, cannot be disentangled from our faith in the field. Facts do not speak for themselves. They take their intellectual authority from their status in a field's ecology. In the political sphere, they get their legitimacy from the authority of their advocates—this authority being awarded by virtue of the advocate's position in a field. So someone always speaks for the facts—someone with interests and goals, background assumptions, prejudices and pieties.

The presumption favoring authority in public discourse should not be confused with authority presumptions inside expert domains. Croasmun argues (this volume) that the norm of consensus undercuts dissent, and Redner (1987) suggests that piety within expert domains precludes scientific progress. Expert domains are not immune to authority, but they achieve balances between prevailing views and pressures for innovation that are unique to their conceptual ecologies. These balances are possible because conceptual stability (preserving the prevailing consensus) and innovation (importing outside ideas) are not—as Toulmin and others put it—activities and attributes of a single audience; they are activities involving different people (Willard 1989a). Big disciplines benefit from a division of labor: within them, we expect to find piety and rebellion, conservatism and progressivism not as Ying-Yang qualities of a single mind but as public positions taken by field actors.

So lamentation must be tempered by appreciation. One does not become modernity's apologist in recognizing that the public sphere is dependent on authority. For many matters, we cannot (or would not) have it otherwise. Whatever the "lost deliberative arts" are, they are not antidotes to our dependence on authority.

In sum, the pedagogical diagnosis of the problem of the public sphere has a history of flamboyant rationales evolving coincidentally with changes in broader philosophical doctrines. The truth's telos idea makes rhetoric the continuation of epistemology by other means.[3] Its pedagogy becomes a union of reason and praxis whose efficacy is taken for granted. Shorn of teleology, the pedagogical rationale is transformed into a political philosophy—a rhetoric of public enfranchisement. The facts of relativity, and especially of authority, should inhibit exaggerations of this rhetoric.

The Epistemic Diagnosis

The epistemic diagnosis of the problem of the public sphere is perhaps already clear by way of contrasts with the epistemological and pedagogical views. It is more relevant to the problem of the public sphere than the epistemological view because it is not hypnotized by the lack of a commensurating discourse. It holds that genuine disagreements are possible, that advocates proceeding competently with the methods of their fields can have nontrivial disputes and that not every disagreement about consequential matters stems from incorrect or unclear expressions or procedural mistakes. And the epistemic view checks the exaggerations of the pedagogical diagnosis: a public fully enfranchised by skills may still be reliant on authority.

The epistemic diagnosis starts with a baffling symptom: there exists no clear picture of the public's epistemic interests. Many writers emphasize the rights of states and of persons, the need of community, or the search for commensurating philosophies. But as one reads Locke, Rousseau, and Hobbes, or Lippmann, Dewey, and Sennett, or Bernstein, Connolly, and Habermas, one sees the problem of the public sphere treated as if it is a philosophical problem (or trivial facsimile thereof), a symptom of an epistemological problem, a matter of selecting the right authorities to define the public's economic interests, or a matter of maintaining reflective awareness while acting within organizations.

Alongside such concerns—or hidden beneath them—is the practical question of the public decision-maker's argumentative stance. We know something of how experts argue; but how should public actors argue? What are their argumentative rights and obligations? When they challenge experts, who has the burden of proof? When experts clash, how does the burden of rejoinder work? If jurisprudence can specify the argumentative relationship between prosecution and defense, can we similarly delineate the stance of the decision-maker vis-à-vis the expert?

These questions are eclipsed by even the most practical approaches. Much of the decision-making literature, for example, expects decision-makers to be pseudo-experts: they must get information, comprehend it, and translate facts into policy. This is a wish list, not an argumentative stance, for the problem of authority intrudes at each step. Is the decision-maker only a questioner whose function is to elicit unfathomable answers, then a poseur who brandishes the experts' popularizations as if they were his or her own, and then a sham decision-maker whose verdicts ratify one expert or another? Are the results the inertia of ongoing policies or the power arrangements of the political community?

Similarly, the "public interest" preoccupies an enormous literature and might be thought to embody the public actor's argumentative stance. But the public interest is not an argumentative stance: it is an enabling premise in one's reasoning—as open to dispute and infused with the authority of disciplines as any other argumentative premise. One might *also* say that the public interest is an ideal perspective public actors may take (and translate into public positions). But still the public interest is not an argumentative stance. A concern for the commonweal does not translate into concrete advice about how public actors can instantiate general interests in particular policies. Both the developer and the environmentalist claim to speak for the common good, so something more concrete is needed to referee their disputes. As disputants and decision-makers get down to particulars, their positions may be equivocally connected to abstract values.

Of course the public interest can be defined so as to include epistemic interests. This distinction requires a normative move: defining the public sphere as an argument field. Such an idealization might clarify the public actor's argumentative stance because to define anything as a field, we must specify its subject matter, problem focus, methods, and relations with other fields. We must, in other words, find some epistemic sovereignty for an abused colony—sovereignty, one hopes, without rancor. The colonial powers—the disciplines—may own what Aristotle calls public knowledge (the facts of war, trade, etc.), but perhaps the public actor still possesses a unique argumentative stance. Defining this stance will be a long process. In this short essay I can only hope to precipitate debate on the matter by suggesting some points of departure.

First the subject matter: is there a public knowledge that transcends the expertise of particular disciplines? I suggest this: public knowledge—what decision-makers must know—is a package of discourse competencies that aim at the appraisal of expert discourse. By appraisal I do not mean deciding whether experts are right or wrong—that is what experts are for—but deciding how expert testimony shall be taken. Such appraisal implies that *public knowledge* includes, inter alia, knowledge about the sociological dynamics of expertise. How are experts designated and monitored by disciplines? How are intradisciplinary meanings, claims, and understandings translated into interdisciplinary or public claims? How do claims that are disputed within a field get translated into public claims (does their controversial status get concealed as they are transformed into public ideas)? Under what conditions do appearances of objectivity, or an expert's ways of insisting upon objectivity, get in the way of evaluating testimony? These questions, in turn, imply comparative questions, for each order of question can be translated into a concrete matter of how two competing disciplines clash (and measure up) in a particular dispute. The decision-maker is not claiming equal epistemic footing with experts but *different* footing. In influencing policy, the experts have to some extent left their expert grounds.

How do we know this is so? The proof brings us to a second point of departure: the principle of *epistemic jurisdiction.* This legal metaphor suggests that the breadth of issues is the basis for the public sphere's special claims. Breadth dilutes authority. The facts of nuclear safety belong to Nuclear Engineering, but nuclear safety is *also* a matter of political expedience, efficiency engineering, administration, and economics. This complex deprives Nuclear Engineering of epistemic hegemony. If the *creationism* v. *evolutionism* dispute carries political, legal, constitutional, pedagogical, and moral implications, then the advocates of either side possess no special claims on the deliberative processes the public sphere should employ in evaluating their dispute. This breadth is definitive of the issues we ordinarily associate with public policy. More often than not, we find decision-makers beset by the competing claims of several fields, the existence of this competition implying that none of the competitors can claim the right to adjudicate the dispute.

The jurisdictional principle dovetails with principles I have defended elsewhere (1987a, 1989b) as central to the public sphere. The *principle of attention* is a distinctively public stance toward the obligations of advocates. It enjoins us to listen to the fields for whom discourse is an open option and suggests that we are not obliged to attend to fields that succeed by virtue of "closure" (preempting outside critique, closing off lines of argument, stipulating ground rules that ensure favorable outcomes). The cost-benefit analyst "closes" by insisting that value judgments be refuted only by claims couched in the language of fiscal costs. Such closure leaves the public and the critic with nothing to say in the face of closed ranks. It allows no weighing of competing claims: decision-makers must opt for the most visible, orthodox, or safe authorities. Closure, in sum, allows experts to tell the public to take it or leave it.

Public decision-making may not have a distinctive methodology. Presumably the principles of sound discussion and debate are as applicable to senators as to academics. But it is worth considering whether public actors might benefit from certain attitudes toward discussion and debate. First, public actors should maximize their chances of capitalizing on the *opposition* among and within expert fields. This goal translates into a need to maximize, clarify, and sharpen opposition. I argue elsewhere (1987a) that the preference for consensus is an epistemic disease that weakens even the best judgmental and veridical methods. But this preference is a deeper pathology outside the disciplines (Willard and Hynes 1989). Expert testimony, for example, may mask the opposition among experts. But decision-makers need not acquiesce to the economies and slogans of popularizations. They can use a field's experts to cut through the facade of consensus in the field's popularizations. The *presumption* is that expert testimony is created by a translation of technical to quasi-technical discourse. Opposition between experts can test the fidelity of the translation.

The need to use opposition to test expert testimony suggests another sort of presumption—one *against* urgency. Cox (1981) defines the public sphere as a field of public policy-making in which issues arise in conditions that seem urgent. The press of events obscures (or seems to outweigh) the need to test claims. Urgency becomes an end in itself. A better view is that urgency is always a claim someone makes—a tactic—which is presumptively inferior to letting opposition flourish. Urgency is not always a shabby tactic for shielding flawed positions, but it always has a masking effect. As mendaciousness is not unfamiliar in public circles, the presumption favoring opposition over urgency seems prudent.

It seems plausible to think that these principles are as binding on the expert as on the decision-maker. Experts *are* public actors when they seek to affect public policies. The responsibilities of experts to the public are often overlooked, even though an expert's judgment may be the decision-maker's best point of leverage for assessing the state of consensus inside the expert's field. My reasoning goes like this: curatorship—one's stewardship of a body of knowledge—entails pedagogical responsibility: this result is because public money gives the expert the office and public trust gives the custodian the authority. These are not gifts but investments. Thus, the expert has teaching responsibilities even while seeking to affect public policies.

Summary

Diseases, Ludwick Fleck says, vary with the terms of diagnosis. So do remedies. The epistemological diagnosis deplores the lack of a commensurating discourse and seeks a remedy in a unifying discourse. The pedagogical diagnosis emphasizes mistakes in public life and seeks a remedy through argument techniques and skills. These two diagnoses, I have argued, are part of the problem. The problem of the public sphere is to some extent an iatrogenic disease. After all, our deliberations about the public sphere are a part of its reality. Defining the public sphere is both a theoretical problem and an ongoing feature of daily life (the jurisdictional principle, for example, implies that the resolution of interfield disputes requires constant adjustment of one's working sense of the public jurisdiction). A faith in commensuration makes for imperialistic deliberation, and a belief that disagreements stem from mistakes yields an inflated belief that one can transcend the diversities, which in fact divide people.

The epistemic diagnosis—though admittedly sketchy here—abandons the goal of commensuration and puts the pedagogical focus on mistakes and skills inside a bigger context. Two aspects (among many) of that larger context have been considered here: relativity as a fact of daily life and the dependence on authority as an unavoidable but problematic feature of ordinary decision-making. Epistemic studies, I should think, must focus on ways of managing these problems. Defining the public's epistemic interests may be a good starting point. It requires, I believe, seeing the public sphere as an argument field—one to be invented from scratch. The first step in building a field is to define its subject matter, methods, and relationships with other fields. I hope that the foregoing makes some headway toward achieving these aims.

If all a philosophy of the public sphere does is recognize the facts of relativity, it will underwrite the practices that deprive the public of power. The retreat to the field—which we have characterized as the proper behavior of actors defending true claims—is epistemologically but not epistemically correct. The retreat shuts off debate, or leaves it at a standstill, because it demands from the public a passive acquiesence to field authority. The philosophy of the public sphere needs substantive claims of its own to be weighed against the particular claims of interested parties. I have thus argued that the substantive knowledge relevant to the public agenda is a knowledge of the sociology of expertise. The guarantors of ordinary knowledge claims are explicit and implicit tapestries of power, politics, authority, prestige, and rationales.

I hope that it is clear that I am not reducing the problem of the public sphere to a need to keep the conversation going. Rorty (1979) by no means argues by slogan, but "keeping the conversation going" has become postmodernism's most waved banner. It is hard to object to this catchphrase, both because it conjures vaguely congenial academic values and because, like a Rorschach inkblot, it can be made to mean almost anything. But surely it matters how the conversation goes. Conversations dominated by authority will not get better by persisting. I have suggested, rather, a focus on the presumptions appropriate to public decision-making and the responsibilities these imply. I am afraid that I have touched only tangentially on what may be the most important of these responsibilities, namely, the expert's pedagogical obligations as a public actor. I believe, though I have not proved it here, that the problem of authority as it manifests itself in the public sphere is an effect of the centrality of authority in intellectual life in general. If so, the study of the dynamics of authority within expert domains may yield cautionary tales for the public decision-maker.

Notes

1. Another diagnosis, the *theological* view, often resembles the epistemological, but focuses, as Rousseau did, on the unifying effects of shared religious values. I discuss the theological diagnosis elsewhere (Willard 1989b) and so ignore it here.

2. Epistemology has admittedly broadened its scope. Some renegade epistemologists (for example, Fuller 1988) advocate a sociological path that would make epistemology resemble epistemics.

3. I owe this quip to William Connolly.

Part IV

The Turn to Critical Advocacy

10

Cultures of Discourse
Marxism and Rhetorical Theory

James Arnt Aune

On November 10, 1837, soon after becoming a student at the University of Berlin, Karl Marx wrote a letter to his father. The letter described the development of Marx's two great loves: for Hegel's philosophy and for his future wife, Jenny von Westphalen. There are at least two items of interest in the letter for the student of rhetoric. First, in the introduction Marx deprecated the love poems he recently sent to Jenny: "All the poems of the first three volumes I sent to Jenny are marked by attacks on our times, diffuse and inchoate expressions of feeling, nothing natural, everything built out of moonshine, complete opposition between what is and ought to be, rhetorical reflections instead of poetic thoughts." Second, he described the writing of a twenty-four-page dialogue, "Cleanthus, or the Starting Point and Necessary Continuation of Philosophy," where in attempting to unite art and science, he was led to the acceptance of the Hegelian system. His philosophical endeavors left him in an agitated state. He sought relief by joining his landlord on a hunting expedition and, on his return, by immersing himself in what he called "positive studies." These "positive studies" included the reading of works on the law of property, criminal law, canon law, and a work on the artistic instincts of animals. He then translated parts of Aristotle's *Rhetoric* (Marx and Engels 1975, 10–21).

It is unclear from the letter or from other writings of Marx what parts of the *Rhetoric* he translated or what effect they had on his work. Nonetheless, I choose this letter for an introduction to a discussion of Marxism and public argument because it serves as a kind of representative anecdote for the reception of rhetoric in the Marxist tradition: if mentioned at all, rhetoric is consigned to the margins of serious discourse, is rigidly separated from both art and philosophy, and is considered, at best, to be a branch of "positive studies." As Kenneth Burke writes, "the Marxist persuasion is usually advanced in the name of no-rhetoric" (Burke 1969, 102), a lesson which Burke no doubt first learned when his venture into Marxist rhetorical theory, "Revolutionary Symbolism in America," was roundly condemned at the Communist Writer's Congress in 1935 (Burke 1935).

The possibility that Marx knew something about the rhetorical tradition is at first sight an intriguing one, but the inevitable conclusion to be drawn from his writings is that the tradition had a negligible influence. To be sure, the historical writings, especially *The Eighteenth Brumaire of Louis Bonaparte* (Marx 1963), display a nearly Ciceronian style, full of antitheses and copia, but the absence of classical notions of invention or audience is rather obvious. In contrast, we know that the father of capitalist political economy, Adam Smith, wrote a series of lectures on rhetoric and that two of the most important nineteenth-century rhetorical theorists, Thomas De Quincey and Richard Whately, wrote books defending free trade.[1] One wonders what a Marxist rhetoric would look like, then and now.[2]

On the other hand, if Marxism has been silent about the rhetorical tradition, the rhetorical tradition has been almost equally silent about Marxism, both as a historical phenomenon and as a theoretical perspective on discourse. Despite Philip Wander's (1983) immensely important work on ideological criticism and Michael Calvin McGee's (1982) ongoing project for a materialist rhetoric, serious discussion of Marxism (as opposed to a sort of eclectic American radicalism) remains limited to a few partisans of political economy or cultural studies, two research traditions notable for their inattention to rhetoric. The term "ideology" has attained quasi-canonical status in rhetorical criticism, but Marx's central focus on class struggle has been thoroughly ignored by rhetorical scholars. Students of social movements in our field virtually have ignored labor, perhaps because many of them came to political consciousness at a time when the working class was no longer in fashion among liberal academics. Perhaps the most impressive work of Marxist rhetorical theory yet produced, Lawrence Grossberg's (1979) "Marxist Dialectics and Rhetorical Criticism," uses the concept of "class" only once, and there it is in the context of a discussion of Stalinism.

At first sight, the substitution of "ideology" for "class" in left academic discourse seems to solve some problems. It eliminates the putative economic determinism of classical Marxism and opens up the possibility of explaining larger patterns of argument in a culture instead of just focusing on a single speech and its effects. The work of Celeste Condit is perhaps the best example of a productive use of the concept of ideology in the study of public argument. One could also point out that substituting "ideology" for "class" also opens up left academic discourse for the analysis of oppression based on race and gender divisions (Condit 1987). It seems curious, however, to claim that an analysis of public discourse based on certain observations about the capitalist mode of production is incomplete or maybe even "patriarchal," when no one has examined seriously how capitalism has affected the theory and practice of rhetoric. Further, substituting "ideology" for "class struggle" as a key term runs the risk of making oppression largely a linguistic or cultural matter. The ambiguous position of academics within the class structure of advanced capitalism makes ideological criticism appealing but scarcely more useful politically than when the Frankfurt School invented it in the 1930s.

The focus of this essay, then, is on the repression of rhetoric in Marxist theory and on the reading of the history of theories of public argument in Marxist terms. A critical "articulation" of Marxism and the rhetorical tradition is perhaps premature.[3] It may well be the case that a commitment to Marxist categories by its nature eliminates a rhetorical understanding of public argument. It may also be the case that a commitment to the rhetorical tradition necessitates that one be either a reformist or a conservative. This essay is intended to be an invitation to dialogue, not the raising of a dogmatic flag. I will proceed by: (1) outlining the communicative dilemma created by certain key silences in the classical texts of Marx and Engels, (2) creating a typology of later Marxist responses to this communicative dilemma, and (3) proposing a rereading of the history of rhetorical theory in Marxist terms.

The Two Marxisms and Marx's Rhetorical Problem

Sometimes it appears that the term "Marxist" is so ambiguous as to be useless, unless one is using it solely for propaganda purposes, as in "The Marxist regime in Nicaragua. . . ." Inasmuch as mainstream historians and social scientists accept many of Marx's once controversial doctrines, why keep using the term? Or, given the tremendous political (and moral) distance between, say, Antonio Gramsci and Joseph Stalin, is it reasonable to argue that both were "Marxists"? These objections aside, I do believe that it is possible to describe the outlines of a Marxist "paradigm," at least as an analytic method. It seems less possible to argue that there exists a specific Marxist *politics*, mainly because Marxism after Marx has realized that Marx lacked a politics (among other things). On the other hand, to suggest that Marxism is simply a method, deserving of a sort of affirmative action treatment in the contemporary university, ignores Marx's own intention, which was, quite simply, "to change the world" (Marx 1972, 145).

At a rather high level of abstraction, the following assumptions are common to the many "Marxisms" (see Heilbroner 1985): (1) "Labor" is a central, if not the central, characteristic of human beings. (2) The mode of production in a given social totality—the level of development of productive forces in addition to the type of work relations that accompany those forces—is a determining factor in establishing that totality's social "being." (3) All hitherto existing societies have been characterized by a class struggle over the control or allocation of the surplus from production. (4) The level of development of the productive forces determines, in the sense of setting boundary conditions for, the sort of class structure and class struggle in a given social system. (5) Because the productive forces tend to develop over time, "history" is generally predictable in terms of the succession of modes of production. (6) That class which controls the mode of production in a given society tends to repress, either through the threat of violence or through promoting a particular set of beliefs in the legitimacy of the existing order, radical alterations in control of the productive forces. (7) Capitalism has outlived its usefulness as a mode of production; that is, it helped develop the productive forces to their currently high level, but its chronic crises, and its wastefulness of natural resources and human talent, mean that it will pass away eventually. (8) The precise mode of capitalism's passing away will vary, depending on the political assumptions of the various schools of Marxism.

Despite the great number of Marxisms, Alvin Gouldner's (1980) division of all hitherto existing Marxisms into "Two Marxisms" is a useful category system. The first is scientific Marxism, and the second is critical Marxism. Followers of the first school would include Lenin, Althusser, and "evolutionary" social democrats such as Eduard Bernstein. These writers view Marxism as science, not critique, and their "canon within the canon" of Marx's writings is the "mature" political economy of *Capital* and not the "ideologized" anthropology of the *1844 Manuscripts*. They stress a deterministic view of ideology, devalue individual experience and action, and emphasize the law-like character of historical change. In contrast, critical Marxists "conceive of Marxism as critique rather than science; they stress the continuity of Marx with Hegel, the importance of the young Marx, the ongoing significance of the young Marx's emphasis on 'alienation,' and are more historicist" (Gouldner 1980, 39). Representative critical Marxists are Gramsci, Sartre, and the Frankfurt School.

Critical Marxism sought to respond to an apparent contradiction in Marx's texts. Gouldner (1980) writes, "The problem is that if capitalism is indeed governed by lawful regularities that doom it to be supplanted by a new socialist society (when the requisite infrastructures have matured), why then stress that 'the point is to change it'? Why go to great pains to arrange capitalism's funeral if its demise is guaranteed by science? Why must persons be mobilized and exhorted to discipline themselves to behave in conformity with necessary laws by which, it would seem, they would in any event be bound?" (32). In other words, Marxism has a rhetorical problem: either the classless society is inevitable and scientifically grounded with individual choice being irrelevant, *or* the classless society comes about through the persuasion of individuals and thus ceases to be grounded in scientific laws of history—laws that, as Kenneth Burke ([1950] 1969b) has pointed out, are a major source of Marxism's rhetorical power in the first place (101). The source of the dilemma is Marx's own failure to create a political theory that would explain how the working class struggles and gains power in or over the state. More precisely, Marx did not explain the psychological and rhetorical prerequisites for revolution.

The Marxist tradition has tended to fill in the gap between what we might call *structure* and *struggle* in roughly four ways:

1. The first is *Leninism*, which is given its quintessential philosophical expression in the work of Lukacs. As Lenin (1961) writes in *What Is to Be Done?*, the working class, left to its own devices, will develop at best trade union consciousness, but never revolutionary consciousness (31–32). Hence the need for a revolutionary vanguard party that anticipates a fully realized class consciousness (Lukacs 1971, 41–42, 51). This party can prepare for revolution and guide the masses at the time of collapse of the capitalist system. In order for the party to be ready for revolution, it must be tightly disciplined, periodically purge itself, and possess a rigidly correct theory of Marxism—concepts that can be summarized by Lenin's wonderfully Orwellian phrase, "democratic centralism." A Leninist party, of course, runs the risk of losing touch with the workers, privileging the role of intellectuals, and eventually becoming totalitarian. The Leninist model of organization also has been notably unsuccessful in advanced industrial societies.

2. A second alternative, which can be traced back to Rosa Luxemburg, and perhaps even further back to Bakunin, does not privilege

the role of the party in fomenting revolution, but rather depends on the spontaneous revolution in the masses themselves, who at the time of capitalist crisis will form naturally the councils to deal with political and economic issues (see Albert and Hahnel 1978). This view is represented also by the early new left, which called for participatory democracy. It also has been influential in the abandonment of what C. Wright Mills (1969) called Marxism's "labor metaphysic" (28). In Herbert Marcuse's (1964) view, for example, the agent of revolution will not necessarily be the industrial working class, but those people marginalized by the status quo—blacks, students, women, homosexuals, for example (256–57). The danger in this version of Marxism is its tendency toward leftist adventurism or toward what Lukacs, in a moment of self-criticism, called "revolutionary messianism." Perhaps a more important limitation is that "new class" theorists from Marcuse to Gouldner were unable to predict the reversion of capitalism to more brutal ideological forms (Reaganism, Thatcherism) after the economic crisis of the 1970s (see Gouldner 1979, 92).

Two other variants of Marxism specifically address problems of communication. The first, the Frankfurt School, views all mass communication in advanced industrial society as inherently manipulative. Perhaps the most popular expression of this view is Christopher Lasch's (1977) *The Culture of Narcissism*, although Horkheimer and Adorno's (1972) *Dialectic of Enlightenment* and Marcuse's (1964) pre–New Left *One-Dimensional Man* remain the most important. The Frankfurt School's position can be distilled into three main propositions: (1) The working class has been bought off by the "safety net" introduced by Keynesian welfare capitalism. (2) The media (or "consciousness industry") have replaced the family as the main agent of socialization, leading to a repressive desublimation of aggressive and erotic instincts. (3) The only legitimate forms of communication are philosophy and high art. Philosophic discourse is critique, "negative thinking," which must be obscure in order to avoid capitulating to the established universe of discourse. High art preserves memories of freedom and happiness or else explicitly condemns the existing world. For Marcuse (1978), Samuel Beckett emerges as the greatest artist of the contemporary period, for he brings a clear message to his audience: put an end to things as they are.

Although Frankfurt Marxism remains the most coherent and intellectually satisfying of all varieties of critical Marxism to date, it too easily lapses into political quietism and elitist rejection of all forms of popular culture. Even Jurgen Habermas, of the Frankfurt School's second generation, shares with Adorno, Horkheimer, and

Marcuse a tendency to reject strategic discourse (what we would call "rhetoric") as inherently manipulative (Habermas 1979, 41).

A fourth and final variant of Marxism has not been articulated fully, as yet, but derives from Antonio Gramsci's (1971) *Prison Notebooks*. Gramsci has had tremendous influence on British cultural studies and on American media critics such as Todd Gitlin (1982) and Douglas Kellner (1982). The first steps toward the appropriation of Gramsci for rhetorical theory have been made by Michael McGee and Martha Martin (1983), and by Frank Lentricchia (1983) in his book on Kenneth Burke. In contrast to Marx, Gramsci believed that capitalism obtained consent (at least in Western societies) through persuasion, its ability to make the status quo seem reasonable and necessary. Lentricchia points out the similarity between Gramsci's idea of "hegemony" (the persuasive domination of the masses by the ruling class) and Kenneth Burke's analysis in *Attitudes Toward History:*

[T]he various "priests" of the pulpit, schools, press, radio, and popular arts, (and we add television), educate the socially dispossessed person to feel "that he 'has a stake in' the authoritative structure that dispossesses him; for the influence exerted upon the policies of education by the authoritative structure encourages the dispossessed to feel that his only hope of repossession lies in his allegiance to the structure that dispossessed him." (Lentricchia 1983, 76–77)

Gramsci's idea of hegemony, especially as interpreted by Gitlin and Kellner, leads to a more optimistic view of mass communication. The task of the intellectual class at the present time is to help construct a counter-hegemony. A counter-hegemony would be based on the following assumptions: (1) Mass communication addresses real human needs for happiness, diversion, and self-assertion but is flawed because those needs are shown to be met only through the purchase of commodities (Gitlin 1982, 452; Kellner 1982, 403). (2) Hegemony is "leaky" in contemporary mass communication because of the contradictory character of liberal capitalism itself (Kellner 1982, 386–87). One could interpret the television series *M*A*S*H*, for example, as reinforcing traditional American values on one hand, while de-legitimating war on the other. (3) The Left should learn how to use mass communication more effectively. As Douglas Kellner (1982) writes, "The left should learn how to produce, or how to participate in, the production of popular television, as well as documentaries, news commentaries, and programs, and political discussion suitable for broadcast media. . . . There must be a cultural/media politics to ensure public access and open new channels of communication" (421).

The neo-Gramscians clearly possess an attitude toward communication that is more congenial to the traditional concerns of rhetorical studies. Most, however, have not addressed the problem of rhetoric and rational argument. They lack a theory of the production of discourse and of audience effects. They also lack a response to the charge of more traditional critics such as Wayne Booth (1974) that concepts such as "ideology" and "hegemony" undercut the possibility of rational argument because of their "motivism" (2–40). A similar charge is made by the Norwegian philosopher Jon Elster (1979), when he attacks the "functionalism" of the Marxist view of ideology in *Ulysses and the Sirens* (28–35).[4]

Terry Eagleton has begun a project for the reconstruction of traditional rhetorical theory along Marxist lines, although it largely is formulated as a critique of the field of English literature. In Eagleton's (1983) *Literary Theory: An Introduction* he argues that "literature" as a privileged concept in the academy is of recent invention. In his view, the rise of departments of English in the nineteenth century was tied to an ideological quest to legitimate the existing class society. The study of literature was seen as a "humanizing" force, one that could replace religion as a prop for the existing order (17–53). In contrast, he says that the earlier study of rhetoric in British and American universities made clear the political thrust of humanistic knowledge. In what is perhaps the most useful definition of rhetoric I have read, Eagleton (1981) writes that rhetoric "is the process of analyzing the material effects of particular uses of language in particular social conjunctures" and that traditional rhetoric was "the textual training of the ruling class in the techniques of political hegemony" (101). He goes on to describe a brief program for the development of a Marxist rhetoric:

As far as rhetoric is concerned, then, a Marxist must be in a certain sense a Platonist. Rhetorical effects are calculated in the light of a theory of the polis as a whole. . . . Since all art is rhetorical, the tasks of the revolutionary cultural worker are essentially threefold: First, to participate in the production of works and events which, within transformed "cultural" media, so fictionalize the "real" as to intend those effects conducive to the victory of socialism. Second, as "critic" to expose the rhetorical structures by which non-socialist works produce political undesirable effects, as a way of combatting what is now unfashionable to call false consciousness. Third, to interpret such works where possible against the grain, so as to appropriate whatever is valuable for socialism. (Eagleton 1981, 113)

It should be clear that I am in basic sympathy with Eagleton's ideas, although they need to be extended and made more relevant to the American experience. One major problem with Eagleton's formulation is that, like most leftist intellectuals, he privileges critique over the teaching of advocacy skills. He also still privileges art and literature over the more humble modes of communication such as public speaking and debate. It is not enough to do Marxist analyses of Richardson and Emily Brontë. Nor is it enough to say, for instance, that Ronald Reagan abuses the ideograph of "family" in order to reinforce existing patterns of economic and sexual oppression. One would need to go on to understand the lived experience of American audiences that predisposes them, often in ways that have nothing at all to do with "false consciousness," to accept family-based arguments. One would also need to show students and politicians how to "steal the symbol" of the family and use it for liberatory purposes (Burke 1984, 328).

If it is the case that Marxism has effaced the role of communication in mediating between social structure and human action and that students of communication have ignored capitalism as a determining force in society, how might we combine both fields' virtues while eliminating some of their vices? It may be that the aporia which Gouldner and others find in classical Marxism may be the result more of confusion over levels of abstraction in social analysis than a failure of Marxism itself. Erik Olin Wright (1985) suggests, in his recent book *Classes,* that Marxist social analysis operates at three levels of abstraction: mode of production, social formation, and conjuncture (9). Further, within each of these three levels, Marx himself moved back and forth between describing an abstract structural map of class relations (as in the first part of *Capital* where he develops a "pure" model of capitalism) and describing concrete conjunctural maps of classes-as-actors (as in the chapter of *Capital* where he describes the battles over the length of the working day or as in the historical writings such as the *Eighteenth Brumaire*). Marx's conjunctural maps are much less "reductive" than his other writings, and it is important to note that neither the critical nor scientific Marxists have given as much weight to them as to the *1844 Manuscripts* or to the first part of *Capital.*

In fitting together Marxism and argumentation, it is necessary to clarify the levels of abstraction at which one is working. In focusing on the mode of production, one wants to isolate the way in which dominant forms of argument relate to forces and relations of production *in the most abstract way.* One can avoid both Booth's critique of Marxian motivism and Elster's refutation of Marxian functionalism if the focus is on argumentative forms. This sort of periodization is no different from that which intellectual historians of rhetoric have already done, except that it provides for greater parsimony of explanation. In focusing on social formation, one traces patterns of argument as they relate to a specific nation or region (as revealed, for instance, in Eugene Debs's appropriation of the images of the American Revolution in his arguments for socialism). In focusing on conjuncture, one evaluates the relationship between text and audience in a concrete rhetorical situation, much as traditional neo-Aristotelian criticism did.

Capitalism, in my view, is ultimately determining only in the sense of establishing general patterns and rules for argument. Not all discourse in a given social formation is conducted in class terms, although it certainly is important to study the ways in which public languages of class are created or inhibited. The rhetorical construction and/or repression of class consciousness in American culture, the rhetorical representation of work relations in the mass media, not to mention the very real needs of American workers to develop rhetorical means to combat the deindustrialization of America and the deskilling of work—all these are potentially rich topics for the critic of American public argument to pursue.

To recast Marxist communication studies in terms of the study of labor and of the often heroic resistance of American workers against capitalist domination seems to me much more productive than the narrow focus on the prison-house of ideology, which many of us inherited from the Frankfurt School. To proclaim as Marcuse did or as more recent poststructuralist Marxists do that we are all imprisoned in a one-dimensional society of spectacle ignores the reality of resistance to capitalism that we have seen in the British miners, American farmers, and Local P-9 in Austin, Minnesota. By maintaining Marx's original dialectical tension between structure and struggle we may be able to avoid the passivity that both scientific Marxism and critical Marxism seem to encourage at their worst moments.

Cultures of Discourse: Rhetoric, Criticism, and Poststructuralism

If the map of the research program implied by classical Marxism makes sense, how can we use it to direct research in the study of communication? The rest of this essay attempts to describe what an analysis of the history of rhetorical theory would look like in mode-of-production terms.

The recent resurgence of rhetorical studies, inside and outside of departments of communication, is simultaneously encouraging and depressing. Arguably, rhetoric shares with Marxism the distinction of being the only research tradition capable of uniting the various disciplines in the university and of combatting the specialization that prevents academic discourse from affecting the public world. (Positivism once served such a function, but at last count even social scientists were hastening to arrange its funeral rites.) Rhetoric, however, in its privileging of symbol-use over labor as the constitutive activity of human beings, risks being coopted by larger forces of domination in our culture. Please note that I am neither impugning the motives of many contemporary rhetoricians (as if they were all covertly in the employ of the National Association of Manufacturers) nor am I arguing that the revival of rhetoric is somehow *functional* in the reproduction of late capitalist economic relations. I am suggesting, rather, that particular stages in the development of a mode of production—in this case capitalism—will create certain social dislocations or class tensions with which given discourses will attempt to cope.

The resurgence of rhetorical studies, whether in its wholesome American form or in its rather sleazy French version, is tied to a common conviction among intellectual elites that the transcendental signifiers of God, Truth, and the Classless Society have failed us. What remains is rhetoric itself, the freeplay of signifiers, which the belatedly canonized Kenneth Burke (1965) tells us to contemplate with dismay and delight as we "huddle, nervously loquacious, at the edge of the abyss" (272). The heroic impulse at the heart of rhetorical studies, however, is too easily subverted into the glorification of power. If, following Gramsci, we can conclude that capitalist hegemony is a persuasive process, it may be possible to read dominant theories of rhetoric as attempts to describe, explain, and occasionally criticize hegemonic techniques. Even when not explicitly or self-consciously "rhetorical," intellectuals and other wielders of power in society always develop cultures of discourse or argumentative grammars. These cultures of discourse exist in an occasionally uneven relationship with economic forces and relations of production, but reciprocally influence and are influenced by them. Cultures of discourse, then, are conventions for the production of discourse and are as historically material as a factory or a Hitler speech.

I will argue that three cultures of discourse are currently competing for the allegiance of rhetorical scholars. The first, which can simply be called "rhetoric," is largely dead in its classical and humanistic forms, especially as it existed in American colleges prior to 1850. The second, the culture of critical discourse (Alvin Gouldner's CCD), has been dominant for many years but is now collapsing under the weight of its own internal contradictions. The third, which lacks an appropriate name, although "the new rhetoric" or even "poststructuralism" may do, while it lacks the political and social influence of the other two cultures of discourse, reflects a society of "spectacle," in which nothing is experienced directly except as a sign.

Traditional rhetoricians can be characterized above all by their nostalgia. S. M. Halloran's important article, "Rhetoric in the American College Curriculum," draws an inspiring picture of American education before the decline of rhetoric. He concludes his essay by contrasting the miserable character of the public debate over AWACS with the intense involvement of the American public in Webster's debates with Hayne and Calhoun (Halloran 1982, 244–62). Halloran is right, of course, that the decline of rhetoric in American universities did parallel the decline of public involvement in politics (although the 1930s certainly come to mind as a counterexample). Nonetheless, he obscures the class character of the decline of traditional rhetoric. Rhetoric declined because it ceased to be an efficient means of education, once the university shifted to a larger, more egalitarian constituency. Rhetoric was a useful tool for a propertied elite, but seemingly less necessary when public discourse became controlled by technical experts.

The culture of discourse or argumentative grammar associated with traditional rhetoric seems to have been based on the following communicative rules. (I rewrite here Gadamer's great synthesis of the rhetorical tradition in the first part of *Truth and Method*, 1975, 10–39.) First, speak in such a way that one embodies the values of one's culture in one's own character. Second, always adapt one's discourse to the common sense of one's listeners. Third, study past rhetorical situations in order to develop a sense of judgment, the virtue of prudence that will generalize to future rhetorical situations. Finally, study great speeches and history and literature in order to develop a sense of timing and taste.

This culture of discourse at its best sacrificed individual ambition to the needs of the community and at its worst, as Eagleton says, was simply a form of training the ruling class in the techniques of textual domination. And yet, rhetoric in its traditional form had to die. It had to be replaced by a new standard of discourse, one more tied to print and to the initially egalitarian drive of capitalism to find new markets. The culture of critical discourse arose to meet technological and economic needs—and it also served as a site of class struggle, since Marxism itself arose within the culture of critical discourse.

Gouldner (1979), in his account of the culture of critical discourse, ties it to the potential rise to power of the new class of humanistic intellectuals and technical intelligentsia (28). I believe that his prediction that this new class will come to power eventually in both the East and the West is invalidated largely by the return of capitalism to earlier and more primitive forms of domination because of the world recession. I also believe that the culture of critical discourse is more a set of formal assumptions about the conduct of public communication than a set of propositions about the public world (despite the notorious difficulties, familiar to every rhetorician, of separating form and content). My point here, however, is less to criticize Gouldner's theory than to use it to characterize the type of speech about speech that replaced rhetoric in intellectual circles.

The rules of the culture of critical discourse as an argumentative grammar can be summarized as follows: (1) Make one's own speech problematic and try to account for its origins. Be reflexive and self-monitoring. (2) Justify claims without reference to the speaker's societal position or authority; in other words, eliminate the classical function of *ethos*. (3) Stand apart from the common sense of the culture in which the speech is occurring, since the common sense of a culture is ultimately a rationalization for that culture's power relations. (4) Thus, privilege theoretical discourse, speech that is relatively context-free (Gouldner 1979, 29). This culture of discourse, which perhaps has its finest expression in Habermas's notion of the ideal speech situation, has been dominant in universities for a long time. The culture of critical discourse is inherently hostile to traditional rhetoric (as the tortured career of rhetorical studies in America's elite universities in the last fifty years or so indicates), even though the culture of critical discourse has become the main standard of speech among theorists of argumentation. The culture of critical discourse helped break down traditional class and race prejudices, the patriarchal family, and religion, but rather than being tied to the needs of Gouldner's new class, it was simply the rhetorical justification for that process which Marx and Engels (1972) so cogently described in *The Communist Manifesto:*

Constant revolutionizing of production, uninterrupted disturbance of all social conditions, everlasting uncertainty and agitation distinguish the bourgeois epoch from all earlier ones. All fixed, fast-frozen relations, with their train of ancient and venerable prejudices and opinions are swept away, all new-formed ones become antiquated before they can ossify. All that is solid melts into air, all that is holy is profaned, and man is at last compelled to face with sober senses, his real conditions of life, and his relations with his kind. (338)

The culture of critical discourse was and is the argumentative grammar that justifies technological revolution, the expansion of markets by giving workers a larger share of profits, and also managerial control over the workplace and over society in general—but not, I must add, at the level of propositional argument, but at the level of form. By translating questions of political practice and class struggle into questions of technical expertise, the culture of critical discourse consolidated the transition of capitalism from anarchic competition to corporate liberalism.

The culture of critical discourse, however, and corporate liberalism itself cannot survive the worldwide crisis of capitalism. It has been replaced in the political realm by the politics of pure image as represented by Ronald Reagan. It has been replaced—or is being slowly replaced—by a new ideology of communication that denies the existence of objective reality, proclaims that everything is constructed rhetorically, and that there is nothing outside the text. Ironically enough, it is the lapsed Marxist Kenneth Burke and the avowed Marxist Jacques Derrida who seem to provide the best ideological justification for the new rhetorical world of late capitalism.

A grossly enlarged conception of rhetoric plays directly into the hands of corporate capitalism, which would just as soon have us believe that mass persuasion is the solution to our collective problems. To assume that all social problems are problems of communication glosses over the presence of real problems that might, at some point, require direct action, even violence. When our most radical rhetoric-as-epistemicists (what we might call left-Burkeians) tell us that even trees are created rhetorically we are offered what Fredric Jameson (1972) described in another context as "the spectacle of a world from which nature as such has been eliminated, a world saturated with messages and information, whose intricate commodity network may be seen as the very prototype of a system of signs" (viii–ix). The new orthodoxy that there is nothing outside the text, nothing outside of rhetoric itself, is the perfect ideological representation of life under late capitalism, in which nothing, it seems, is experienced outside of its media images.

It seems silly, however, to claim that poststructuralism is somehow "functional" in preserving capitalist domination. It makes more sense to indict poststructuralism's current influence in the academy as a distraction from more productive uses of rhetorical theory. It is silly, too, to claim that late capitalism has created a seamless web of ideological images—Marx himself wrote books and participated in the labor movement in order to dispel the myth that capitalism is an eternal and natural type of social order. My contention in this essay has been that a revitalized conception of traditional rhetoric, one informed by Marxist theory and practice, may be of some use in advancing, if not the Revolution, at least a more humane practice of public argument. I want to conclude by summarizing the main themes of my overall argument in the context of some theses toward a Marxist rhetorical theory.

1. The Marxist representative anecdote of human beings as producers rather than simply as symbol-users may help correct the "trained incapacity" or "occupational psychosis" of rhetorical theory. By foregrounding the role of labor in constructing our human world, a Marxist approach to communication may help revitalize the criticism of public discourse.

2. By foregrounding class struggle rather than public consensus, a Marxist rhetorical theory may be better able to explain broad historical shifts in rhetorical practice and pedagogy than do existing theoretical alternatives.

3. Traditional rhetoric, in privileging of common sense as a starting point for the construction of enthymemes, may provide a needed corrective to Marxism's tendency to view the common sense of a culture merely as a rationalization of that culture's relations of domination.

4. Uniting Marxism's traditional concern for economic democracy with rhetoric's traditional (if at times ambiguous) concern for political democracy may provide a narrative structure for a new politics, one that views revolution as a struggle against racial, sexual, and economic oppression and against the specialized languages of expertise, which have characterized "liberal" reform in this century. Marxism needs to correct rhetoric's avoidance of the category of labor in the construction of the social world, while rhetoric needs to correct Marxism's one-sided focus on labor at the expense of other forms of domination.

The preceding four points are perhaps too facile a sketch of a theory that needs further justification, revision, and empirical validation. I have tried to make a case, at a rather high level of abstraction, for the connection of developments in rhetorical theory with developments in modes of production. The next step is to develop longitudinal analyses of public discourse within a given social formation, using Marxist categories. As I suggested earlier, even traditional public address study has largely ignored the rhetoric of the American labor movement. Given what might be called "American exceptionalism," it still remains to be proved empirically that Marxist categories can illuminate the development of languages of labor and class in the United States. But the attempt must be made.

What Marxism has taught us, in admittedly flawed ways, is that human beings have the potential to build a heroic society. What students of rhetoric and communication can give Marxism is a more humane way of bridging the critique of ideology with political action. The ultimate point is that audiences, when presented with the contradictions inherent in their social systems, have a choice about the ideological narratives to which they will subscribe or which they will create. That these narratives may not be limited to the banal yet frightening ones of the White House or the Kremlin depends on our ability to extend our imaginative range. As Marx (1975) himself wrote, "Every emancipation is a restoration of the human world and of human relationships to man himself" (240).

Notes

I am grateful to Joli Jensen, John Rodden, M. S. Piccirillo, and the members of my seminar on Marxism and Communication Studies at the University of Virginia (Spring 1986) and the University of Iowa (Summer 1986) for conversations that helped me clarify the ideas presented in this chapter.

1. Marx, of course, cites Smith's economic and ethical writings in *Kapital*; he also cites De Quincey's *The Logic of Political Economy*; Whately was professor of political economy at Oxford from 1829 to 1831. One sign of the remarkably insular character of much scholarship in the history of rhetorical theory is that rhetoricians write about Smith, De Quincey, and Whately as if rhetoric were the only interest of these theorists.

2. By "rhetoric" here I mean a comprehensive rhetorical theory; for a more limited, practical rhetoric, see the work of Angelica Balabanoff and Willkie (1974).

3. See Ryan 1982 for a useful explication of the metaphor of "articulation," a term from metallurgy referring to the joining of two distinct metals. The nightmare side of my current project is that rhetoric and Marxism may be related more like two magnets opposing one another.

4. I first started reading Elster at the beginning of the final revision of this essay; were I to redraft the project from the bottom up I would make Elster's work central, including also his *Making Sense of Marx* (1985). Elster opens up the prospect of a Marxism without functionalist explanation, a prospect, alas, that most Marxist students of communication, whether in political economy or cultural studies, have yet to consider.

11

The Rhetorical Tradition, Modern Communication, and the Grounds of Justified Assent

G. Thomas Goodnight

A journey to the South always prompts me to reflect on the contrast between patterns of life rooted in different places. My present residence is Chicago, a city perched on the edge of an endless prairie. So different is North Carolina from this vast metropolis that the beautiful forests and towns seem part of another land, suggesting that life here somehow is comported differently. I do not mean to say that my impressions derive from the usual contrast between the South as a place of tradition and the North of change; even though my university, Northwestern, with its starkly modern buildings thrown up against Lake Michigan, demands a tempo of life much different from that invited by the harmonious Georgian architecture and stately grounds of Wake Forest. There is much in the South that is changing, even to embrace the national capital, the very hub of contemporary power. Moreover, it is becoming evident that the builders of our great northern cities had in mind the perpetuation of a tradition of sorts in synchronizing factories, transportation, and living quarters on a massive scale. My feelings of distance and familiarity arise from much simpler observations of people and place and climate. It is as if no way has yet been found in the South to convert the land into mere lots, and time has not been fully materialized into schedules. In the slow, unhasty rhythms of mannered speech, silence itself seems to be comported differently, allowing ample space for conversation and thought. My memories of the South are infused with this sense of spaciousness. There seems to be room enough for work and leisure, technology and mystery, modernity and tradition. It is with these sentiments in mind that I turn to a discussion of the rhetorical tradition and modern communication in the United States.[1]

The specific question that brings us together is as simply constructed as it is difficult to answer: "When, if ever, is assent justified?" My own credentials for essaying an answer are modest indeed, especially when compared to those whose social function it is to advise routinely on when it is appropriate to say "yes" or "no." A preacher admonishes our behavior by appealing to the certainties announced in spiritual doctrine. A politician impresses us with the urgency and responsibility of choice by rendering apparent the exigencies of the times. A scientist uses measurement to quantify the factual composition of substances and requests provisional belief on the grounds of impartiality and methodical care. A philosopher asks assent to a program of perpetual questioning in the pursuit of knowledge. Lacking the faith of a parson, the ardor of a politician, the accouterment of a scientist, and the patience of a philosopher, I have but the avocation of a rhetorician to fashion an answer. And rhetoric is a most untrustworthy art. In fact, Ambrose Bierce (1911) once described oratory—one of the few recognized offsprings of rhetoric—at its best as "A tyranny tempered by stenography" and its worst as "A conspiracy between speech and action to cheat the understanding" (93). Bierce was writing at the close of the nineteenth century, a time when citizens only had to contend with traditional persuasion from the lyceum, pulpit, bar, and stump. The massing of technology and the struggles among competing ideologies in the twentieth century have made the problem of creating a shared community of discourse much more difficult.

The purpose of this discussion is to uncover some of the complexities faced when trying to construct grounds upon which valid and knowledgeable assent can be articulated. Statements inviting affirmation always raise questions of individual choice and collective preference, testing how the grounds for valid, legitimate, truthful, and moral communication can be constructed. The study will bring into focus contrasting assumptions about building such grounds by reflecting on the differences between an older rhetoric, a tradition of public discourse transposed onto the democratic soils of a new world (Bitzer 1978, 1980, 1981), and a modern communications industry that utilizes, even while it supplants and erodes, limited rhetorical practices and articulate publics. It will be argued that assent can find appropriate grounds within a public sphere where a widening tradition of free speech renders interests articulate, prioritizes actions, and engages active audiences. By contrast, industrially produced modern communication severely limits grounds for justified assent by circumscribing communication practices. The essay will attempt to explain how problems within the traditional understanding of the public imparted impetus to its own erosion, and to suggest ways to reopen the public sphere to more vital and humane communication practices in the contemporary world.

The Rhetorical Tradition and the Public Sphere

To understand the problems of justified assent within the purview of American culture, it is necessary to take up the question of the rhetorical tradition. Even in early America, where individualism was celebrated as a creed and personal achievement a duty, some common domain was necessary to discuss the things that could be done only if they were done together. Essential to the democratic tradition were the rights of free speech and assembly creating the common space necessary for people to get together and to decide upon the instruments of self-governance and actions appropriate to the common good. The public assembly became a place for speaking on matters where authorities conflicted, jurisdictions needed clarification, and common interests were unclear. Its discourse was the art of rhetoric practiced by all who were permitted to communicate an opinion on matters of community concern, including most significantly opinions about the nature of appropriate influence itself. Precisely because the question of how best to influence opinion and fashion assent was important to the commonweal, there has never existed an agreed-upon, hegemonic philosophy of public discourse (Sullivan 1982, 9); rather, each new generation of American "gamblers" and "opportunists" have had to work out successive solutions to the problem of justified choice and action (Commanger 1950, 12).

The antecedents of this conflicted tradition are rooted in classical Greece, where in a great dispute over the nature of education and politics, ethics and self-interest, rhetoric and philosophy there was created a body of arguments that has influenced the development of Western culture for two millennia (Jaeger 1939). Recall that it was the Sophists who defined man to be the measure of all things, finding justified assent in the arguments of the marketplace rather than in the entrails of signs sent from the gods (J. Poulakos 1987, 97–102). Plato's observation of the life of Socrates revealed another path. On it, justified assent was only possible by turning attention away from the chatter of the crowd and toward the truth (Black 1958, 361–74). Such a turn could not be accomplished by going to the multitudes and twisting words to fit popular standards, perceptions, and concerns. True belief could be tested only by those capable of refined thought in the privacy and freedom of personal discussion. Isocrates offered yet a third position, finding the wellspring of rhetoric neither in public pleading nor in privatized truth (T. Poulakos 1987, 39–44). Emphasizing the necessity of education and the benefits of cultural enlightenment, Isocrates found in persuasion the materials necessary to create and preserve a culture capable of providing grounds for its own coherent action. Aristotle's work seems to go even further. Rhetoric as a process gives effective voice to the truth as it joins theoretical knowledge with the practical arts in deliberative action (Hunt 1965, 144–59). Speech could be secured in a standard of ethical, truthful decisions because the orator must engage and confront the critical reasoning powers of audiences.

Each position in the debate, of course, was extended to arguments about public life, each vying for ascendancy. That the heritage of classical Greece comprises a constellation of unresolved discursive problems bearing upon ethics and politics rather than a unified body of cultural truths to be appropriated by philosophical inquiry is a fact that has been recognized insufficiently. As the cultural institutions of the West developed, issues relevant to the classical Paideia were replayed even as its particular concerns were superseded by the evolution of empire and Christianity. The original turbulence of a community grounded in the logos of the street and public assembly gradually gave way to disengagement of the individual from a public world, and then to social rule by prerogatives of class and institution (Habermas 1973).

United States history begins with a rupture in the lineal descent from classical times. In a single stroke, the American revolution sought to insulate the nascent democracy from European institutions and values and to celebrate the "new man." In the new world, freedom of speech and conscience were to guarantee people a right to a say; freedom of assembly, access to forming audiences; and equality, attention to the worth of what was said rather than belief accorded to those with preordained status. The democratic experiment was—and still is—closely tied to the assumptions of the classical rhetorical tradition. Therein justified assent is not a question that can be answered by following the rules of any cultural institutions or by developing a code from an abstract philosophy. Rather, what is brought into play is a complex of arguments, opinions about the issues of the day, that can bring to the test questions concerning the relationships among effective, truthful, valid, moral, and authentic discourse. The only secured boundaries are those which require that all arguments are permitted to be voiced and put to the test of discussion and debate.

Early Americans seemed to emulate the discursive practices of the classical world in a homespun, pioneer manner. In part, the tradition of public discourse demanded a departure from the constraints of the Old World. No longer could appropriate public choice be reduced to the authority of spokespersons representing the institutional dogmas of class and religion, monarchical and military institutions. Crafted in Constitutional documents and supported by the institutional political structure, the United States preserved a broad domain for individual choice, initiative, and decision. Thus was the public sphere protected from domination by social institutions. Indeed, some of the prejudices that survived in the New World, limiting the status of the autonomous person, were assaulted in the nineteenth century and were mitigated as the public sphere expanded (Kraditor 1965).

At the same time, the neoclassical presuppositions about human influence made free assent simpler and more complex: simpler because the conflicting opinions of institutional spokespersons were reduced to the common status of private interest or personal belief, hence demanding that anyone speaking for the public produce the better argument; more complex because now the individual had the responsibility not only to listen and decide but also to weigh conflicting views about what constitutes appropriate bases for communication per se. Only if the interests of the individual could be reconciled with and affiliated to those of the community by discourse could democracy itself be sustained. However imperfect the distribution of liberty might have been and however uncertain and troubled the development of the public sphere, still the direction of progress was clear. A better society could be assured to the extent that a discursively competent public could be achieved and sustained.

William James (1969), traveling abroad in Europe at the time of the Dreyfus trial, expressed the nineteenth-century American's convictions as well as anyone.

The breath of the nostrils of all these big institutions is crime—that is the long and short of it. We must thank God for America; and hold fast to every advantage of our position. Talk about corruption! It is a mere flyspeck of superficiality compared with the rooted and permanent forces of corruption that exist in the European states. The only serious permanent force of corruption in America is party spirit. All the other forces are shifting like the clouds, and have no partnerships with any permanently organized ideal. Millionaires and syndicates have their immediate cash to pay, but they have no entrenched prestige to work with, like the church sentiment, the army sentiment, the aristocracy and royalty sentiment, which here can be brought to bear in favor of every kind of individual and collective crime—appealing not only to the immediate pocket of the persons to be corrupted, but to the ideals of their imagination as well. . . . My dear Mack, we "intellectuals" must all work to

keep our precious birthright of individualism, and freedom from these institutions. Every great institution is perforce a means of corruption—whatever good it may also do. Only in the free personal relation is the full ideality
to be found. (100–01)

The point James makes is unmistakable. Whenever rhetoric is
grounded in the prerogatives of social order and the "sentiments" of
its various institutions, the causes of truth and justice cannot be
voiced and the individual stands unprotected. Of course, democracy
is fallible, but reliance on force of the better argument is more trustworthy in the long run than activity arranged by institutional allegiance and abetted by social prejudice. "Damn it, America doesn't
know the meaning of the world corruption compared with Europe!
Corruption is so permanently organized here that it isn't thought of
as such—it is so transient and shifting in America as to make an
outcry whenever it appears," James concludes in postscript (100).
The task he and other turn-of-the-century pragmatists set was to
guard and to protect the public sphere. Their view: As the community of interested partisans grew wider and as its discussions became
more enlightened, the greatest number of opinions in reciprocal
tests of reason could produce the greatest good for all. Even as the
notion of the public sphere was influenced by classical cultural values, problems arose on two fronts to challenge the viability of the
public.

Justified Assent and Materialized Discourse

From the point of the first democratic revolution onward, a complex set of distinctive tensions concerning the ethical and political
constitution of personal and public speech marked American history.
The formulations of political opinion within the public sphere rendered within American history stem from a formal rejection of many
of the most fundamental cultural and institutional presuppositions
characterizing custom and thought in Western Europe. As James Boyd
White writes: "In separating from Great Britain and setting up their
own government, Americans claimed the freedom and the power to
remake their world. That claim was of course not absolute, and a
constant question at the time was how much of the old to change,
how much to save. Nevertheless, what was proposed, and perhaps
achieved, in America was nothing less than the self-conscious reconstitution of language and community to achieve new possibilities for
life" (White 1984, 231). And yet, the habits of mind and heart that

constitute the allegiance of peoples and nations are never entirely exorcised.

Problems of class and culture, religion and secularization, work and capital, representation and interest were carried forward in the struggle to accommodate diverse nationalities and races in a new world. So long as the frontier promised room for all divergent opinions, no matter how unlikely or unorthodox, the democratic myth could be preached unimpaired; but, as free land was taken up and the frontier closed, the promise of institutionalized urban living on massive scales threw into relief the most haunting aspects of the American dream; namely, that institutional forces and segmented interests could dominate communities and coerce individuals, thereby reducing all public discourse to the garbing of power. Paradoxically, as the pragmatists sought ways to affirm and adapt the public sphere to the exigencies of twentieth-century life, uncertainty spread concerning the capacity of public discourse to provide an arena for valid communication (Dewey 1927).

If American social thinkers grew uneasy about the great democratic experiment, nineteenth-century political events on the European continent did not provide encouragement for the viability of a vital, cooperative public sphere. Out of the turbulent revolutions in Europe and burgeoning industrialization emerged the rhetorics of modernity. Going back as far as Rousseau, human conduct was reduced to an epiphenomenon within society or a romantic gesture against it. In this "modern" view, public discourse was only a product of social conformity and ignorance, standing in need of correction and in the way of truth (Habermas 1973). Rather than taking up the public discussion on its own terms within a common vocabulary, modern thinkers collapsed the public sphere to ideology, then compressed personal and public life into mutually reenforcing signs of illusion and error. The result was a distinctively solitary modern consciousness "consequent to the disestablishing of communal reality" (Gablik 1984, 31).

The undermining of the public sphere bore fruit in the great wars of this century. The radical left, for example, pressed art itself into the cause of revolutionary service. Painting, sculpture, writing, indeed anything wrought by human hands either supported the cause or was part of the reactionary regime. If the left politicized aesthetics, the right responded by aestheticizing politics (Benjamin 1969, 241–42). In the totalitarian spectacles of the National Socialist State, the Nazis converted the excitement of politics into a macabre form of mass art, a grotesque congeries of rallies, torchlight parades, and military displays that solidified, for a time, authoritarian power.

For the left, the human is a species being, a creature who shapes and is shaped by human beliefs and works, and remains a malleable object of social influence. Conversely, for the right, as a creature of the supreme state and a subject of the people's will, human beings are constant targets for imagined disloyalties and programs of reconstruction.

To comprehend the complexity that the negation of the public sphere adds to political address, one need only think of a relatively simple object like a house. At first glance, a house seems to offer no intrinsic rhetorical problem. There are no complicated questions of assent attached to a personal dwelling place. Or are there? In the commune movement, occupation of a house was converted into a sign of attachment to private property, and a commitment to privacy itself was interpreted as a betrayal of revolutionary values. So, too, in Nazi Germany, the house became an object of social significance as public decorations of group affiliation were demanded, and homes that did not belong were marked as well. The home stood open for inspection as a sign of good faith in the benevolence of the party and state in either case.

If a simple dwelling place can be taken as a tacit assent to one grand scheme of life or another, it is easy to see how the complexity of rhetoric begins to grow. Of course, in a democratic society the relative adequacy of housing may be taken as evidence that more or less public action is required. Concern for the homeless may lead to greater public involvement and sacrifice. In some views, however, all features of life are materialized into signs of the societal processes at work rather than exigencies to be prioritized and resolved. Where there can be no meaningful space apart to appraise problems and discuss opinions—no personal sphere of choice connected to judgment and obligation, or public sphere in which shared commitments are forged—questions of justified public assent become moot and are supplanted by either revolutionary praxis or reactionary purge.

Even though the problems of immigration, industrialization, and mass living tested the viability of democratic values, and though some American intellectuals and social movements especially during the Great Depression took up in varying degrees a search for alternatives, political movements by and large sought to reform rather than abolish the public sphere (Hofstadter 1955, 306). The rhetorical tradition in the United States was to receive its most significant challenge neither from dissent at home nor from a competing ideology but from a new, unforeseen and unusual source of persuasion and power—the alliance of government and technology in creating the mass audience.

Justified Assent and the Communications Industry

A distinctively modern rhetoric took root in the United States in the first quarter of the twentieth century. Even as American political philosophers and social reformers—the progressives—worked to widen the circle of social problems that could be addressed as public issues to secure urban life and take advantage of the tools of technology for the commonweal, the relationship between the public sphere and the democratic actor became more tenuous because of a new, unlikely institution, the mass media. Out of humble beginnings—partisan newspapers and traveling medicine shows, chautauqua and sales catalogs, wild west circuses and pulp novels—emerged a new, powerful organization that flourished by putting the materials of public discourse to technological use. Indeed, once the mass media came into being, traditional concerns for public opinion as a measure of civil liberty "ceased to exist" (Persons 1958, 374). Like the communication practices of the political extremes, the mass media began to build social cohesion on unprecedented scales by materializing the instruments of social communication.

Originally fueled by the opportunity to expand markets through warping habits of customer spending, aided by the need to produce universal support for what was thought might be an unpopular war (World War I), shaped by advertising research and economic models, the modern mass media grew to influence, dominate, and control the important channels of public communication in the United States. Public communication, once the product of meetings with fellow citizens at the town hall, lecture, church social, the local press, and other community forums, was commodified, turned into a product that is concocted, processed, and delivered without the intervention of traditional publics. Thus, the public actor was demoted to the "wise public relations counselor" who dealt in "mental images and stereotypes" to "amplify" or "articulate" the prejudices of the masses for his client (Bernays 1965; Persons 1958, 376).

So diverse are the instruments of technology used by the mass media and so complex are its organizations, formats, regulations, and changes, that it would be oversimplification to attribute its workings to any one rhetorical base. Yet, the rhetoric that does seem to provide some commonality for many media practices and products seems to remain that of an industrial vision of communication. Many mass media scholars say that the mass media industry *is* "big business" and "an adjunct of an industrial order" (Voelker and Voelker 1975: 7, 13; Hiebert et al. 1974, 51). Some even lament that such an orientation results in undervaluing "public service" (Sandman et al. 1972, p. 8). Few consider how industrial values circumscribe the very bases of human communication by delimiting the public sphere.

Consider the premises of an industrial vision of communication. As in any industrial process, mass media products are fashioned out of raw, material resources; yet, unlike industries that mine the earth, plant the land, and fish the seas, all converting the fruits of nature for the uses of mankind, the communications industry finds in the modeled psyches of human beings the material of its raw resources. Like the communication practices produced by the political extremes, it strives to materialize fully the conditions of discourse. Unlike its counterpart, the mass media industry is not inherently attached to any particular program of human improvement, other than ensuring that the mass audience approaches maximum, regularized habits of consumption—consuming media products, which in turn stimulate greater needs for more material consumption (Frye 1975, 403).

The mass audience as such comprises no particular people but all individuals collectively considered—a parody of a perfect political democracy. Humanity is appraised as a group of living organisms, and like any collectivity of living things, its habits of consumption and excretion, needs for energy and rest, can be described, predicted, and stimulated. Whatever it says or does can be reduced to its manifestations, mapped, subjected to manipulation, and directed. Further, since all living things are influenced by the environment and learn to adapt to its changes over time, so the mass audience can be shaped by any stimuli, if powerful, frequent, and prolonged enough. All that is needed is the time and control necessary to alter the habitat. The results of this view, among other things, are that the vast panorama of human history is reduced to glamorous, episodic encounters; the array of cultures to on-site locations; and the complexities of urban life to banal authority rituals ubiquitously exemplified in shoot-outs and car chases.

To say that the media industry provides a symbolic habitat that envelopes the public sphere is not to say that its products are everywhere the same. Of course, the mass media do take into account market segments. Just as mining engineers recognize different mineral deposits, the media isolate different sets of associations that characterize a particular age group or socioeconomic class. Moreover, there is no single theory of psychology or sociology that dominates the media—no settled view of human nature that would offer vortices of judgment. Just as prospectors use different combinations of techniques to discover nature's hidden riches, the media experiment with different brands of knowledge produced by the academy.

Of course, it would be too cynical to say that the industrial model of mass communication has triumphed completely. Occasionally, there appear works of artistic integrity, significant thought, and political importance that contravene the industrial communication model. But as the mass media industry itself becomes ever more attached to an industrial/economic model by linking success to ratings, and as ratings themselves reduce the public actor to data point, and the public to data aggregates, the homogenization of the mass media continues to erode the public sphere. At a minimum, popular ratings create incentives for standardization that reduce risk (Klein 1972). Once gold is found in an untapped formation of audience attention, producers rush in to dig it out until the resource is exhausted.

Arguably, an industrial model of mass media communication is not the worst available. Certainly, other organizing metaphors have significant problems, like the much abhorred authoritarian model where the truth in media is judged according to a communications service for the dominant regime—a model, too, that is permeable to industrial values. Moreover, it would be luddism to conclude that technology is a barrier to public communication per se and equally foolish to essay that public discourse was perfected in rural, pioneer America. Neither Utopian scheming nor nostalgic longing furnishes an adequate picture of the situation. But the point that should neither be compromised nor forgotten is that the air waves are the property of the PUBLIC. While the mass media industry gains much currency by pretending to stand for the public—to provide a medium in which its interests and views can be articulated—its own production values are not only insufficiently supportive of public discourse but are in many ways antithetical to it. When communication is processed to suit the industrial vision of a public realm, the common domain of community discourse is transformed from an arena of advocate and audience to a market of salespersons and customers, thereby transforming the public sphere from a place where ideas are aired out to a supermarket where associations are picked up.

The discourse of a public sphere is linked inextricably to the conflicted rhetorical tradition. Rhetoric brings to the surface and resolves for purposes of prudent choice conflicts among valid-illegitimate, authentic-inauthentic, effective-ineffective, informed-uninformed, good-bad, and pleasing-painful speech. To generate thoughtful involvement, public communication must invite its concerned participants to formulate and authenticate their own discourses. When speech is prepackaged, stuffed into monolithic, institutionalized settings, and chopped up to meet the requirements of production formats arranged according to industrial values, the public is cheated and responds with inattention or indifference—displaying the key qualities of a mass audience. At its optimal, rhetoric is that art which permits people to shape for themselves truthful, valid, authentic, effective, and prudent choice through sharing and refining opinions. When the sources of opinion-making are removed from ordinary contingencies, dialogue dies and public participation becomes tenuous— if it is ever born at all.

When the public no longer remains in control of its own channels of communication and means of producing discourse, the potential for exploitation grows. The television programming made possible by some recent deregulation signals the results. Cartoon makers in the last few years have worked on whole new methods to gull children. I do not refer to traditional sophisticated, scientifically constructed, expensive commercials crafted to separate a child from a nickel, but to those that now merge worlds of fantasy with habits of consumption. Crafting programs that appeal to children's fantasies of power and aggression (male) and security and acceptance (female), toy manufacturers now fabricate imaginary worlds on the edge of oblivion, where heroic warriors fight their way to extinction, and set these apocalyptics side by side with warm, fuzzy fantasies of social acceptance and playful ease among collapse and oblivion. The program itself functions as a long commercial for the toys to be sold, and the world of fantasy and consumption become a seamless web of participation. Of course, the computer-formatted violence is pasted over with a moral at the end of the story, a mouthing of platitudes that suggest that prosocial values are nice—especially with sufficient aggression to back them up.

The critique of television is nothing new, nor are its defenses (Rosten 1977). But in this case one finds a special example of how public interest—even to the minimal extent of giving children a fair shot to evaluate a product on its own merits—is discarded. As children are collectivized into data and psychologically manipulated, they are trained to be good consumers. What is true for the young is true for any market segment. So, the members of the mass audience will eventually become only the socially vulnerable, those who are either too habituated or too poor to flee relentless exploitation.

To craft a culture of discourse with enough depth of understanding, capacity for feeling, breadth of experience, and tolerance for intelligent response—in short, to enable people to participate in the production of their own symbolic life—takes time, effort, and risk. To recover the public sphere means that those who participate in communication must have some responsibility for producing and ability to fashion messages of consequence to a community (Dewey 1927, 184). Only in this way can the mass be transformed to audiences, and receivers to spokespersons. So long as the mass media dominate public space, public culture in American life remains at most a thin reality and a remote potential. To generate rich, interesting, and lively acts of communication, the public itself first must have some immediate stake in the production of its own communication processes.

The Problem of Critique

Modern views of communication have utilized technology to extend the powers of social persuasion even as such practices compress the space in which people can fashion the grounds of justified assent. To shape a community of opinion that sustains the capacity of a group to come to good decisions and take prudent action requires practices of communication that can be validated in the very process of communicating. The mass media industry, with its closed formatting, scientized means of invention, and need to control public channels, works to remove the processes of crafting communication from the public sphere. Necessarily, mass media production exists in parasitic relationship to human communication—selecting, imitating, exploiting, and eroding the creations of personal and political discourse to meet the needs of its own form of life. This observation is not new. There exists a long tradition of dissatisfaction with mass media products and practices. Although critique has been venomous and sustained, there exists a peculiar problem in coming to terms with mass media productions in such a way as to preserve or expand alternatives.

If the premise is correct that the mass media industry creates symbolic habitats that indifferently absorb all public discourse, then the grounds upon which criticism can be constructed and from which it must speak are tenuous indeed. Put bluntly: if the public sphere is co-opted, then there is no place in which an alternative can be incubated, and no hope of constructing grounds upon which common, justified assent can be fashioned. This problem seems not to bother critics who regularly hurl assaults at the media; but, however strident the dissent, it disempowers itself either by rooting public address in a rigid ideological base outside the public sphere, or by giving itself over to co-option by talking within existing "public" parameters. Thus critique can be ignored because of its ideological intractability or transformed into an episode where the media industry appears to purify its own practices. Such ideological opponents as Weaver (1948) and Marcuse (1964) offer far-ranging critiques of the media, which remain out of contact with the sources of influence because celebrating high culture or raising consciousness both leave the critic without contact requisite to *argue* alternatives. On the other hand, when the *Miami Herald* sends reporters to camp outside a presidential candidate's bedroom window, the media not only attract attention by gathering material for salacious headlines but also ride the crest of attention for weeks by discussing whether their own practices have gone too far. Neither of these critical practices has a sufficiently viable rhetorical base. So contemporary critics conclude that all opinion is but the struggle for power (Carey 1982, 30, 32), and this conclusion, paradoxically, validates media practices and continues to erode the capacity of criticism to revive the public sphere.[2]

An alternative to these dilemmas may be found in critically examining the rhetorical constitution of communication practices. The rhetorical tradition, examined at the outset of the essay, suggests that communication is not a univocal, material phenomenon, but rather a self-constituting aspect of culture, which emerges out of distinctive but complementary practices of constituting human relationships. Critique may preserve contact with all communication, yet move deeply enough to make more than ephemeral suggestions, by uncovering and putting into perspective contemporary discursive practices in light of their rhetorical presuppositions and values. Such criticism would (1) uncover dominant rhetorical assumptions governing the invention of communication systems or discursive regimes; (2) describe the functioning of those systems or the structure of regimes by decoding discourse and other symbolic artifacts (that is, reading communication products in terms of deduced inventional schematics); (3) interpret the discourse in frameworks pertaining to forms of life obfuscated by its selective representation; (4) expose the "surrogate" qualities of such depictions, thereby providing difference and room for alternative discourse; (5) suggest supplementary rhetorical values that might inform more satisfactory communication practices; and (6) recover from communication practices those exemplars of discourse that break from the routine and reinvigorate the public sphere.

Toward the end of building an effective basis for critique, I wish to focus attention on the rhetorical construction of a basic component of human communication, the "public opinion." In adducing critique, I wish to examine how public opinion is popularly regarded by the mass media—as an index of individual belief that can be aggregated to define public sentiment by the public opinion poll (Leirserson 1968, 188; Glynn and Mcleod 1982, 773)—and describe the limitation of this orientation. Then I wish to bring back into view an alternative view of human opinion from a bygone age—namely, the convergence of personal and public truth in a person's last words. The alternative view, together with its own limitations, might help provide an alternative basis for crafting public communication and modifying contemporary practices.

The Public Opinion Poll

The authority of surveyed public opinion emerges from a complicated, paradoxical view of the role of speech in the life of a democracy. As a principle, free speech is praised, its rights protected, and self-governance through force of the better argument taught as a social value. In practice, the opinion of any single individual is held to have little legitimate content, unless expressing the beliefs and interests of one (or of a special-interest group). "That is your opinion," it is often said as a means of discounting a statement by relegating expression to the domain of subjective belief and special interest. Thus, all statements of collective purpose, goals, values, social needs, and common opportunities are in principle attributable to the strategic, the manipulative, the pose or guise of power; and where power is the rule, discourse is defined by the process of compromise among interests. In the supposition that any statement of shared goals or beliefs is a compromise waiting the right moment to settle for less or gain more, political speech is reduced to posturing, a show for the public's benefit. The only accurate meaning of political speech is entailed in its effects, which can be known by indexing approval and disapproval of various interests—and subsequently disassembling responses demographically by audience characteristics. Thus, the opinion poll provides the chart of public will, and it remains only for political speech to steer a course around all obstacles.

Whereas opinion polls are now taken as the primary measure of public assent, I am not sure that they do not disintegrate what they purport merely to measure. Notice that in a survey the beliefs of no single individual matter. Notice, too, that the aggregated beliefs are not an index of present opinion but refer to the past—the time at which a person's political views are formulated into a constrained transaction (Whitney 1975, 420). Present beliefs include reflection on what the survey might find, and in that sense the sampling inevitably confounds its accuracy with its own effects. Even as an index of recently held opinion, a marker freezing the ongoing dialectic of public discussion, the survey rarely provides knowledge of the depth of commitment or knowledge derived to make an informed judgment (Beard 1943, 311). Moreover, the evolution of contexts that invite reshaping, even reformulation, of opinion are left undisclosed even if the surveyor has guessed rightly the important questions on the public agenda. The result of these features is that the survey cannot refer to a live ongoing world where people converse in dialogue and make judgments, a public world; rather, the survey measures societal predispositions, a world in which norms, however incomplete, contradictory, and changing, are fitted on demand into a surveyor's idea about what important choices ought to be and how they can be expressed. Recognizing limitations of the traditional model, Glynn and Mcleod (1982) argue that the definition of public opinion should be changed from "a collection of individual expressions to the summation of perceptions about what others in the society believe" (773).

Given the tendency of polls to tap into general, attributed, passing perceptions, it is not surprising to find that polls often mirror general desires to have the best and avoid the worst, rather than an articulated public agenda (Zukin 1981, 369–70). The "public" is said to want to decrease the budget deficit and increase government programs, to get richer and solve problems of social distribution, to increase arms and solve the nuclear problem, and so on. As the public itself comes to see the survey as a lever for pushing requests, rather than as an exigence inviting choice among priorities, the discriminatory power of "public opinion" itself tends to evaporate. As a result, attention turns away from the "issues"—as these come to be seen as superficial indicators—and toward the images of leaders and their own public relations problems, as politicians seek to avoid making mistakes that would register declines in the polls and take advantage of the personal liabilities of their adversaries. Even as the polls offer information about how "the public" feels about a candidate's latest misstatement, miscue, or misfortune, it contributes to obscuring the means of judgment and undercutting the possibility of public discourse. Noting the distortive nature of polling and its affinity to mass media production, Earl Shorris (1982) concludes: "For the sake of the illusion of power the press has inflated the importance of the polls to such a degree that the political nature of the nation may be permanently changed and the ability of government to exercise its constitutional function permanently damaged" (35).

The assumption that public opinion can be freed from risk and scientifically accumulated depends upon a paradox: members of the public are attributed derived views on matters important to themselves, yet also are expected to state naively preference without considering the poll as an instrument of persuasive power. Surveyors expect public opinion to be surrendered for free and stated without strategic considerations of risk. But, there is no proof to indicate that people act in such an innocent manner, and as surveys become a more ubiquitous part of American life, it would be incorrect to fail to take into account increasing sophistication of the public in putting the proper "spin" on replies. Simultaneously, sampling elevates the aggregate of opinion to a truth that cannot be grounded, while demoting the status of any one person's ideas to a measured relationship to an ungrounded norm (Shorris 1982, 35). Thus, public opinion sampling distorts communication, placing experts in the position of power and authority while restricting the capacity of discourse to form community. When the agenda of discussion is not held in common (the agenda being the "opinions" interchanged between interviewer and respondent), it is an open question as to who may be the naive social actor.

Last Words

The assumption that public opinion can be determined by the unreflective check of a box or a yes-no to an anonymous telephone call is at odds with the long history of controversy concerning opinion, truth, and politics. What aroused Socrates' ire was the deceit of those who were so skilled in deception that they could not realize they were deceiving themselves. Machiavelli saw in the complexities of the court the exquisite elaboration of self-interest disguised as the public good. So history records many occasions when public assent was a mask for personal disbelief. In a world where illusion sometimes is protected as truth, and the consequences of public statements are unknown, opinion-making usually is accompanied by risk. At best, public expressions can only provide a partial indicator of a person's personal beliefs. Indeed, it was a popular conceit of ages gone by that only in a person's last words could some measure of truth concerning publically stated views be ascertained.

Of a person's last words, Montaigne wrote:

[T]he resolution and confidence of a well-ordered mind should never be accredited to a man until we have seen him play the last and, doubtless, the most difficult act of his drama. In all the rest there may be disguise, whether it be that those fine reasonings of philosophy are in us only conventionally, or that the things happen, not proving us to the quick, permit us to keep always a serene demeanour. But in this last scene between Death and ourselves, there is no more feigning, we must talk plainly, we must show what there is good and unspotted in the bottom of the pot:

For then at last words of truth come from the depths of the breast; the mask is torn off; reality remains (Horace)

It is thus that all the other acts of our lives must be put to the touch and tested by this last stroke. It is the masterday, it is the day that is the judge of all other days. It is the day, says one of the ancients, which is to pass judgment on all my past years. I postpone until death the trial of the fruit of my studies. We shall see then whether my words come from the lips or the heart. (Montaigne 1946, 101)

Montaigne's admonition is sombering, and out of place in the American rhetorical tradition, which views speech as a lively art that ever expands partisan views. Indeed, it even might be considered bad taste to subject the last words of the dying to critical scrutiny; but inspecting the utterance of opinions from the point of view of finality is necessary, for only such analysis can provide an antidote to the world projected by the survey, a place where all opinion is indexed arbitrarily for the moment in the process of unlimited change. From the alternative perspective, it is clear that one's own beliefs are not transparent. Beliefs seem to be what they are, tentative or unshakable, but in meeting life's trials, reversal and transformation are the constant partners of adherence and preservation. At any time, the depth of a single opinion, much less its relationship to all personal knowledge, may not be directly accessible or even clearly apparent to one asked to espouse a preference or judgment.

As valuable as Montaigne's views are in reminding us that all opinion carries with it a risk in its expression, there is something antiquated in his evaluation. In fact, Montaigne seems to realize that even death may not settle anything. Of one of the ancients whose lifetime of work was shattered on a final day, he writes: "And it would seem that Fortune precisely watches for the last day of our life, in order to show her power to overturn in an instant what she has built up in long years, and makes us cry, like Laberius: Surely I have lived to-day one day longer than I should have lived" (100). It is a short step from giving final words an ultimate place in revealing the meaning of a life to no place at all. In the fields of Flanders, the youth of Europe discovered that there may not be much difference between dying well and simply dying. The last words prompted by an indifferent fate may be no more significant than the routines of daily gossip.

Montaigne's consideration of the end of days does suggest a valuable lesson about the nature of communication. Prevailing models of societal communication invite people to live in a survey world where discourse can be scissored into its component parts, then industrially reconstituted for mass dissemination. For example, Schramm (1972, 16–29) reduces communication to a "process" wherein a "source" (a human being, a group of people) "encodes" (writes, acts, sings, cries, speaks) a "signal" (poem, oration, painting, play) for a "decoder" (an interpreter, a machine) thereby reaching a destination (a human being, a mass audience). Dominick (1983, 23) extends this analytic to categorize human communication as distinguished by three settings: interpersonal, machine-assisted interpersonal, and mass. In this view, there is neither need nor room for a public space. The arts of discourse are reduced by the simple notation that sometimes "transmitting" is done from person to person without the aid of a machine (interpersonal communication) and sometimes with (mass communication) (Sandman, Rubin, and Sachsman 1972, 4).

The personal elements of a communication, those which from the point of view of the individual or a community may be the most important, varied, and surprising, are reduced by this orientation to a uniform sameness, as all discourse is materialized fully into its processes. Whitney (1975) goes so far as to claim, for example, that: "The Mona Lisa, the Sistine Chapel, Venus De Milo, the Colosseum, and the Great Pyramid are all mass media of historical times" (406). Once the industrial model is accepted, culture is flattened, and the self-constituting power of human endeavor is consigned to Romanticism, mysticism, or worse. Communication study—which might speak to the puissant paradoxes and fruitless contradictions between personal and public speech—uncritically enfolds all human conduct into versions of the natural world, which somehow is claimed to be known: Like other animals, humans adapt. This is a law of nature, and a social fact. What may be theorized from a species standpoint, however, is not confirmed from the perspective of any one person's communications that, as Montaigne reminds us, are particularized in the end by uniqueness and finality.

Each person is allotted only so many words to say, only so many gestures, glances, thoughts, or strokes of the pen. Just as these words grow from and into a social world, so they are shadowed by limits and termination. In every talk that is struck up, just as surely as there was the first moment of greeting there will be the last of goodbye. Conversation among old friends, I believe, is valued uniquely because it affirms a continuity that overcomes, for the time being, the limitations of design and accident through sustaining a personal relationship. There is a risk to talk that struggles to overcome absences in time and space. One may speak with an old friend, and in an instant's pause, discover that there is nothing more to be said; that for some odd reason "last words" have been spoken. What once provided a continuing dialogue may disappear just as mysteriously as it began. In the course of a life, there are many departures, and it may not be apparent, except in the perspective provided by retrospection, when communication with another person, a social group, or a whole way of life has come to an end.

In this light, the choice to express an opinion or to listen to another is endowed with a dignity commensurate with the human condition. To talk with others, even in the throws of heated argument or a shared silence, is to do them and oneself honor. Words may be arbitrary. They can be scooped up for commodification or disbursed by ideological critique, but they are all people have to move together back from the abyss of time. This rhetorical world is existential, but it is not made of the material that promotes philosophical alienation; for rhetoric crafts a bridge among people, even if they can share no identifiable meaning or purpose but only a common time. At its best, rhetoric can serve to allow us to open a common past, to move toward a future not yet arrived, and to fashion—out of fleeting moments—a present that endures.

Just as rhetoric enables each person to share a personal world, so it contains the possibility of a viable public sphere. Hannah Arendt (1958) has written: "The basic error of all materialism in politics . . . is to overlook the inevitability with which men disclose themselves as subjects, as distinct and unique persons, even when they wholly concentrate upon reaching an altogether worldly, material object" (183). The realm of politics may be reduced to the materials of persuasion—images, signs, and symbols, all regarded as communication commodities; but, in the comportment of community life is disclosed telling visions of what audiences are, enabling and constraining what they may become.[3] So long as rhetorical criticism retains the capacity to penetrate and freeze the flow of images and to uncover better versions of communication, the public abides as a potential of all discourse—even in an era that strives to mediate it out of existence.

Conclusion

The question of justified assent was never to be answered simply within the rhetorical tradition. The grounds upon which assent can be built have been complicated still further by the political philosophies, institutions, and technologies of communication in the modern world. Yet, the rhetorical tradition, by virtue of its location of political action in community and allegiance to maintaining arenas of open expression, provides the grounds for people to debate openly and call for agreement worthy of commitment. The expansion and preservation of the rhetorical tradition may be either subverted or confirmed by the communication practices of a society.

In the main, America celebrates rhetoric as a comic art of subversion (Duncan 1962). In comic drama, beliefs expressed by opinion seem the property of the individual, yet are always capable of change, modification, disguise, and recovery—depending upon the needs of the situation, the inventiveness of the speakers, and the gullibility of audiences. Public discourse always plays the parts of overstatement and understatement in the service of partisanship. Thus, the public is treated to contests where personalities wrestle one another vigorously for the fans' allegiance, knowing that these bellicose protestations of difference will be transformed ritually into proofs of unity. Surveys and polls platform the stage on which these biannual and quadrennial dramas are played out, and the mass media fill the public sphere with compelling stories replete with goofs and mistakes as well as stinging jabs and timely comebacks. Fortune rules the outcome. As useful as these rituals are in maintaining charity requisite to allowing difference, there is another side to the rhetorical tradition, and it is forgotten at great expense.

Rhetoric is sometimes a tragic art, even in a democracy. Desperation and despair, loss and reconciliation must find a voice, if the human condition is to be expressed fully (Langer 1953). Public choices, however comically enacted, are fated to affect those excluded from the game, and the interests of the excluded may never be accorded a part equal to the risks that are taken in the public's name. The instruments of the mass media seek to guarantee the consumer an uninterrupted flow of marketable communication products, thereby endorsing a comic world. However powerful, no media can assure either that the voices of those who are not massed will be heard or that what those marginalized have to say is unimportant for the common good. The world's destitute and impoverished, the generations yet unborn who will live in a world shaped by present deeds, the culture with ways that are different from our own, the localities that are drained of resources and left to ruin—indeed, all nonconsuming human aggregates are rarely permitted to speak for themselves; nor can the mass media hire spokespersons without converting alternative points of view into passing opinions reduced by the peculiarities of formatting requirements. So, this century continues to see the explosive growth of the instruments of mass transmission and the tragic silence, fragmentation, and alienation of publics who might be heard.

It may be the case that the dominance of the mass media over the public sphere will some day be a historical artifact. Certainly, the tendency of technology is to make the vehicles of communication cheaper, more varied, and ubiquitous. The growing diversity of new communications technology suggests that the comic frame, essential to the formation and preservation of the public, may yet be strengthened by local adaptation and use. Bagdikian (1975) says: "If we are wise, we shall make this kind of facility plentiful, so that every neighborhood, every community, every school district will have many channels, often vacant, so that it becomes easy and inexpensive to circulate information, ask questions and get a response on the items of social and political need at the grass roots—communications that are now impossible in systems that have relatively few one-way channels addressing everyone in thousands of square miles" (417). The evolution of local cable systems and experimental use of video technology seems to suggest that Bagdikian's rhetorical vision may not be merely an empty dream.

Ironically, it is possible that the burgeoning diversity of technologies simply will reproduce mass communication on a local scale. So long as industrial values dominate orientations to human communication, technology remains the master and not the servant of personal and public discourse. This essay has tried to provide a corrective for this orientation by examining opinion as it emerges from and returns to a personal sphere of life. All people—theorists and technicians, politicians and citizens—speak from the limited perspective of a time and place, and all perform the work of coming to terms with the potential and responsibility of a living generation. Each generation, as it breaks from the past and invents the future, struggles to fashion its own activities from the available materials of discourse and instruments of technology. Yet all are limited, even defined, by the manner in which human communication evolves in dialogue with those forever silenced and those yet to speak.

To acknowledge the existential risk involved in essaying even the most fleeting opinion is to return to the enterprise of assent-making a stature commensurate with preserving human dignity and improving human life. To no small extent, the survival of democratic values may depend upon the capacity of publics not only to read and criticize mediated messages but also to become competent in the arts of communication, which, in part, requires the innovative use of new technologies to realize the capacity of the rhetorical tradition. How we comprise our own communication in engaging the voices of others yet to be heard will define that tradition and create the available grounds for fashioning justified assent for this generation and others to come.

Notes

1. The essay is revised from an address delivered at the Wake Forest Conference on Argumentation. The author wishes to express his thanks to Michael Hyde for his post-modern suggestions.
2. The critical program I have in mind is not dissimilar from Kenneth

Burke's analysis of attitudes toward history (1937); however, in an era when history seems to have been subordinated to immediacy, I think that it is necessary to probe attitudes toward communication.

3. For an example of the creative link between the personal sphere and the public sphere, see Warren's essay on feminist's formulations on critical theory and practice (1987).

References

Albert, M., and R. Hahnel. 1978. *Unorthodox Marxism*. Boston: South End Press.

"Anatomy of an Informer—Part 2." 1975. *Akwesasne Notes* 7 (Early Winter): 10–13.

Annis, D. 1978. "A Contextualist Theory of Epistemic Justification." *American Philosophical Quarterly* 15: 213–19.

Apel, K. 1979. "Types of Rationality Today: The Continuum of Reason between Science and Ethics." In *Rationality To-Day.* Edited by T. F. Geraets. Ottawa: University of Canada Press.

Arendt, Hannah. 1958. *The Human Condition*. Chicago: University of Chicago Press.

Aristotle. 1954. *Rhetoric*. Translated by W. R. Roberts. New York: Modern Library.

_____. 1977. *Poetics*. Translated by G. Else. Ann Arbor: University of Michigan Press.

Arkeketa, M. 1973. "Oklahoma People Still Traveling on the Trail of Tears: A Personal Statement from Tulsa." *Akwesasne Notes* 5 (Early Autumn): 21.

Arkin, W., and R. Fieldhouse. 1985. *Nuclear Battlefields: Global Links in the Arms Race*. Cambridge: Ballinger Publishing.

Arnold, Carroll C. 1970. "Perelman's New Rhetoric." *Quarterly Journal of Speech* 56: 87–92.

_____. 1986. "Foreword." In *Communication and Knowledge*, by Richards A. Cherwitz and James W. Hilkins, ix–x. Columbia: University of South Carolina Press.

Bagdikian, Ben H. 1975. "How Communications May Shape Our Future Environment." In *Mass Media: Forces in Our Society.* Edited by F. H. Voelker and L. A. Voelker, 412–19. New York: Harcourt Brace Jovanovich.

Balthrop, V. W. 1984. "Culture, Myth, and Ideology as Public Argument: An Interpretation of the Ascent and Demise of 'Southern Culture.'" *Communication Monographs* 51: 339–52.

Barthes, Roland. 1982. "Inaugural Lecture, College de France." In *Barthes Reader.* Edited by Susan Sontag. New York: Hill and Wang.

Bartley, William Warren III. 1987. "Philosophy of Biology versus Philosophy of Physics." In *Evolutionary Epistemology, Rationality, and the Sociology of Knowledge.* Edited by Gerard Radnitzky and William Warren Bartley III, 7–45. LaSalle, Ill.: Open Court.

Beard, Charles Austin. 1943. *The Republic: Conversations on Fundamentals.* New York: Viking Press.

Beiner, Ronald. 1983. *Political Judgment.* Chicago: University of Chicago Press.

Bellah, R. N., et al. 1985. *Habits of the Heart.* Berkeley: University of California Press.

"Bellecourt Explains AIM Goals." 1973. *Wassaja* 1 (April/May): 7.

Benjamin, Walter. 1969. *Illuminations.* Translated by Harry Zohn. Edited by Hannah Arendt. New York: Shocken Books.

Bennett, W. L. 1977. "The Ritualistic and Pragmatic Bases of Political Campaign Discourse." *Quarterly Journal of Speech* 63: 219–38.

———. 1980. "Myth, Ritual, and Political Control." *Journal of Communication* 30: 166–79.

———. 1981. "Assessing Presidential Character: Degradation Rituals in Presidential Campaigns." *Quarterly Journal of Speech* 67: 310–21.

Benson, Thomas. 1974. "Rhetoric and Autobiography: The Case of Malcolm X." *Quarterly Journal of Speech* 60: 1–13.

Berlo, D. 1960. *The Process of Communication: An Introduction to Theory and Practice.* Chicago: Holt, Rinehart & Winston.

Berman, M. 1982. *All That Is Solid Melts into Air.* New York: Simon & Schuster.

Bernays, Edward L. 1965. *Biography of an Idea: Memoirs of a Public Relations Counsel, Edward L. Bernays.* New York: Simon & Schuster.

Bernstein, Richard J. 1971. *Praxis and Action.* Philadelphia: University of Pennsylvania Press.

———. 1983. *Beyond Objectivism and Relativism: Science, Hermeneutics, and Praxis.* Philadelphia: University of Pennsylvania Press.

Bierce, Ambrose. 1911. *The Devil's Dictionary.* New York: T. Y. Crowell.

Bitzer, Lloyd F. 1968. "The Rhetorical Situation." *Philosophy and Rhetoric* 1: 1–14.

———. 1978. "Rhetoric and Public Knowledge." In *Rhetoric, Philosophy, and Literature: An Exploration.* Edited by Don M. Burks, 167–94. West Lafayette, Ind.: Purdue University Press.

———. 1980. "Functional Communication: A Situational Perspective." In *Rhetoric in Transition: Studies in the Nature and Uses of Rhetoric.* Edited by Eugene E. White, 21–38. University Park: Pennsylvania State University Press.

————. 1981. "Political Rhetoric." In *Handbook of Political Communication*. Edited by Dan D. Nimmo and Keith R. Sanders, 225–48. Beverly Hills: Sage Publications.

Black, Edwin. 1958. "Plato's View of Rhetoric." *Quarterly Journal of Speech* 44: 361–74.

————. [1965] 1978. *Rhetorical Criticism: A Study in Method*. Madison: University of Wisconsin Press.

————. 1970. "The Second Persona." *Quarterly Journal of Speech* 56: 109–19.

Blair, Carole. 1987. "The Statement: Foundation of Foucault's Historical Criticism." *Western Journal of Speech Communication* 51: 364–83.

Bocock, R. 1974. *Ritual in Industrial Society: A Sociological Analysis of Ritualism in Modern England*. London: George Allen & Unwin.

Bokeno, R. Michael. 1987. "The Rhetorical Understanding of Science: An Explication and Critical Commentary." *Southern Speech Communication Journal* 52: 285–311.

Bonjour, L. 1985. *The Structure of Empirical Knowledge*. Cambridge: Harvard University Press.

"Book Reviews." 1978. *Akwesasne Notes* 10 (Late Spring): 33.

Booth, Wayne C. 1961. *The Rhetoric of Fiction*. Chicago: University of Chicago Press.

————. 1974. *Modern Dogma and the Rhetoric of Assent*. Notre Dame: University of Notre Dame Press; paper edition, Chicago: University of Chicago Press.

Bormann, Ernest G. 1973. "The Eagleton Affair: A Fantasy Theme Analysis." *Quarterly Journal of Speech* 59: 143–59.

"Bringing Vietnam Home." 1975. *Akwesasne Notes* 7 (Early Winter): 4–5.

Brinton, Alan. 1985. "On Viewing Knowledge as Rhetorical." *Central States Speech Journal* 36: 270–81.

Brockreide, W., and D. Ehninger. 1960. "Toulmin on Argument: An Interpretation and Application." *Quarterly Journal of Speech* 46: 44–53.

Brummett, Barry. 1976. "Some Implications of 'Process' or 'Intersubjectivity': Postmodern Rhetoric." *Philosophy and Rhetoric* 9: 21–51.

————. 1980. "Intersubjectivity or Critical Rationalism?" Unpublished manuscript.

————. 1981. "A Defense of Ethical Relativism as Rhetorically Grounded." *Western Journal of Speech Communication* 45: 286–98.

————. 1982. "On to Rhetorical Relativism." *Quarterly Journal of Speech* 68: 425–30.

————. 1984. "Consensus Criticism." *Southern Speech Communication Journal* 49: 111–24.

————. 1986. "Professor Cherwitz in the Prison House of Language." *PRE/TEXT* 7: 91–98.

Bruner, E. M. 1986. "Ethnography as Narrative." In *The Anthropology of Experience*. Edited by V. W. Turner and E. M. Bruner, 139–55. Urbana, Ill.: University of Illinois Press.

Bryan, David. 1983. "Cultural Relativism—Power in Service of Interests:

The Particular Case of Native American Education." *Buffalo Law Review* 32: 643–95.

Bryant, Donald C. 1973. "Rhetoric: Its Functions and Its Scope *Rediviva.*" In *Rhetorical Dimensions in Criticism.* Edited by D. C. Bryant. Baton Rouge: Louisiana State University Press.

Burgess, Parke. 1985. "The Dialectic of Substance: Rhetoric vs Poetry." *Communication Quarterly* 33: 105–12.

Burke, Kenneth. [1931] 1968. *Counter-Statement.* Berkeley: University of California Press.

———. 1935. "Revolutionary Symbolism in America." In *American Writer's Congress.* Edited by Henry Hart, 87–93. New York: International Publishers.

———. 1937. *Attitudes toward History.* Los Altos, Calif.: Hermes Press.

———. [1945] 1969a. *A Grammar of Motives.* Englewood Cliffs, N.J.: Prentice Hall. Reprint, Berkeley: University of California Press.

———. [1950] 1969b. *A Rhetoric of Motives.* Englewood Cliffs, N.J.: Prentice-Hall. Reprint. Berkeley: University of California Press.

———. [1953] 1968. *Counter-Statement.* 2d ed. Los Altos, Calif.: Hermes Publications. Reprint. Berkeley: University of California Press.

———. 1965. *Permanence and Change.* 2d ed. Indianapolis: Library of the Liberal Arts.

———. 1973. "The Philosophy of Literary Form." In *The Philosophy of Literary Form.* Berkeley: University of California Press.

———. 1984. *Attitudes Toward History.* Berkeley: University of California Press.

Burns, Edward McNall. 1957. *The American Idea of Mission: Concepts of National Purpose and Destiny.* New Brunswick, N.J.

Butler, G. 1983. *Eagle Wing Press,* January 7.

Caldicott, Helen. 1986. "Nuclear Madness: Excerpts from Helen Caldicott's Farewell Speech." *National Women's Studies Association Perspectives* 4: 2–4.

Campbell, Karlyn Kohrs. 1972. "Richard M. Nixon." In *Critiques of Contemporary Rhetoric,* chapter 4. Belmont, Calif.: Wadsworth Publishing Co.

Campbell, Paul N. 1972. *Ritual/Rhetoric: A Study of the Communicative and Aesthetic Dimensions of Language.* Belmont, Calif.: Dickenson Publishing Co.

———. 1975. "The *Personae* of Scientific Discourse." *Quarterly Journal of Speech* 61: 391–405.

Carey, James W. 1982. "The Mass Media and Critical Theory: An American View." In *Communication Yearbook,* Vol. VI. Edited by Michael Burgoon, 18–33. Beverly Hills: Sage Publications.

Carleton, Walter M. 1978. "What Is Rhetorical Knowledge? A Response to Farrell—And More." *Quarterly Journal of Speech* 64: 313–28.

Cassirer, Ernst. [1944] 1975. *An Essay on Man: An Introduction to a Philosophy of Human Culture.* Reprint. New Haven, Conn.: Yale University Press.

———. 1946. *Language and Myth.* Translated by S. Langer. New York: Dover Publications.

———. [1955–57] 1975–77. *Mythical Thought.* Vol. 2 of *The Philosophy of Symbolic Forms.* Translated by R. Manheim. Reprint, New Haven, Conn.: Yale University Press.

Castaneda, C. 1974. *The Teachings of Don Juan.* New York: Simon & Schuster.

Cathcart, R. S. 1978. "Movements: Confrontation as Rhetorical Form." *Southern Speech Communication Journal* 43: 233–47.

Chavers, D. 1983. "Around the Campfire: BIA Lawbreakers." *Eagle Wing Press,* January 22.

Cherwitz, Richard A. 1984. "Rhetoric as Epistemic: A Conversation with Richard A. Cherwitz." *PRE/TEXT* 5: 197–235.

Cherwitz, Richard A., and James W. Hikins. 1982. "Toward a Rhetorical Epistemology." *Southern Speech Communication Journal* 47: 135–62.

———. 1983. "Rhetorical Perspectivism." *Quarterly Journal of Speech* 69: 249–66.

———. 1986. *Communication and Knowledge.* Columbia: University of South Carolina Press.

Chisholm, R. 1978. "On the Nature of Empirical Evidence." In *Essays on Knowledge and Justification.* Edited by G. S. Pappas and M. Swain, 253–78. Ithaca, N.Y.: Cornell University Press.

Codrington, R. H. 1891. *The Melanesians.* Oxford: Clarendon Press.

Collingridge, D., and C. Reeve. 1986. *Science Speaks to Power: The Role of Experts in Policy-Making.* New York: St. Martin's Press.

Commanger, Henry Steele. 1950. *The American Mind: An Interpretation of American Thought and Character Since the 1880's.* New Haven: Yale University Press.

Condit, Celeste M. 1987. "Democracy and Civil Rights: The Universalizing Influence of Public Argumentation." *Communication Monographs* 54: 1–18.

Conley, T. M. 1978. "'Logical Hylomorphism' and Aristotle's Koinoi Topoi." *Central States Speech Journal* 29: 92–97.

———. 1984. "The Enthymeme in Perspective." *Quarterly Journal of Speech* 70: 168–87.

Conrad, Joseph. [1907] 1982. *The Secret Agent.* New York: Penguin Books.

Corcoran, F. 1983. "The Bear in the Back Yard: Myth, Ideology, and Victimage Ritual in Soviet Funerals." *Communication Monographs* 50: 305–20.

Cox, J. Robert. 1981. "Investigating Policy Argument as a Field." In *Dimensions of Argument.* Edited by G. Ziegelmueller and J. Rhodes, 126–42. Annandale: Speech Communication Association.

Cox, J. Robert, and Charles Arthur Willard. 1982. "The Field of Argumentation." In *Advances in Argumentation Theory and Research.* Edited by J. Robert Cox and Charles Arthur Willard. Carbondale and Edwardsville: Southern Illinois University Press.

———, eds. 1982. *Advances in Argumentation Theory and Research.* Carbondale: Southern Illinois University Press.

Crick, Bernard. 1982. *In Defense of Politics*. New York: Penguin Books.

Croasmun, Earl. 1987. ". . . To Cherwitz and Brummett." *PRE/TEXT* 8: 273–77.

Croasmun, Earl, and R. A. Cherwitz. 1982. "Beyond Rhetorical Relativism." *Quarterly Journal of Speech* 68: 1–16.

"Crow Dog from Prison." 1976. *Akwesasne Notes* 8 (Early Spring): 14.

Davenport, Edward. 1987. "The New Politics of Knowledge: Rorty's Pragmatism and the Rhetoric of the Human Sciences." *Philosophy of the Social Sciences* 17: 377–94.

Davidson, D. 1973–74. "On the Very Idea of a Conceptual Scheme." *Proceedings and Addresses of the American Philosophical Association* 47: 5–20.

Davis, G. 1985. "Hearings, Dept. of Defense Authorization for Appropriations for Fiscal Year 1986." *Communications on Armed Services, U.S. Senate* 99: 1. Washington, D.C.: Government Printing Office.

D.C. Wounded Knee Defense Committee. 1975. *West River Times, East River Echo* 1 (August).

Dearin, Ray. 1986. "Justice and Justification in the New Rhetoric." In *Practical Reasoning in Human Affairs: Studies in Honor of Chaim Perelman*. Edited by J. Golden and J. Pilotta, 155–86. Dordrecht: Reidel.

Delia, Jesse G. 1970. "The Logic Fallacy, Cognitive Theory, and the Enthymeme: A Search for the Foundations of Reasoned Discourse." *Quarterly Journal of Speech* 56: 140–48.

Devine, Phillip E. 1987. "Relativism, Abortion, and Tolerance." *Philosophy and Phenomenological Research*. 48: 131–38.

Dewey, John. [1927] 1954. *The Public and Its Problems*. New York: Henry Holt. Paper edition, Chicago: Swallow Press.

Dolan, M. 1986. "Crusade on Drugs Urged by Reagans." *Los Angeles Times*, September 15, pt. I.

Dominick, Joseph R. 1983. *The Dynamics of Mass Communication*. New York: Random House.

Douglas, M. [1970, 1973] 1982. *National Symbols: Explorations in Cosmology*. London: Barrie & Rockliff: The Cresset Press. Reprint, New York: Pantheon Books.

Duncan, Hugh Danziel. 1962. *Communication and Social Order*. New York: Oxford University Press.

Durkheim, Emile. [1915] 1965. *The Elementary Forms of the Religious Life*. Translated by J. W. Swain. Reprint, New York: Free Press.

Eagleton, Terry. 1981. *Walter Benjamin Or, Towards a Revolutionary Criticism*. London: Verso.

———. 1983. *Literary Theory: An Introduction*. Minneapolis: University of Minnesota Press.

Eco, Umberto. 1976. *A Theory of Semiotics*. Bloomington: Indiana University Press.

———. 1983. *The Name of the Rose*. New York: Harcourt Brace Jovanovich.

"Economic History of the Hau de Nau Sau Nee." 1977. *Akwesasne Notes* 9 (Autumn): 12–15.

Edmondson, Ricca. 1984. *Rhetoric in Sociology*. London: Macmillan Press.

Edwards, Bruce L. 1986. *A Rhetoric of Reading: C. S. Lewis's Defense of Western Literacy.* Provo: Center for the Study of Christian Values in Literature.

Ehninger, D. 1968. "Validity as Moral Obligation." *Southern Speech Journal* 23: 215–22.

———. 1977. "On Inferences of the 'Fourth Class.'" *Central States Speech Journal* 28: 157–62.

Eliade, M. [1957] 1959. *The Sacred and the Profane: The Nature of Religion.* Translated by W. R. Trask. Reprint, New York: Harcourt, Brace, & World.

———. [1958] 1965. *Rites and Symbols of Initiation: The Mysteries of Birth and Rebirth.* Translated by W. R. Trask. Reprint, New York: Harper & Row.

———. [1963] 1968. *Myth and Reality.* Translated by W. R. Trask. Reprint, New York: Harper & Row.

———. 1985. "Masks: Mythical and Ritual Origins." In *Symbolism, the Sacred, and the Arts.* Edited by D. Apostolos-Cappadona, 64–71. New York: Crossroad.

Eliot, George. *Daniel Deronda.* New York: A. L. Burt.

Elliott, Robert C. 1982. *The Literary Persona.* Chicago: University of Chicago Press.

Elsbree, L. 1982. *The Rituals of Life: Patterns in Narratives.* Port Washington, N.Y.: Kennikat Press.

Elster, Jon. 1979. *Ulysses and the Sirens.* Cambridge: Cambridge University Press.

———. 1985. *Making Sense of Marx.* Cambridge: Cambridge University Press.

Emery, Edwin, Phillip H. Ault, and Warren K. Agee. 1971. *Introduction to Mass Communications.* New York: Dodd, Mead & Company.

Erikson, Erik. 1963. *Childhood and Society.* 2d ed. New York: W. W. Norton.

———. 1968. *Identity, Youth and Crisis.* New York. W. W. Norton.

Farrell, Thomas B. 1976. "Knowledge, Consensus, and Rhetorical Theory." *Quarterly Journal of Speech* 62: 1–14.

———. 1977. "Validity and Rationality: The Rhetorical Constituents of Argumentative Form." *Journal of the American Forensics Association* 13: 142–49.

———. 1978a. "Political Conventions as Legitimation Ritual." *Communication Monographs* 45: 293–305.

———. 1978b. "Social Knowledge II." *Quarterly Journal of Speech* 64: 329–34.

———. 1982a. "A Quiet Observation." *Quarterly Journal of Speech* 68: 430–31.

———. 1982b. "Knowledge in Time: Toward an Extension of Rhetorical Form." In *Advances in Argumentation Theory and Research.* Edited by J. R. Cox and C. A. Willard. Carbondale: Southern Illinois University Press.

Farrell, Thomas B., and G. T. Goodnight. 1981. "Accidental Rhetoric: The Root Metaphors of Three Mile Island." *Communication Monographs* 48: 271–300.

Finkelstein, Leo, Jr. 1981. "The Calendrical Rite of the Ascension to Power." *Western Journal of Speech Communication* 45: 51–59.

Fisher, W. R. 1978. "Toward a Logic of Good Reasons." *Quarterly Journal of Speech* 64: 376–84.

_____. 1980. "Rationality and the Logic of Good Reasons." *Philosophy and Rhetoric* 13: 121–30.

_____. 1981. "Good Reasons: Fields and Genre." In *Dimensions of Argument: Proceedings of the Second Summer Conference on Argumentation.* Edited by G. Ziegelmueller and J. Rhodes, 114–25. Annandale, Va.: Southern Communications Association.

_____. 1987. *Human Communication as Narration: Toward a Philosophy of Reason, Value, and Action.* Columbia: University of South Carolina Press.

Flanders, T. 1983. "Seven Levels of Life, (part IV)." *Eagle Wing Press,* January 23.

Fornell, Gordon. 1985. "Hearings, Dept. of Defense Authorization for Appropriations for Fiscal Year 1986." *Comm. on Armed Services, U.S. Senate* 99: 1. Washington, D.C.: Government Printing Office.

Fortenbaugh, W. W. 1974. "Aristotle's *Rhetoric* on Emotions." Reprinted in *Aristotle: The Classical Heritage of Rhetoric.* Edited by K. V. Erickson. Metuchen: Scarecrow Press.

Foss, Sonja K., and Ann Gill. 1987. "Michel Foucault's Theory of Rhetoric as Epistemic." *Western Journal of Speech Communication* 51: 384–401.

Foucault, Michel. 1983. "The Subject and Power." In *Michel Foucault: Beyond Structuralism and Hermeneutics,* 2d ed. Edited by H. L. Dreyfus and P. Rabinow. Chicago: University of Chicago Press.

Frank, David A. 1981. "*Shalom Achshav*—Rituals of the Israeli Peace Movement." *Communication Monographs* 48: 164–82.

Frentz, T. S., and Thomas B. Farrell. 1976. "Language-Action: A Paradigm for Communication." *Quarterly Journal of Speech* 62: 333–49.

Freud, Sigmund. [1953–66] 1975a. "Obsessive Actions and Religious Practices." In *The Standard Edition of the Complete Psychological Works of Sigmund Freud.* Edited by J. Strachey, in collaboration with A. Freud, with the assistance of A. Strachey and A. Tyson, 24 vols., 9: 115–27. Reprint, London: Hogarth Press.

_____. [1953–66] 1975b. "Totem and Taboo." In *The Standard Edition of the Complete Psychological Works of Sigmund Freud.* Edited by J. Strachey, in collaboration with A. Freud, with the assistance of A. Strachey and A. Tyson, 24 vols., 13: ix–161. Reprint, London: Hogarth Press.

Frost, J. 1974. "A Rhetorical Analysis of Wounded Knee II, 1973." Paper presented at the 43rd annual meeting of the Central States Speech Association, Milwaukee, Wisconsin, April.

Frye, Northrop. 1975. "Communications." In *Mass Media: Forces in Our Society.* Edited by F. H. Voelker and L. A. Voelker, 402–06. New York: Harcourt Brace Jovanovich.

Fuller, Steve. 1988. *Social Epistemology.* Bloomington: University of Indiana Press.

_____. 1989. "Beyond the Rhetoric of Antitheory: Towards a Revisionist Interpretation of Critical Legal Studies." In *Rhetoric in the Human Sciences.* Edited by Herbert W. Simons, 133–51. London: Sage Publications.

Fuller, Steve, and Charles A. Willard. 1987. "In Defense of Relativism: Rescuing Incommensurability from the Self-Excepting Fallacy." In *Argumentation: Perspectives and Approaches.* Edited by F. H. van Eemeren, R. Grootendorst, J. A. Blair, and C. A. Willard. Dordrecht: Foris.

Gablik, Suzi. 1984. *Has Modernism Failed?* New York: Thames & Hudson.

Gadamer, H. 1975. *Truth and Method.* Translated by Garrett Barden and John Cumming. New York: Seabury Press.

Gallagher, Kenneth. 1984. "Rorty on Objectivity, Truth, and Social Consensus." *International Philosophical Quarterly* 24: 111–24.

"Garden Plot—'Flowers of Evil.'" 1975. *Akwesasne Notes* 7 (Early Winter): 6–7.

Gay, V. P. 1979. *Freud on Ritual: Reconstruction and Critique.* American Academy of Religion Dissertation Series. Edited by H. G. Little, Jr., no. 26. Missoula, Montana: Scholars Press.

Geach, P. T. 1976. *Reason and Argument.* Berkeley: University of California Press.

Geertz, C. 1973. *The Interpretation of Cultures.* New York: Basic Books.

Gitlin, Todd. 1982. "Prime Time Ideology: The Hegemonic Process in Television Entertainment." In *Television: The Critical View,* 3rd ed. Edited by Horace Newcomb, 507–32. New York: Oxford University Press.

Glynn, Carroll J., and Jack M. Mcleod. 1982. "Public Opinion Communication Processes and Voting Decisions." In *Communication Yearbook,* Vol. VI. Edited by Michael Burgoon. Beverly Hills: Sage Publications.

Goffman, Erving. 1967. *Interaction Ritual: Essays on Face-to-Face Behavior.* Garden City, N.Y.: Anchor Books.

Gold, Ellen Reid. 1978. "Political Apologia: The Ritual of Self-Defense." *Communication Monographs* 45: 306–16.

Goodnight, G. Thomas. 1982. "The Personal, Technical, and Public Spheres of Argument: A Speculative Inquiry into the Art of Public Deliberation." *Journal of the American Forensic Association* 18: 214–27.

Goody, J. 1977. "Against 'Ritual': Loosely Structured Thoughts on a Loosely Defined Topic." In *Secular Ritual.* Edited by S. F. Moore and B. G. Myerhoff, 25–35. Amsterdam: Van Gorcum & Comp. B.V.

Gouldner, Alvin. 1979. *The Future of Intellectuals and the Rise of the New Class.* New York: Seabury Press.

———. 1980. *The Two Marxisms.* New York: Oxford University Press.

Graff, Gerald. 1978. "The Politics of Anti-Realism." *Salmagundi* 42: 4–30.

Grainger, R. 1974. *The Language of the Rite.* London: Darton, Longman & Todd.

Gramsci, Antonio. 1971. *The Prison Notebooks: Selections.* Translated by Quintin Hoare and Geoffrey Nowell Smith. New York: International Publishers.

"Great Lakes: Alexian Brothers Break Contract with Menominees." 1975. *Akwesasne Notes* 7 (Early Autumn): 16.

Gregg, Richard B., and Gerard A. Hauser. 1973. "Richard Nixon's April 30, 1970 Address on Cambodia: The 'Ceremony' of Confrontation." *Speech Monographs* 40: 167–81.

Grice, H. P. 1975. "Logic and Conversation." In *Syntax and Semantics,* vol.

3, *Speech Acts.* Edited by P. Cole and J. Morgan. New York: Academic Press.

Grimaldi, William M. A. 1972. *Studies in the Philosophy of Aristotle's Rhetoric.* Wiesbaden: Franz Steiner Verlag.

Grimes, R. L. 1982. *Beginnings in Ritual Studies.* Lanham, Md.: University Press of America.

Gronbeck, B. E. 1978. "The Functions of Presidential Campaigning." *Communication Monographs* 45: 268–80.

———. 1982. "On Classes of Inference and Force." In *Explorations in Rhetoric: Studies in Honor of Douglas Ehninger.* Glenview, Ill.: Scott, Foresman.

Gross, Alan G. 1983. "Analogy and Intersubjectivity: Political Oratory, Scholarly Argument and Scientific Reports." *Quarterly Journal of Speech* 69: 37–46.

Grossberg, Lawrence. 1979. "Marxist Dialectics and Rhetorical Criticism." *Quarterly Journal of Speech* 65: 235–49.

Gupta, Shefali. 1974. *Between Skepticism and Rationalism.* Calcutta: Scientific Book Agency.

Habermas, Jurgen. 1970. "On Systematically Distorted Communication." *Inquiry* 13: 205–18.

———. 1971. *Knowledge and Human Interests.* Translated by Jeremy J. Shapiro. Boston: Beacon Press.

———. 1973. *Theory and Practice.* Translated by John Viertel. Boston: Beacon Press.

———. 1979. *Communication and the Evolution of Society.* Translated by Thomas McCarthy. Boston: Beacon Press.

———. 1984. *The Theory of Communicative Action: Reason and the Rationalization of Society.* Translated by Thomas McCarthy. Boston: Beacon Press.

———. 1987. *The Philosophical Discourse of Modernity.* Cambridge: M.I.T. Press.

Halloran, S. M. 1982. "Rhetoric in the American College Curriculum." *PRE/TEXT* 3: 244–69.

Hample, D. 1981. "What Is a Good Argument?" In *Dimensions of Argument: Proceedings of the Second Summer Conference on Argumentation.* Edited by G. Ziegelmueller and J. Rhodes, 875–93. Annandale, Va.: Speech Communication Association.

Hardwig, J. 1973. "The Achievement of Moral Rationality." *Philosophy and Rhetoric* 6: 171–85.

Harman, Gilbert. 1980. *Change in View: Principles of Reasoning.* Cambridge: M.I.T. Press.

Harpine, William D. 1985. "Can Rhetoric and Dialectic Serve the Purposes of Logic?" *Philosophy and Rhetoric* 18: 96–112.

Hartung, Frank E. 1954. "Cultural Relativity and Moral Judgments." *Philosophy of Science* 21: 118–26.

Haskell, T. L. 1984. *The Authority of Experts.* Bloomington: Indiana University Press.

Heath, R. L. 1979. "Kenneth Burke on Form." *Quarterly Journal of Speech* 65: 392–404.

Heilbroner, R. 1985. *Marxism For and Against*. New York: Norton.

Hekman, Susan J. 1986. *Hermeneutics and the Sociology of Knowledge*. South Bend: University of Notre Dame Press.

Hesse, M. 1980. *Revolutions and Reconstructions in the Philosophy of Science*. Brighton: Harvester Press.

Hiebert, Ray Eldon, Donald F. Ungurait, and Thomas W. Bohn. 1974. *Mass Media: An Introduction to Modern Communication*. New York: David McKay.

Hikins, James W. 1981. "George Campbell and Immanuel Kant on Synthetic *A Priori* Judgments." Paper delivered at the convention of the Speech Communication Association.

Hikins, James W., and Kenneth S. Zagacki. 1988. "Rhetoric, Philosophy, and Objectivism: An Attenuation of the Claims of the Rhetoric of Inquiry." *Quarterly Journal of Speech* 74: 201–28.

Hilgartner, S., R. Bell, and R. O'Connor. 1982. *Nukespeak*. New York: Penguin Books.

Hilpinen, R. 1982. "Rescher's Theory of Cognitive Systematization." In *Praxis and Reason: Studies in the Philosophy of Nicholas Rescher*. Edited by R. Almeder, 28–53. Lanham, Md.: University Press of America.

Hirsh, E. D., Jr. 1982. "The Politics of Theories of Interpretation." *Critical Inquiry* 9: 235–47.

Hoban, J. L., Jr. 1980. "Rhetorical Rituals of Rebirth." *Quarterly Journal of Speech* 66: 275–88.

Hochmuth [Nichols], M. 1952. "Kenneth Burke and the 'New Rhetoric.'" *Quarterly Journal of Speech* 38: 133–44.

Hofstadter, Richard. 1955. *The Age of Reform: From Bryan to F.D.R.* New York: Vintage Books.

Hogan, J. Michael. 1987. "Apocalyptic Pornography and the Nuclear Freeze: A Defense of the Public." Summer conference on Argumentation, Alta, Utah.

Hollihan, Thomas A., Patricia Riley, and Keith Freadhoff. 1986. "Arguing for Justice: An Analysis of Arguing in Small Claims Court." *Journal of the American Forensic Association* 22: 187–95.

Hollinger, Robert. 1985. "Practical Reason and Hermeneutics." *Philosophy and Rhetoric* 18: 113–22.

"Hoopa Tribe Demands Removal of Federal Officers." 1978. *Wassaja* 6 (October/November): 6.

Horkheimer, M., and T. W. Adorno. 1972. *The Dialectic of Enlightenment*. Translated by John Cumming. New York: Herder and Herder.

Hunt, Everett Lee. 1965. "Plato and Aristotle on Rhetoric and Rhetoricians." In *Readings in Rhetoric*. Edited by Lionel Crocker and Paul A. Carmack, 144–59. Springfield: Charles C. Thomas.

Hyde, Michael J., and C. R. Smith. 1979. "Hermeneutics and Rhetoric: A Seen but Unobserved Relationship." *Quarterly Journal of Speech* 65: 347–63.

Jaeger, Werner. 1939. *Paideia: The Ideals of Greek Culture*. Vol. I. Translated by Gilbert Highet. New York: Oxford University Press.

James, William. 1969. *The Letters of William James.* Vol. II. Edited by Henry James. Boston: Atlantic Monthly Press.

Jameson, Fredric. 1972. *The Prison-House of Language: A Critical Account of Structuralism and Russian Formalism.* Princeton: Princeton University Press.

Japp, Phyllis M. 1985. "Esther or Isaiah?: The Abolitionist-Feminist Rhetoric of Angeline Grimke." *Quarterly Journal of Speech* 71: 335–48.

Jasinski, J. 1986. "A Pragmatic Account of Rhetorical Force." *Belfast Working Papers in Language and Linguistics* 8: 124–44.

_____. 1987a. "The Feminization of Liberty and the Ambiguity of Power." Paper presented at the Speech Communication Association Convention, Boston.

_____. 1987b. "Liberty and Power in Nineteenth-Century Public Argument: A Foucaultian Analysis of Jacksonian Rhetoric." In *Argument and Critical Practice: Proceedings of the Fifth SCA/AFA Conference on Argumentation.* Edited by J. W. Wenzel. Annandale, Va.: Speech Communication Association.

_____. 1988. "Ideology, Reflection, and Alienation in Rhetorical and Argumentative Practice." *Journal of the American Forensic Association* 24: 207–17.

Jerry, E. Claire. 1987. "Rhetoric as Epistemic: Implications of a Theoretical Position." In *Visions of Rhetoric: History, Theory and Criticism.* Edited by Charles W. Kneupper, 119–31. Arlington, Tex.: Rhetoric Society of America.

Johnstone, Henry W., Jr. 1970. *The Problem of Self.* University Park: Pennsylvania State University Press.

Jung, C. G. [1966] 1977a. *The Archetypes and the Collective Unconscious.* Vol. 9, pt. 1 of *The Collected Works of C. G. Jung.* Edited by H. Read, M. Fordham, and G. Adler. Translated by R. F. C. Hull. Bollingen Series 20. 2d ed. Reprint, Princeton: Princeton University Press.

_____. [1966] 1977b. *Two Essays on Analytical Psychology.* Vol. 7 of *The Collected Works of C. G. Jung.* Edited by H. Read, M. Fordham, and G. Adler. Translated by R. F. C. Hull. Bollingen Series 20. 2d ed. Reprint, Princeton: Princeton University Press.

Kahn, Herman. 1965. *On Escalation: Metaphors and Scenarios.* New York: Frederick A. Praeger.

Karon, L. 1976. "Presence in the New Rhetoric." *Philosophy & Rhetoric* 9: 96–111.

Kaufer, David S. 1979. "The Ironist and Hypocrite as Presidential Symbols: A Nixon-Kennedy Analog." *Communication Quarterly* 27: 20–26.

Keane, C. 1983. "Native Americans Say They Learned to Kill Vietnamese Not Talk to Them." *Wassaja* 10 (March/April): 7.

Keith, William M., and Richard A. Cherwitz. 1989. "Objectivity, Disagreement, and the Rhetoric of Inquiry." In *Rhetoric in the Human Sciences.* Edited by Herbert W. Simons, 195–210. London: Sage Publications.

Kekes, John. 1976. *A Justification of Rationality.* Albany: State University of New York Press.

Kellner, Douglas. 1982. "TV, Ideology, and Emancipatory Popular Culture."

In *Television: The Critical View,* 3rd ed. Edited by Horace Newcomb, 386–421. New York: Oxford University Press.

Kills Straight. 1973. "Respected, Not Ignored." *Wassaja* 1 (July): 3.

Kirkpatrick, Walter G. 1981. "Bolingbroke and the Opposition to Sir Robert Walpole: The Role of a Fictitious *Persona* in Creating an Audience." *Central States Speech Journal* 32: 12–22.

Klein, Paul. 1972. "The Television Audience and Program Mediocrity." In *Mass Media and Society: Introduction.* Edited by Alan Wells. Mountain View, Calif.: Mayfield Publishing.

Klumpp, J., and T. A. Hollihan. 1979. "Debunking the Resignation of Earl Butz: Sacrificing an Official Racist." *Quarterly Journal of Speech* 65: 1–11.

Kraditor, Aileen S. 1965. *The Ideas of the Women's Suffrage Movement, 1890–1920.* New York: Columbia University Press.

LaFlesche, F. 1925. *The Osage Tribe: Rite of Vigil.* 39th Annual Report of the Bureau of American Ethnology. Washington, D.C.: Smithsonian Institution.

Lake, R. A. 1983. "Enacting Red Power: The Consummatory Function in Native American Protest Rhetoric." *Quarterly Journal of Speech* 69: 127–42.

Lake, R. A., and C. M. Keough. 1985. "Exploring the Boundaries of Technical and Social Knowledge: A Case Study in Arbitration Arguments." In *Argument and Social Practice: Proceedings of the Fourth SCA/AFA Conference on Argumentation.* Edited by J. R. Cox, M. O. Sillars, and G. B. Walker, 483–96. Annandale, Va.: Speech Communication Association.

Lakoff, George, and Mark Johnson. 1980. *Metaphors We Live By.* Chicago: University of Chicago Press.

Lame Deer, J., and R. Erdoes. 1972. *Lame Deer, Seeker of Visions.* New York: Simon & Schuster.

Lang, Berel. 1975. "Space, Time, and Philosophical Style." *Critical Inquiry* 2: 263–80.

Langer, Susanne K. 1953. *Feeling and Form: A Theory of Art.* New York: Scribner.

————. [1957] 1973. *Philosophy in a New Key: A Study in the Symbolism of Reason, Rite, and Art.* 3d ed. Reprint, Cambridge, Mass.: Harvard University Press.

Lasch, Christopher. 1977. *The Culture of Narcissism.* New York: Norton.

————. 1978. "Recovering Reality." *Salmagundi* 42: 44–47.

Leach, Edmund R. 1968–79. "Ritual." In *International Encyclopedia of the Social Sciences.* 18 vols. Edited by D. L. Sills, 13: 520–26. New York: Macmillan and Free Press.

Leff, Michael C. 1978. "In Search of Ariadne's Thread: A Review of the Recent Literature on Rhetorical Theory." *Central States Speech Journal* 29: 73–91.

————. 1983a. "The Topics of Argumentative in Invention in Latin Rhetorical Theory from Cicero to Boethius." *Rhetorica* 1: 23–44.

————. 1983b. "Topical Invention and Metaphorical Interaction." *Southern Speech Communication Journal* 48: 214–29.

_____. 1985. "Recovering Aristotle: Rhetoric, Politics, and the Limits of Rationality." *Quarterly Journal of Speech* 71: 362–72.

Leff, Michael C., and D. E. Hewes. 1981. "Topical Invention and Group Communication: Towards a Sociology of Inference." In *Dimensions of Argument: Proceedings of the Second Summer Conference on Argumentation.* Edited by G. Ziegelmueller and J. Rhodes, 770–89. Annandale, Va.: Speech Communication Association.

Lehrer, K. 1978. "Systematic Justification: Selections from *Knowledge.*" In *Essays on Knowledge and Justification.* Edited by G. S. Pappas and M. Swain, 289–308. Ithaca, N.Y.: Cornell University Press.

Leiserson, Avery. 1968. "Public Opinion." *International Encyclopaedia of the Social Sciences.* Vol. 13. Edited by David L. Shills. New York: Macmillan and Free Press.

Lenin, V. I. 1961. *What Is to Be Done?* Translated by Joe Fineberg and George Hanna. New York: International Publishers.

Lentricchia, Frank. 1983. *Criticism and Social Change.* Chicago and London: University of Chicago Press.

"Let Us Act to Re-empower the People." 1983. *Akwesasne Notes* 15 (Late Winter): 23.

Lippmann, Walter. 1922. *Public Opinion.* New York: Macmillan.

_____. 1955. *The Public Philosophy.* New York: Mentor Books.

_____. 1963. "The Dilemma of Liberal Democracy." In *The Essential Lippmann.* Edited by C. Rossiter and J. Lare, 3–46. New York: Vintage.

_____. 1982. "The World Outside and the Pictures in Our Heads." In *Perspectives on Mass Communications.* Edited by Warren K. Agee, Phillip H. Ault, and Edwin Emery, 6–7. New York: Harper & Row.

Lodge, David. 1977. *The Modes of Modern Writing: Metaphor, Metonymy, and the Typology of Modern Literature.* Ithaca: Cornell University Press.

Lucey, K. 1976. "Toward Scales of Epistemic Appraisal." *Philosophical Studies* 29: 169–79.

Lukacs, Georg. 1964a. "In Search of the Bourgeois Man." In *Essays on Thomas Mann.* New York: Merlin Press.

_____. 1964b. "The Playful Style." In *Essays on Thomas Mann.* New York: Merlin Press.

_____. 1964c. "The Tragedy of Modern Art." In *Essays on Thomas Mann.* New York: Merlin Press.

_____. 1971. *History and Class Consciousness.* Translated by Rodney Livingstone. Cambridge, Mass.: M.I.T. Press.

Lyne, John, and Henry F. Howe. 1986. "'Punctuated Equilibria': Rhetorical Dynamics of a Scientific Controversy." *Quarterly Journal of Speech* 72: 132–47.

Lyotard, Jean-François. 1984. *The Postmodern Condition: A Report on Knowledge.* Translated by Geoff Bennington and Brian Massumi. Minneapolis: University of Minnesota Press.

McCarthy, Thomas. 1978. *The Critical Theory of Jurgen Habermas.* Cambridge and London: M.I.T. Press.

McCloskey, Donald N. 1983. "Notes on the Character of Argument in Modern Economics." In *Argument in Transition.* Edited by D. Zarefsky,

M. O. Sillars, and J. Rhodes. Annandale, Va.: Speech Communication Association.

———. 1985. *The Rhetoric of Economics.* Madison: University of Wisconsin Press.

McCloud, Janet. 1977. "A Tribute to Native Women Warriors." *Akwesasne Notes* 9 (Summer): 27.

McGee, Michael Calvin. 1980. "The 'Ideograph': A Link between Rhetoric and Ideology." *Quarterly Journal of Speech* 66: 1–16.

———. 1982. "A Materialist's Conception of Rhetoric." In *Explorations in Rhetoric: Studies in Honor of Douglas Ehninger.* Edited by Raymie E. McKerrow. Glenview, Ill.: Scott, Foresman.

McGee, Michael Calvin, and John R. Lyne. 1987. "What Are Nice People Like You Doing in a Place Like This? Some Entailments of Treating Knowledge Claims Rhetorically." In *The Rhetoric of the Human Sciences: Language and Argument in Scholarship and Public Affairs.* By John S. Nelson, Allan Megill, and Donald N. McCloskey, 381–406. Madison: University of Wisconsin Press.

McGee, Michael Calvin, and Martha A. Martin. 1983. "Public Knowledge and Ideological Argumentation." *Communication Monographs* 50: 47–65.

MacIntyre, Alasdair. 1984. *After Virtue.* Notre Dame, Ind.: University of Notre Dame Press.

McKeon, Zahava Karl. 1982. *Novels and Arguments: Inventing Rhetorical Criticism.* Chicago: University of Chicago Press.

McKerrow, Raymie E. 1976. "Rhetorical Validity: An Analysis of Three Perspectives on Reasoning." *Journal of the American Forensic Association* 13: 133–41.

———. 1982. "Rationality and Reasonableness in a Theory of Argument." In *Advances in Argument Theory and Research.* Edited by R. Cox and C. A. Willard, 105–22. Carbondale: Southern Illinois University Press.

———. 1986a. "Case Studies in Field Theory: An Introduction." *Journal of the American Forensic Association* 22: 185–86.

———. 1986b. "Pragmatic Justification and Perelman's Philosophy of Rhetoric." In *Practical Reasoning in Human Affairs: Studies in Honor of Chaim Perelman.* Edited by J. Golden and J. Pilotta, 207–26. Dordrecht: Reidel.

———. 1987a. "Rescher's Plausibility Thesis and the Justification of Arguments: A Critical Appraisal." In *Argumentation: Across the Lines of Discipline: Proceedings of the Conference on Argumentation, 1986.* Edited by F. Van Eemeren, R. Grootendorst, J. A. Blair, and C. A. Willard, 317–22. Dordrecht: Foris.

———. 1987b. "Coherentism and Contextualism and the Process of Justification." In *Argument and Critical Practices: Proceedings of the Fifth SCA/AFA Conference on Argumentation.* Edited by J. W. Wenzel, 215–21. Annandale, Va.: Speech Communication Association.

Mackin, Jim. 1987. "Meaning and Knowledge in a Pragmatic Theory of Rhetoric." Paper delivered at the Speech Communication Association Convention.

McKinney, Ronald J. 1987. "Sartre and the Politics of Deconstruction." *Philosophy and Social Criticism* 13: 327–41.

Mann, Thomas. [1948] 1966. *Dr. Faustus.* Translated by H. T. Lowe-Porter. New York: Modern Library.

———. [1927] 1969a. *The Magic Mountain.* Translated by H. T. Lowe-Porter. New York: Vintage Books.

———. [1953] 1969b. "The Making of *The Magic Mountain.*" In *The Magic Mountain.* Translated by H. T. Lowe-Porter. New York: Vintage Books. Originally published in *Atlantic Monthly,* January 1953.

———. 1982. *Thomas Mann: Diaries, 1918–1939.* Edited by Herman Kesten. New York: Abrams.

"Mapuches Continue Their Struggle." 1975. *Akwesasne Notes* 7 (Early Winter): 38–39.

Marcuse, Herbert. 1964. *One-Dimensional Man: Studies in the Ideology of Advanced Industrial Society.* Boston: Beacon Press.

———. 1978. *The Aesthetic Dimension: Toward a Critique of Marxist Aesthetics.* Boston: Beacon Press.

Maria, S., and M. C. Mohawk. 1977. "Brainwashing." *Akwesasne Notes* 9 (Summer): 31.

Marx, Karl. 1963. *The Eighteenth Brumaire of Louis Bonaparte.* New York: International Publishers.

———. 1972. "Theses on Feuerbach." In *The Marx-Engels Reader.* Edited by Robert C. Tucker. New York: Norton.

———. 1975. "On the Jewish Question." In *Early Writings.* Translated by Rodney Livingston and Gregor Benton. New York: Vintage Books.

Marx, Karl, and Frederick Engels. 1972. *The Communist Manifesto.* In *The Marx-Engels Reader.* Edited by Robert C. Tucker. New York: Norton.

———. 1975. *Collected Works.* Vol. 1. New York: International Publishers.

Mead, George Herbert. [1934] 1962. *Mind, Self, and Society from the Standpoint of a Social Behaviorist.* Vol. 1 of *Works of George Herbert Mead.* Edited by C. W. Morris. Reprint. Chicago: University of Chicago Press.

Mencken, H. L. 1955. "On Being an American." In *Prejudices.* Edited by J. T. Farrell. New York: Vintage Books.

"Menominee Defense." 1976. *Spirit of the People* 1 (March): 1, 3.

Miller, Thomas P. 1987. "Communication and Knowledge: Theorizing in a World Beyond Language." *Rhetoric Society Quarterly* 17: 433–46.

Mills, C. Wright. 1969. "The Politics of Responsibility." In *The New Left Reader.* Edited by Carl Oglesby. New York: Grove Press.

Mohawk, J. 1982. "Building a Traditional Resistance to Western Penetration." *Akwesasne Notes* 14 (Early Winter): 6–8.

Montaigne, Michel de. 1946. *The Essays of Montaigne.* Translated by George B. Ives. New York: Heritage Press.

Moore, S. F., and B. G. Myerhoff, eds. 1977. *Secular Ritual.* Amsterdam: Van Gorcum & Comp. B.V.

Moorehead, Warren K. 1914. *The American Indian in the United States, 1850–1914.* Andover, N.J.: Andover Press.

Moser, R. 1985. *Empirical Justification.* Dordrecht: Reidel.

Muller, F. M. n.d. "Persona." From "The Open Court." Vol. I, No. 20, n.p. Typescript.

Munz, Peter. 1987. "Philosophy and the Mirror of Rorty." In *Evolutionary Epistemology, Rationality, and the Sociology of Knowledge.* Edited by Gerard Radnitzky and William Warren Bartley III, 345–98. LaSalle, Ill.: Open Court.

Musil, Robert. 1980. *The Man without Qualities.* Translated by Eithne Wilkins and Ernst Kaiser. New York: Perigee Books. Originally published in English in 1953.

NASC News. n.d. Vol. 1, no. 2.

Native American Solidarity Committee. n.d. [Untitled leaflet concerning grand juries.] St. Paul, Minn.: n.p. Photocopy.

Nelson, John S. 1987. "Stories of Science and Politics: Some Rhetorics of Political Research." In *The Rhetoric of the Human Sciences: Language and Argument in Scholarship and Public Affairs.* Edited by John S. Nelson, Allan Megill, and Donald N. McCloskey, 198–220. Madison: University of Wisconsin Press.

Nelson, John S., and Allan Megill. 1986. "Rhetoric of Inquiry: Projects and Prospects." *Quarterly Journal of Speech* 72: 20–37.

Nelson, John S., Allan Megill, and Donald N. McCloskey. 1987. *The Rhetoric of the Human Sciences: Language and Argument in Scholarship and Public Affairs.* Madison: University of Wisconsin Press.

O'Keefe, B. J. 1988. "The Logic of Message Design: Individual Differences in Reasoning about Communication." *Communication Monographs* 55: 80–101.

O'Keefe, Daniel J. 1982. "The Concepts of Argument and Arguing." In *Advances in Argumentation Theory and Research.* Edited by J. Robert Cox and Charles Arthur Willard. Carbondale: Southern Illinois University Press.

———. 1985. "Argument Criticism and Willardian Skepticism." *Journal of the American Forensics Association* 21: 196–205.

"Opening Statements at Wounded Knee Trials." 1974. *Akwesasne Notes* 6 (Early Spring): 17.

Opler, Morris E. 1941. *An Apache Life-Way.* Chicago: University of Chicago Press.

Oravec, Christine. 1981. "John Muir, Yosemite, and the Sublime Response: A Study in the Rhetoric of Preservationism." *Quarterly Journal of Speech* 67: 245–58.

Orr, C. Jack. 1978. "How Shall We Say: 'Reality Is Socially Constructed through Communication'?" *Central States Speech Journal* 29: 263–75.

Osborn, Michael. 1963. "The Functions and Significance of Metaphor in Rhetoric Discourse." Dissertation, University of Florida.

———. 1967. "Archetypal Metaphor in Rhetoric: The Light-Dark Family." *Quarterly Journal of Speech* 53: 115–26.

———. 1977. "The Evolution of the Archetypal Sea in Rhetoric and Poetic." *Quarterly Journal of Speech* 63: 347–63.

———. 1982. "Metaphor: A Summary and Position Paper." Unpublished.

Osborn, M., and D. Ehninger. 1962. "The Metaphor in Public Address." *Speech Monographs* 39: 223–34.

Park, W. Z. 1938. *Shamanism in Western North America*. Evanston, Ill.: Northwestern University Press.

Patterson, Orlando. 1973–74. "Guilt, Relativism, and Black-White Relations." *American Scholar* 43: 123–32.

Payne, Keith. 1984. "What If We 'Ride Out' a Soviet First Strike?" *Washington Quarterly* 7: 85–92.

Peacock, J. L. 1975. *Consciousness and Change: Symbolic Anthropology in Evolutionary Perspective*. New York: John Wiley & Sons.

Peltier, L. 1982. "An Open Letter to National A.I.M. Leadership." *Eagle Wing Press*, November 17, 20.

Perelman, Chaim, and L. Olbrechts-Tyteca. [1969] 1971. *The New Rhetoric: A Treatise on Argumentation*. Translated by J. Wilkinson and P. Weaver. Notre Dame, Ind.: University of Notre Dame Press.

Persons, Stow. 1958. *American Minds: A History of Ideas*. New York: Holt, Rinehart & Winston.

"Pine Ridge After Wounded Knee: The Terror Goes On." n.d. *Akwesasne Notes* 7 (Early Summer 1975): n.p. In *Pine Ridge, June, 1975*. Compiled by American Indian Movement. St. Paul, Minn.: n.d., n.p. Photocopy.

Popper, Karl. 1963. *Conjectures and Refutations*. New York: Basic Books.

———. 1976. "Reason or Revolution?" In *The Positivist Dispute in German Sociology*. Edited by Theodor W. Adorno et al., 288–300. New York: Harper & Row.

Poulakos, John. 1987. "Sophistical Rhetoric as a Critique of Culture." In *Argument and Critical Practices*. Edited by Joseph Wenzel, 97–102. Annandale, Va.: Speech Communication Association.

Poulakos, Takis. 1987. "Recovering the Voices of the Text: Rhetorical Criticism as Ideological Critique." In *Argument and Critical Practices*. Edited by Joseph Wenzel, 39–44. Annandale, Va.: Speech Communication Association.

Powers, W. K. 1977. *Oglala Religion*. Lincoln: University of Nebraska Press.

Putnam, Hilary. 1981. *Reason, Truth, and History*. Cambridge: Cambridge University Press.

Railsback, Celeste Condit. 1983. "Beyond Rhetorical Relativism: A Structural-Material Model of Truth and Objective Reality." *Quarterly Journal of Speech* 69: 351–63.

Rarick, David L., M. B. Duncan, D. G. Lee, and L. W. Porter. 1977. "The Carter Persona: An Empirical Analysis of the Rhetorical Visions of Campaign '76." *Quarterly Journal of Speech* 63: 258–73.

Rathbun, John W. 1969. "The Problem of Judgment and Effect in Historical Criticism: A Proposed Solution." *Western Speech* 33: 146–59.

Ray, J. W. 1978. "Perelman's Universal Audience." *Quarterly Journal of Speech* 64: 361–75.

Reagan, R. 1984. "Text of the Second Reagan-Mondale Debate." *Washington Post*, October 22.

Redner, H. 1987. "Pathologies of Science." *Social Epistemology* 1: 215–47.

"Reign of Terror Continues in S. Dakota." 1975. *Akwesasne Notes* 7 (Early Autumn): 4–9.

Reik, T. [1946] 1958. *Ritual: Psycho-Analytic Studies*. Vol. 1 of *The Psycho-*

logical Problems of Religion. Translated by D. Bryan. New York: Farrar, Straus & Co. Reprint. New York: International Universities Press.

Rescher, N. 1976. *Plausible Reasoning.* Amsterdam: Van Gorcum.

———. 1977. *Dialectics: A Controversy-Oriented Approach to the Theory of Knowledge.* Albany: State University of New York.

———. 1979. *Cognitive Systematization.* Totowa: Rowman and Littlefield.

———. 1980. *Induction.* Pittsburgh: University of Pittsburgh Press.

———. 1982. *Empirical Inquiry.* Totowa: Rowman and Littlefield.

Ricoeur, P. 1977. *The Rule of Metaphor.* Toronto: University of Toronto Press.

Rojas, J. C. 1976. "Native People in Guatemala Need Our Help!" *Akwesasne Notes* 8 (Early Spring): 3–5.

Rorty, Richard. 1979. *Philosophy and the Mirror of Nature.* Princeton: Princeton University Press.

Ross, A., and S. Most. 1976. "A.I.M. Seeking New Strength in Spiritual Roots of the Indians." *Kansas City Times,* September 2, sec. C.

Rosten, Leo. 1977. "The Intellectual and the Mass Media: Some Rigorously Random Remarks." In *Mass Media Issues: Articles and Commentaries.* Edited by Leonard L. Sellers and William L. Rivers. Englewood Cliffs, N.J.: Prentice-Hall.

Rowland, R. C. 1981. "Argument Fields." In *Dimensions of Argument: Proceedings of the Second Summer Conference on Argumentation.* Edited by G. Ziegelmueller and J. Rhodes, 56–79. Annandale, Va.: Speech Communication Association.

———. 1982. "The Influence of Purpose on Fields of Argument." *Journal of the American Forensics Association* 18: 228–45.

———. 1985. "On Argument Evaluation." *Journal of the American Forensics Association* 21: 123–32.

———. 1987. "Narrative: Mode of Discourse or Paradigm?" *Communication Monographs* 54: 264–74.

Rushing, Janet Hocker. 1985. "'E.T.' as Rhetorical Transcendence." *Quarterly Journal of Speech* 71: 188–203.

Rushing, Janet Hocker, and Thomas S. Frentz. 1980. "'The Deer Hunter': Rhetoric of the Warrior." *Quarterly Journal of Speech* 66: 392–406.

Ryan, M. 1982. *Marxism and Deconstruction: A Critical Articulation.* Baltimore: Johns Hopkins University Press.

Sandman, Peter M., David M. Rubin, and David B. Sachsman. 1972. *Media: An Introductory Analysis of American Mass Communications.* Englewood Cliffs, N.J.: Prentice-Hall.

Sayers, Sean. 1985. *Reality and Reason.* Oxford: Basil Blackwell.

Scheer, R. 1983. *With Enough Shovels.* New York: Vintage Books.

Scheffler, I. 1967. *Science and Subjectivity.* New York: Bobbs-Merrill.

Schramm, Wilbur. 1972. "How Communication Works." In *Mass Media and Society.* Edited by Alan Wells, 16–29. Palo Alto, Calif.: Mayfield Publishing.

Schweder, R. 1986. "Untitled Review." *New York Times Book Review* 39.

Scott, Robert L. 1964. "Some Implications of Existentialism for Rhetoric." *Central States Speech Journal* 15: 267–78.

_____. 1967. "On Viewing Rhetoric as Epistemic." *Central States Speech Journal* 18: 9–17.

_____. 1976. "On Viewing Rhetoric as Epistemic: Ten Years Later." *Central States Speech Journal* 27: 258–66.

_____. 1988. "Non-Discipline as a Remedy for Rhetoric? A Reply to Victor Vitanza." *Rhetoric Review* 6: 233–37.

Scult, A. 1979. "Rhetoric and Magic: A Comparison of Two Types of Religious Action." In *Rhetoric 78: Proceedings of "Theory of Rhetoric: An Interdisciplinary Conference."* Edited by R. L. Brown and M. Steinmann, Jr., 321–38. Minneapolis: University of Minnesota Center for Advanced Studies in Language, Style, and Literary Theory.

Searle, J. R. 1969. *Speech Acts.* London: Cambridge University Press.

Seaton, James. 1980. "Dialectics: Freedom of Speech and Thought." *Journal of the History of Ideas* 41: 283–92.

Shaughnessy, J. D., ed. 1973. *The Roots of Ritual.* Grand Rapids, Mich.: Eerdmans.

Shorris, Earl. 1982. "Market Democracy." In *Perspectives on Mass Communication.* Edited by Warren K. Agee, Phillip H. Ault, and Edwin Emery, 34–38. New York: Harper & Row.

Simons, Herbert W. 1985. "Chronicle and Critique of a Conference." *Quarterly Journal of Speech* 71: 52–64.

_____. 1989. "Kenneth Burke and the Rhetoric of the Human Sciences." In *The Legacy of Kenneth Burke.* Edited by Herbert W. Simons and Trevor Melia, 3–27. Madison: University of Wisconsin Press.

Sloane, Thomas O. 1965. "The Persona as Rhetor: An Interpretation of Donne's *Satyre III.*" *Quarterly Journal of Speech* 51: 14–27.

Smith, C. R., and D. M. Hunsaker. 1972. *The Bases of Argument.* Indianapolis: Bobbs-Merrill.

Socolow, R. H. 1976. "Failures of Discourse: Obstacles to the Integration of Environmental Values into National Resource Policy." In *When Values Conflict.* Edited by L. H. Tribe, C. S. Schelling, and J. Voss, 1–34. Cambridge: Ballinger.

Solmsen, Friedrich, ed. 1954. *The Rhetoric and the Poetics of Aristotle.* Translated by W. R. Roberts and I. Bywater. New York: Modern Library.

Solomon, M. 1983. "Villainless Quest: Myth, Metaphor, and Dream in 'Chariots of Fire.'" *Communication Quarterly* 31: 274–81.

Solomon, Robert C. 1973. "Emotions and Choice." *Review of Metaphysics* 27: 20–41.

_____. 1977. *Introducing Philosophy.* New York: Harcourt, Brace, Jovanovich.

Special Issue: Review Symposium on Argument Fields. 1982. *Journal of the American Forensic Association* 18: 191–258.

Spitzer, Leo. 1946. "Note on the Poetic and the Empirical 'I' in Medieval Authors." *Traditio* 4: 414–22.

"A Statement from John Trudell." 1975. *Akwesasne Notes* 7 (Early Autumn): 14.

Stelzner, H. 1977. "Ford's War on Inflation: A Metaphor That Did Not Cross." *Communication Monographs* 44: 284–97.

Stich, S. P., and R. Nisbett. 1984. "Expertise, Justification, and the Psychology of Inductive Reasoning." In *The Authority of Experts*. Edited by T. L. Haskell. Bloomington: Indiana University Press.

Stumbo, B. 1986. "A World Apart." *Los Angeles Times Magazine*, June 15, 10–21.

Sullivan, William M. 1982. *Reconstructing Public Philosophy*. Berkeley: University of California Press.

Swanson, David L. 1977. "A Reflective View of the Epistemology of Critical Inquiry." *Communication Monographs* 44: 207–19.

Thompson, W. R. 1975. *Aristotle's Deduction and Induction: Introductory Analysis and Synthesis*. Amsterdam: Rodopi N.V.

Toulmin, Stephen E. [1958] 1974. *The Uses of Argument*. Cambridge: Cambridge University Press.

———. 1972. *Human Understanding*. Princeton: Princeton University Press.

Trent, Judith S. 1978. "Presidential Surfacing: The Ritualistic and Crucial First Act." *Communication Monographs* 45: 281–92.

Tsipis, Kosta. 1983. *Arsenal*. New York: Simon & Schuster.

Tucker, Charles O., and Gerald L. Wilson. 1980. "Confrontation Rhetoric in Institutional Settings: A Rational Process." *Central States Speech Journal* 31: 42–51.

Turner, F. W. III, ed. 1974. *The Portable North American Indian Reader*. New York: Viking Press.

Turner, Victor R. 1969. *The Ritual Process: Structure and Anti-Structure*. New York: Aldine Publishing.

———. 1974. *Dramas, Fields and Metaphors: Symbolic Action in Human Society*. Ithaca, N.Y.: Cornell University Press.

———. 1980. "Social Dramas and Stories about Them." *Critical Inquiry* 7: 141–68.

"Two Warriors Die: But Struggle Goes On." 1976. *Akwesasne Notes* 5 (Early Spring): 16–18.

Underhill, R. M. 1965. *Red Man's Religion*. Chicago: University of Chicago Press.

van Eemeren, F. H., and R. Grootendorst. 1983. *Speech Acts in Argumentative Discussions*. Dordrecht: Foris Publications.

Van Gennep, A. 1960. *The Rites of Passage*. Translated by M. B. Vizedom and G. L. Caffee. Chicago: University of Chicago Press.

Van Matre, L. 1986. "Eurythmics' Style Isn't Skin Deep." [Pasadena, Calif.] *Star-News Plus*, August 20, sec. A.

Vasaly, Ann. 1985. "The Masks of Rhetoric: Cicero's *Pro Roscio Amerino*." *Rhetorica* 3: 1–20.

Vatz, Richard L. 1973. "The Myth of the Rhetorical Situation." *Philosophy and Rhetoric* 6: 154–61.

Voelker, Francis H., and Ludmila A. Voelker, eds. 1975. *Mass Media: Forces in Our Society*. New York: Harcourt Brace Jovanovich.

Voices from Wounded Knee, 1973. 1974. Rooseveltown, N.Y.: Akwesasne Notes.

von Wright, Georg Henrik. 1972. "Wittgenstein on Certainty." *Problems in the Theory of Knowledge*, 47–60. The Hague: Martinus Nijhoff.

Wallace, K. 1963. "The Substance of Rhetoric: Good Reasons." *Quarterly Journal of Speech* 49: 239–49.

Wander, Philip. 1983. "The Ideological Turn in Modern Criticism." *Central States Speech Journal* 34: 1–18.

_____. 1984. "The Third Persona: An Ideological Turn in Rhetorical Theory." *Central States Speech Journal* 35: 197–216.

_____. 1985. "The Place of Morality in the Modern World." In *Argument and Social Practice: Proceedings of the Fourth SCA/AFA Conference on Argumentation.* Edited by R. Cox, M. Sillars, and G. Walker, 323–49. Annandale, Va.: Speech Communication Association.

Ware, B. L., and W. A. Linkugel. 1982. "The Rhetorical Persona: Marcus Garvey as Black Moses." *Communication Monographs* 49: 50–62.

Warnick, Barbara. 1983. "A Rhetorical Analysis of Episteme Shift: Darwin's *Origin of the Species.*" *Southern Speech Communication Journal* 49: 26–42.

_____. 1987. "The Narrative Paradigm: Another Story." *Quarterly Journal of Speech* 73: 172–82.

Warren, Helen. 1987. "The Truth Lies Somewhere Between the Two: Feminist Formulations on Critical Theory and Practice." In *Argument and Critical Practices.* Edited by Joseph Wenzel. Annandale, Va.: Speech Communication Association.

Watt, Ian. 1957. *The Rise of the Novel.* Berkeley: University of California Press.

_____. 1979. *Conrad in the Nineteenth Century.* Berkeley: University of California Press.

Weaver, R. A. 1982. "Acknowledgment of Victory and Defeat: The Reciprocal Ritual." *Central States Speech Journal* 33: 480–89.

Weaver, Richard M. 1948. *Ideas Have Consequences.* Chicago: University of Chicago Press.

Weiler, Michael. 1985. "Political Pluralism and Ideological Argument." In *Argument and Social Practice: Proceedings of the Fourth Annual SCA/AFA Conference on Argumentation.* Edited by J. Robert Cox, Malcolm O. Sillars, and Gregg B. Walker, 277–88. Annandale, Va.: Speech Communication Association.

Weimar, Walter B. 1979. *Notes on the Methodology of Scientific Research.* Hillsdale, N.J.: Lawrence Erlbaum Associates.

_____. 1983. "CCR Is Not Completely Confused Rhetoric (and There Is No Need to 'Pan' It)." In *Absolute Values and the Creation of the New World,* Vol. II, 1101–18. New York: International Cultural Foundation Press.

Weiss, T. B. 1975. "Media Speaks with Forked Tongue: The Unsuccessful Rhetoric of Wounded Knee." Paper Presented at the 61st Annual Meeting of the Speech Communication Association, Houston, Texas, December.

Wenzel, J. W. 1982. "In Defense of Criticism." Paper presented at a Meeting of the Speech Communication Association, Louisville, Kentucky.

"'When in the Course of Human Events': An Interview with Carter Camp." 1973. *Akwesasne Notes* 5 (Early Autumn): 11.

White, James Boyd. 1984. *When Words Lose Their Meaning: Constitutions and Reconstitutions of Language, Character, and Community.* Chicago: University of Chicago Press.

Whitney, Frederick C. 1975. *Mass Media and Mass Communications in Society.* Dubuque, Iowa: William C. Brown.

"Who We Are." 1976. *Spirit of the People* 1 (April): 4.

Willard, Charles Arthur. 1978. "A Reformulation of the Concept of Argument: The Constructivist/Interactionist Foundations of a Sociology of Argument." *Journal of the American Forensic Association* 14: 121–40.

————. 1981. "The Status of the Non-Discursiveness Thesis." *Journal of the American Forensic Association* 17: 190–214.

————. 1982a. "Argument Fields, Sociologies of Knowledge, and Critical Epistemology." Paper presented at a meeting of the Speech Communication Association, Louisville, Kentucky.

————. 1982b. "Argument Fields." In *Advances in Argumentation Theory and Research.* Edited by J. R. Cox and Charles Arthur Willard, 24–77. Carbondale: Southern Illinois University Press.

————. 1983a. *Argumentation and the Social Grounds of Knowledge.* University, Ala.: University of Alabama Press.

————. 1983b. "The Balkanization of Knowledge and the Problem of the Public Sphere." Paper presented at the Wake Forest Conference on Argumentation in Winston-Salem, North Carolina, November.

————. 1985. "Cassandra's Heirs." In *Argument and Social Practice: Proceedings of the Fourth SCA/AFA Conference on Argumentation.* Edited by R. Cox, M. Sillars, and G. Walker, 16–34. Annandale, Va.: Speech Communication Association.

————. 1987a. "Valuing Dissensus." In *Argumentation: Across the Lines of Discipline.* Edited by F. H. van Eemeren, R. Grootendorst, J. A. Blair, and C. A. Willard, 145–57. Dordrecht: Foris.

————. 1987b. "Argumentation et le Principe Social du Reconnaissance." Paper for *Argumentation et Signification.* Cerisy La Salle, France.

————. 1989a. *A Theory of Argumentation.* Tuscaloosa: University of Alabama Press.

————. 1989b. "The Balkanization of Knowledge and the Problem of the Public Sphere." Unpublished manuscript. University of Louisville.

Willard, Charles Arthur, and T. J. Hynes. 1989. "Valuing Dissensus." Unpublished manuscript. University of Louisville.

Willkie, R. W. 1974. "The Marxian Rhetoric of Angelica Balabanoff." *Quarterly Journal of Speech* 60: 450–58.

Windes, Russell, and Arthur Hastings. 1965. *Argumentation and Advocacy.* New York: Random House.

Wright, Erik Olin. 1985. *Classes.* London: Verso.

Wright, George T. 1960. *The Poet in the Poem.* Berkeley: University of California Press.

Wright, Michael. 1985. "National Security's New Insiders." *New York Times Magazine,* March 3.

Zarefsky, David. 1976. "Argument as Hypothesis-Testing." Paper delivered at the convention of the Speech Association Convention.

————. 1977. "President Johnson's War on Poverty—The Rhetoric of Three 'Establishment' Movements." *Communication Monographs* 44: 352–73.

————. 1981. "Reasonableness in Public Policy Argument: Fields as Institutions." In *Dimensions of Argument: Proceedings of the Second Summer Conference on Argumentation.* Edited by G. Ziegelmueller and J. Rhodes, 88–100. Annandale, Va.: Speech Communication Association.

———. 1982. "Persistent Questions in the Theory of Argument Fields." *Journal of the American Forensic Association* 18: 191–203.

Zukin, Cliff. 1981. "Mass Communication and Public Opinion." In *Handbook of Political Communication.* Edited by Dan D. Nimmo and Keith R. Sanders, 359–90. Beverly Hills: Sage Publications.

Contributors

James Arnt Aune is Assistant Professor of Speech Communication at St. Olaf College. Aune has written extensively on rhetoric and contemporary critical theory.

J. Robert Cox is Associate Professor of Speech Communication at the University of North Carolina at Chapel Hill. Co-editor of *Advances in Argumentation Theory and Research* (with Charles Arthur Willard), Cox pursues argument not only as critical practice but also in practice as an advocate for the Sierra Club.

Earl Croasmun is Assistant Professor of Speech Communication at the University of Georgia. He is a frequent critic of consensus theory, and his work has appeared in the *Quarterly Journal of Speech* and *Pre/Text*.

G. Thomas Goodnight is Associate Professor of Communication Studies at Northwestern University. As a proponent of nuclear criticism, Goodnight has published widely on critical issues relative to various "publics."

Michael David Hazen is Associate Professor of Speech Communication at Wake Forest University.

James Jasinski is Assistant Professor of Speech Communication at Southern Illinois University at Carbondale. He is a 1986 winner of the Speech Communication Association dissertation award (from Northwestern University).

Charles Kauffman is Assistant Professor of Communication Studies and Director of Debate at Northwestern University. An authority on argument and classical rhetoric, Kauffman has published primarily in *Philosophy and Rhetoric.*

Randall A. Lake is Associate Professor in the Department of Communication Arts and Sciences and Director of Debate at the University of Southern California. His scholarly interests include contemporary argumentation practices and criticism. He has published in *The Quarterly Journal of Speech, Communication Monographs,* and *Signs.*

Raymie E. McKerrow is Professor of Speech Communication at the University of Maine at Orono. Editor of *Explorations in Rhetoric,* McKerrow is a former editor of the *Journal of the American Forensic Association.*

Donn W. Parson is Associate Professor of Communication Studies at the University of Kansas. Most recently as editor of *American Forensics in Perspective,* Parson has long been an important figure in American forensics.

Robert C. Rowland is Assistant Professor of Communication Studies and Director of Debate at the University of Kansas. Rowland is author of *The Rhetoric of Menachem Begin: The Myth of Redemption Through Return.*

Michael Weiler is Assistant Professor of Communication Studies at Emerson College. A student of ideology and criticism, Weiler has written on American contemporary political rhetoric.

Charles Arthur Willard is Associate Professor of Communication at the University of Louisville. Author of *Argumentation and the Social Grounds of Knowledge,* Willard was co-editor of *Advances in Argumentation Theory and Research* (with J. Robert Cox). His most recent book is *A Theory of Argumentation.*

David Cratis Williams is Assistant Professor of Speech Communication in the Division of Language and Literature, Northeast Missouri State University.

Index

Absolute certainty, 42
Absolutism, 41
Abstraction, 165
Action, 20, 29, 30; purposive, 10; appropriate, 18; symbolic, 54, 70, 73; political, 171
Actors, 151; social, 64; public, 151; democratic, 181
Acts: symbolic, 60–64; rhetorical, 70; instrumental, 71; ritual, 72
Address: political, 180; public, 180, 185
Affairs, contingent, 141
Analogy, 94
Analytic epistemology, 31
Annis, D., 21, 24
Anomie, 135
Anticipation, 55
Antitheory, 41
Apodictic claims, 31
Applied formalism, 3, 4, 14 (n. 1). *See also* Analytic epistemology
Appropriate actions, 18
Appropriateness of claim, 58
A priori values, 44
Archetype, 88 (n. 1); metaphor, 62
Arendt, H., 192
Arguing, 9, 11; as a communication practice, 6; by form, 114
Argument, 43, 81, 91, 92, 104, 108, 110, 114, 115, 120, 124, 126, 128, 129; in-use, 3; practice, 5, 11; social condi-

tions of, 8; field, 11, 139, 152; dominant forms of, 12; validity of 29; commensurability of, 43; topical, 55; nondiscursive, 83; distance, 99; public, 99, 119, 158, 170; type I, 104, 105; type II, 105; fictional, 106; messages, 109; of unrejoined advocates, 110; dialogic, 111; deliberative, 115; criticism, 120, 130; evaluation, 124–34 passim; critic, 126; fields of, 127; consistent, 128; counter-, 128; quality, 130; pedagogy, 143; techniques and skills, 152; rational, 164; rhetorical, 164. *See also* Debate; Logic; Reasoning
Argumentation, 93, 119; epistemic merit of, 121
Argument Theory: normative dimension of, 2, 3, 8
Argumentative: movement, 56; form, 65, 165; stance, 149; grammar, 168–69
Aristotle, 54, 55–57, 93–94, 122, 141–42, 157; *Rhetoric*, 68 (n. 6)
Arnold, C., 3
Art: high, 162; tragic, 193
Assembly, public, 176
Assent, 1, 2, 32, 53, 70, 83, 91–92; rational, 2–3; justified, 3, 12, 174–76, 185, 192; idealist criteria for, 4; systematic, 17, 32; producing force, 65;

Corrigible nature, 20
Cost-benefit analysis, 138–39, 150
Counterarguments, 128
Crisis: epistemic, 119; capitalist, 162
Critic, 150; task of the, 3; argument, 126
Critical: practice, 6, 10, 14; reason, 43; thinking, 126; Marxism, 160–62, 166; Marxist, 165; discourse, 167–70
Criticism, 12, 22, 48, 130, 192; ideological, 12; perception, 22; argument, 120, 130, rhetorical, 192
Critique, 13, 162, 186; postmodern, 145; of ideology, 171; of television, 184
Culture, 186; postmodern, 2; of discourse, 167–68, 184; public, 185

Dancing, 71
Davidson, D., 138–40
Debate, 43, 124; sound, 151. See also Argument
Debord, G., 1
Decision-maker, 148, 150
Decision-making, 22–23, 119, 126, 143–44, 147; literature, 149; public, 151, 153
Deconstructionist, 48
Delia, J., 67 (n. 3)
Deliberative: rhetoric, 14, 144; argument, 115
Democracy, 177–78
Democratic: humanism, 112; myth, 179; actor, 181
Demonstration, 82
Derrida, J., 170
Descartes, R., 4
Dewey, J., 1, 11
Dialectic, 113–14, 132
Dialectical: terms, 112; process, 124, 126
Dialogic argument, 111
Difference, tolerance of, 44
Differences, substantive, 144
Direct realism, 46–47
Disagreements, genuine, 148
Discourse: practical, 12; intercultural, 36; intergroup, 36; propositional, 67 (n. 2); Native American, 75–76; poetic, 82; rational, 134; expert, 145; specialized, 145; technologized, 145; public, 147, 159, 168, 181, 185, 193–94; commensurating, 148, 152; appraisal of expert, 149; technical, 151; quasi-technical, 151; strategic, 163;

critical, 167–70; cultures of, 167–68, 184; shared community of, 174; hegemonic philosophy of, 175; arts of, 191. See also Messages; Text
Discursive, 73, 81, 94; praxis, 8; practices, 13; forms, 74, 95; claim, 83
Discursively, 70
Discussion: sound, 151; personal, 176
Disputes: interfield, 10, 152, rational resolution of, 119
Dissent, 35, 185; dissenters, 37
Distancing effect, 100
Dominant: forms of argument, 12; rhetorical assumptions, 186
Domination, 167, 169; capitalist, 170. See also Hegemony; Power
Doubt, 120; systematic, 17
Durkheim, E., 69

Eagleton, T., 12, 164; privileges critique over teaching advocacy skills, 165
Eco, U., 108–109
Ehninger, D., 29
Eliade, M., 69
Elite, 99; scientific, 100; technical, 100; political, 146. See also Expert
Elites, 143
Eloquence, 55
Elster, J., 164
Emotion, 57
Emotional form, 63
Enacted claim, 83
Enlightenment, 1
Enthymeme, 67 (n. 3), 81, 171
Enthymemic reasoning, 121
Epistemic, 125; rhetoric, 4; justification, 5, 20–22; procedures, 6; practices, 9; concern, 11; pessimism, 42, 45; crisis, 119; relativity, 119, 143–44; merit of argumentation, 121; diagnosis, 148, 152; interests, 149; jurisdiction, 150
Epistemological, 5, 136; issues, 34; belief, 45; diagnosis, 151
Epistemology, 9, 34, 46, 49, 136, 148, 153 (n. 2); analytic, 31; consensus, 35; rhetorical, 35; foundational, 48
Ethical: standards, 36; belief, 38, 42, 45; pessimism, 45
Evaluation, 120–21; interfield, 120; argument, 124–27, 131, 134; universally applicable standards for, 127; purpose-centered view of, 130; probabilistic nature of, 132. See also Commensurability

Human: fallibility, 41; reason, 45; agent, 75; beings as producers, 171; communication, 191; dignity commensurate with the human condition, 192
Humanism, democratic, 112
Humanistic intellectuals, 168
Humanitarian value, 45
Hume, D., 133
Husserl, E., 4

Idealism, 114
Idealist, 11
Ideal speech situation, 169
Identification, 63–64, 78
Ideological: criticism, 12; narratives, 172; rigid base, 185
Ideology, 35, 45, 158–60, 164, 179; prison house of, 166; of communication, 170; critique of, 171. *See also* Consciousness
Images, 63–64
Implicit messages, 105
Incommensurability, 137
Incommensurabilities, 141
Incommensurable, 140. *See also* Differences
Incomprehension gulf, 146
Individual conduct, 29
Induction, 27–28; serves as regulative function, 28. *See also* Inferential; Logic
Industrial: societies, 161–62; values, 181; model of mass communication, 182–83; vision of communication, 182. *See also* Capitalist; Corporate
Industry, mass media, 182, 185
Inferencing, 7, 9, 54–55
Inferential: deep structure, 55; leap, 56; theory, 56; form, 57–64 passim; criterion, 58; topoi, 58. *See also* Induction; Logic
Infinite regress, 126
Informal logic, 11, 14 (n. 3), 121, 129, 130, 133–34, 143. *See also* Enthymeme; Reasoning
Inquiry: rhetoric of, 33–34, 39, 48; realist rhetoric of, 43, 46
Institution, prerogatives of, 176
Instrumental, 72–73, 82, 84; rationality, 22; acts, 71; ritual, 72
Instrumentally, 81
Intellectuals, new class of humanistic, 168
Intelligentsia, 168

Interest: self, 64, 141; public, 149, 184
Interests, segmentation of, 11
Intercultural discourse, 36
Interfield: disputes, 10, 152; arenas, 24; evaluation, 120
Intergroup discourse, 36
Intersubjective validation, 35
Intersubjectivity, 36, 38, 42, 45, 60. *See also* Consensus
Invariant standards, 133
Invention, 14
Irrational, 110
Irrationalism, romantic, 103
Irrationalist, 53
Isocrates, 176
Issues, breadth of, 150

James, W., 177–78
Johnson, M., 96
Judgment: practical, 19; probabilistic, 103
Jurisdiction, epistemic, 150
Jurisdictional principle, 152
Justification, 31–32, 39; epistemic, 5, 20–22; pragmatic, 5–6, 17–22, 29, 31; assessment of, 24
Justificationism, 10, 126; Perelman's sense of, 20
Justified: assent, 3, 12, 174–76, 185, 192; consensus, 103

Kellner, D., 163
Knowledge, 48, 103; propositional, 6; expert, 11, 129, 134 (n. 1); social, 60, 121; comparisons to expert, 127; technical, 134 (n. 1); fragmentation of, 137; balkanization of, 141; *sophia*, 141; public, 149; personal, 190

Labor, 160, 167
Lakoff, G., 96
Langer, S., 72, 94
Language, 47–48, 108–109
Leff, M., 33, 55, 56, 61, 68 (n. 4)
Left, 163
Legalistic model, 23
Legitimacy of claim, 58
Legitimate, 60
Lenin, V. I., 44, 161
Leninism, 161. *See also* Marxism
Lentricchia, F., 11
Liberalism, corporate, 170
Linkugel, W. A., 74
Literacy, rhetorical, 65

Literature, 8
Logic: formal, 3; informal, 11, 14 (n. 3), 121, 129–30, 133–34, 143; philosophic, 103; ordinary, 121, 126; syllogistic, 128. *See also* Induction; Inferential; Rational; Reasoning
Logical prose, 92
Logicians, informal, 128
Lukacs, G., 112
Luxemburg, R., 161
Lyne, J., 48

McCloskey, D. N., 41
McGee, M. C., 48, 158
Mackin, J., 47
Magic, 72
Majoritarianism, 37
Mana, 72
Mann, Thomas, 112
Marginalized, 193
Marx, K., 157, 172
Marxism, 12, 158, 160, 162, 165, 168; critical, 160–62, 166; scientific, 160, 166. *See also* Critical; Critique; Frankfurt School
Marxist, 159; critical, 165; scientific, 165; rhetorical theory, 171
Mask, 74
Mass: communication, 162, 182–83, 194; audience, 180, 182, 184; media, 181, 186, 193; industry, 182, 185; homogenization of, 183
Masses, 162
Material criterion, 58
Material theory, 56
Mead, G. H., 75
Media, mass, 181–86 passim, 193
Megill, A., 34
Messages: explicit, 105; implicit, 105; argument, 109. *See also* Discourse; Text
Metaphor, 8, 61, 68 (n. 7), 92–101 passim, 146–47; dead, 8, 96; feminization, 61; archetypal, 62; military, 78; faded, 96, 101; escalation, 98, 102 (n. 3). *See also* Form
Methodological rationality, 29
Miller, T. P., 47
Minority, 35
Modernism, 2
Modernity, 135, 144, 147; rhetorics of, 179. *See also* Postmodernism
Modern rhetoric, 181
Moral: purpose, 13; rationality, 29, 31

Moral-practical reason, 13
Moser, R., 30
Motivational forms, 64
Motivism, 12
Mundane, 8; world, 6
Mystification, 59, 66
Myth, 69, 88 (n. 1)

Narrative: fictional, 104; forms, 109; ideological, 172. *See also* Novels
Narrator, 106–107, 109
Native American: protest rhetoric, 70, 78; discourse, 75–76; activist movement, 80
"Nazi examples," 44. *See also* Fascism
Negative thinking, 162
Nelson, J. S., 34, 48
Neo-Aristotelianism, 2
Neo-Aristotelians, 81
New rhetoric, 18
Nietzsche, F., 3
Nondiscursive, 57, 63, 121; argument, 83
Nonfoundationalist, 21
Nonrelativism, 40, 44
Normative, 6, 10–11, 13; argumentation, 2–3, 8; dimension, 4, 8; adherence of audiences, 4
Novels, 104–107; realistic, 112; form, 115. *See also* Fiction; Narrative
Nuclear: war, 98; weapons, 100; policies, 101

O'Keefe, B. J., 140
Objective, 54; reality, 40–41, 170
Objectivism, 46–47; rhetorical, 33
Objectivist, 48; rhetorical, 48
Objectivity, 68 (n. 8)
Olbrechts-Tyteca, L., 19, 54, 92–93, 101, 116 (n. 2)
Ontological, 38, 46
Opinion, *doxa*, 141, 190–91; public, 186, 188
Opposition, 151
Oppression, 171
Organic unity, 30
Orr, C. J., 35, 41
Osborn, M., 62

Paradoxes, self-referential, 34
Party, 162
Payne, K., 97–100
Pedagogical, 136; diagnosis, 147–48, 152; rationale, 148

About the Series

STUDIES IN RHETORIC AND COMMUNICATION
General Editors:
E. Culpepper Clark, Raymie E. McKerrow, and David Zarefsky

The University of Alabama Press has established this series to publish major new works in the general area of rhetoric and communication, including books treating the symbolic manifestations of political discourse, argument as social knowledge, the impact of machine technology on patterns of communication behavior, and other topics related to the nature or impact of symbolic communication. We actively solicit studies involving historical, critical, or theoretical analyses of human discourse.